LANSING LAMONT

Day of Trinity

Atheneum   *New York*

1985

TO ADA

And to the memory of my brother,
Seaman 1/C Thomas William Lamont,
missing in action April 1945 while on submarine war patrol
in the waters off Japan

Library of Congress Cataloging in Publication Data
Lamont, Lansing.
Day of Trinity.

Bibliography: p.
Includes index.
1. United States. Army. Corps of Engineers.
Manhattan Engineer District. 2. Atomic bomb—New Mexico
—Los Alamos—History. 3. Los Alamos (N.M.)—
Description. I. Title.
QC773.A1L3 1985   623.4'5119   84–45635
ISBN 0–689–70686–3 (pbk.)

ACKNOWLEDGMENTS

I wrote this book in the hope of giving general readers for the first time a full and understandable account of one of the climactic occasions in the history of man: the explosion of the first atomic bomb.

This is a story of great scientific achievement and of the scientists who accomplished it. But my book is not a scientific primer on the atomic age. It is, rather, a story of men and women and what they went through to build and test the weapon that has changed life on earth.

For help in telling this story, I am indebted to many persons.

I should like to start with my wife, who, despite the strains of managing four children in the frequent absence of her husband, managed to read and offer critical advice as the manuscript progressed. To Mary Vreeland and her husband, Colonel Frederick F. Vreeland, I proffer special thanks for their aid in preparing the manuscript and proofreading. To my colleagues at *Time*—especially Hugh Sidey, John Steele, Jerry Hannifin and Charles J. V. Murphy—who gave me encouragement and advice, I am most grateful. To Charles Bracelen Flood and Arthur Hendrick, two old Saint Bernards who succored me in differing ways, a warm toast. The same, and more, to my late mother and father, who cheered me on from beginning to end. And to Michael Bessie and Tom Stewart of Atheneum, my sincerest appreciation for their unflagging enthusiasm.

Acknowledgments

A number of government officials have helped me in this endeavor, and to them I am indebted. I want to thank particularly Richard G. Hewlett, chief historian of the U.S. Atomic Energy Commission, who has been a reliable guide on paper and over the telephone throughout this writing. Also, Charles L. Marshall and Murray L. Nash of the AEC's classification division; Duncan Clark, chief public information officer; and two hospitable members of the AEC's Los Alamos public information office, John V. Young and Earl Zimmerman. I should also like to thank Ted Sherwin, public affairs officer for the Sandia Corporation in Albuquerque, and Herbert McGushin, deputy director of the United States Information Agency's press office in Washington.

To Colonel (Ret.) Gerald R. Tyler and two former members of that dauntless and often misunderstood security brigade, Frederick B. Rhodes and Thomas O. Jones, my thanks. Their recollections have added color and cloak-and-dagger seasoning to this yarn. To Dr. Ralph Lapp, who generously reviewed my manuscript for scientific accuracy, I express sincere appreciation. And to William L. Laurence, who supplied me with books, rare insight and a newspaperman's stirring sense of history, my deep gratitude.

Finally, this book could not have been written without the co-operation and patience of those very busy gentlemen who built the atomic bomb and who gave of their time and wisdom toward the preparation of this narrative. They are legion, but principally I am beholden to the late Lieutenant General Leslie Groves, on whom I imposed far too often; to the late Dr. Robert Oppenheimer, who gave me a long and memorable interview at Princeton; and to Dr. Kenneth Bainbridge of Harvard, who has been generous and painstaking in his assistance. Also, I could not have relived the days and hours before Trinity as seen through the eyes of the GI's without the aid of Leo Jercinovic and Louis Jacot of Albuquerque, two lively and perceptive friends with an unerring ear for the many little humors and ironies of that event.

I cannot overlook the following scientists whose accounts to me of Trinity have added substantially to this book: Harry Allen, Robert Van Gemert, Ralph Carlisle Smith, Wright Langham and Joseph McKibben of Los Alamos; Luis Alvarez and Emilio Segrè of Berkeley; Robert Bacher of the California Institute of Technology; Julian Mack of the University of Wisconsin; Samuel Allison and Herbert L. Anderson of the University of Chicago; George Kistiakowsky of Harvard; Cyril Smith of the Massachusetts Institute of Technology; Philip Morrison and Hans Bethe of Cornell; and Donald Hornig, George Weil and Stafford Warren of Washington, D.C.

To all these men, and to their dedicated colleagues, I extend my deepest thanks. Forty years ago they watched the fruit of their labors shatter the dawn above Trinity and usher in the nuclear age. They have brought this story to life, as no one else could, for those of us who may never comprehend the mysteries of the atom but who can appreciate the human foibles and fragilities which led to that memorable day.

FOREWORD

TWENTY years have elapsed since *Day of Trinity* was first published in 1965 and became an immediate best seller.

That original edition told the story of how the world's first atomic bomb was built and tested under extraordinary wartime secrecy conditions. Nothing, of course, has happened since to change the facts of that story. But that same edition also assessed the long-term consequences of the Trinity test, the era it created, through the very limited perspective of just two intervening decades.

Now, another two decades later in 1985, the United States and Russia have undergone a succession of changes in their leadership; both superpowers have witnessed an epoch of dazzling innovation in nuclear weaponry; the arms race has spiraled to unprecedented levels of potential destruction. The Trinity scientists, whose views were recorded for publication in 1965, have since enlarged on or in some cases altered their thinking about the birth of the atomic era and their role in it. The whole atomic weapons industry, from Los Alamos to the military-political complex in Washington, has undergone profound changes in doctrine and technology. Public opinion, too, these past twenty years has significantly matured in its awareness of and concern over the dangers of nuclear war.

This new edition was produced to reassess the impact of that historic test from the longer perspective of four decades. The narrative of the events leading up to the test, the dramatic account of the test itself, remain untouched. A new final section has been written, however, bringing the reader up to date on what of importance has transpired during these last decades in the politics, technology and human understanding of the atomic bomb and the arms competition. More than two dozen of the original core of Trinity scientists who built the first bomb have been reinterviewed. The author revisited Los Alamos, the Trinity test site, the Sandia weapons laboratory in Albuquerque, and talked with informed government sources at the Department of Energy in Washington and with foreign affairs experts in New York.

On the fortieth anniversary of the Trinity explosion in July 1945 the publishers have released this modern edition of *Day of Trinity*. They have done so not only because the story of that first unforgettable test is as relevant today as it was twenty years ago. They have done so with the hope of informing a new generation of readers about the genesis of mankind's ultimate weapon and how we have managed to arrive years later at this critical hour in world history when, in Pope John Paul II's words, only through a conscious choice and then deliberate policy can humanity survive.

Finally, this new edition has been written to assuage once more the doubts voiced in a letter to the author from Robert Oppenheimer shortly after the first edition of *Day of Trinity* appeared. He concluded: "It is just possible, I suppose, that the whole episode seems so remote, so vastly overtaken by the times, and so hopelessly romantic, that no one will care to read about it. But I would not be sad if this were to prove wrong."

L.L.
January 1985

CONTENTS

ILLUSTRATIONS

MAPS AND DIAGRAM DESIGNED BY GUY FLEMING

The interior of the implosion-type device tested at Trinity
PAGE 176

FOLLOWING PAGE 176

Maj. Gen. Leslie R. Groves and Dr. J. Robert Oppenheimer
(Marie Hansen, *Life*)

Klaus Fuchs
(Keystone)

Tech. Sgt. Leo M. Jercinovic

Manhattan Project leaders: General Groves, Dr. James B. Conant, Dr. Vannevar Bush
(George Skadding, *Life*)

Dr. George B. Kistiakowsky
(*Life*)

Dr. Enrico Fermi
(Los Alamos Photographic Laboratory)

Base Camp at Trinity
(Los Alamos Photographic Laboratory)

The shot tower at Trinity
(Los Alamos Photographic Laboratory)

The test bomb arrives at Trinity
(Los Alamos Photographic Laboratory)

Opening session of the Potsdam Conference
(U.S. Army Photograph)

Explosion of the world's first atomic bomb
(5 photographs from Los Alamos Photographic Laboratory, 6th from Los Alamos Scientific Laboratory)

A "Fat Man" plutonium bomb
(Los Alamos Scientific Laboratory)

Nagasaki after the bomb had fallen
(George Silk, *Life*)

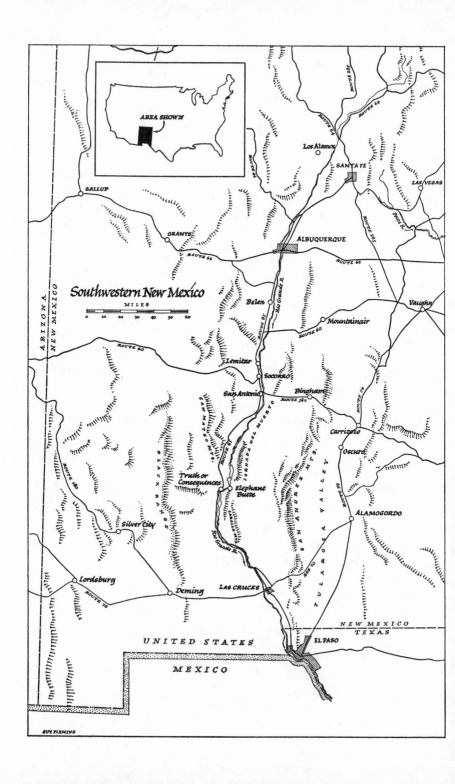

AREA SHOWN

Southwestern New Mexico

MILES
0 10 20 30 40 50 60

GUY FLEMING

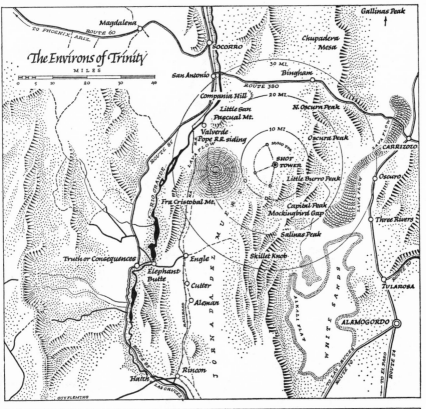

The Environs of Trinity

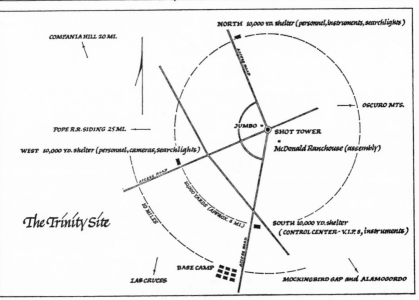

The Trinity Site

I

Prelude

D AWN, July 16, 1945, 5:29:35 Mountain War Time. The countdown had reached Zero minus ten seconds.

In those milliseconds before the most awesome weapon devised by man created its first terrifying sunrise, the only sound on the desert wastes of southern New Mexico was the mating buzz of a colony of spadefoot toads. And, if one strained for it, the distant drone of a B-29 bomber.

There had been a downpour earlier, and the toads had left their subterranean burrows in the gravelly sand of the Jornada del Muerto to fill the rain-choked hollows across the desert with their staccato song. The bomber far above them was groping its way along the mountainous west rim of the test site, seeking in those final seconds the searchlight beam that would indicate the steel tower where the bomb rested.

To the east the sky was clearing. A finger of gray crept over Little Burro and Oscura peaks. To the west, where the Fra Cristobal Range runs down to meet an ancient lava flow, solid overcast still blotted out the half-moon. A gentle ground wind caressed the sleeping yucca bushes and murmured through the drenched arroyos streaking the desert floor. The temperature was climbing the sixties.

Ten thousand yards south of the tower, in a timbered shelter clogged with weird dials and consoles, men counted off the seconds and froze in their thoughts. The shelter, code-named "Baker," faced the tower behind a massive

3

earthwork bunker. It was the central control point for the first atomic bomb test.

The war was in its sixth year. Germany had surrendered two months earlier. Japan was reeling under the combined air and naval bombardment of the U.S. Third Fleet. The Big Three—the United States, Britain, and the Soviet Union —were meeting in Potsdam to sort out the postwar future.

Across the Pacific, troop convoys were on the move. The invasion of Japan had been planned for four months later. Estimated casualties for American troops alone ranged from half a million up. The Japanese could be counted on to wage a ferocious defense of their homeland. Their dead, plus those of the Allies, might exceed the million mark.

The world was weary of slaughter. It was ready for a way, almost any way, to stop it—swiftly, decisively, and if possible forever.

In the doorway of the South-10,000-yard shelter, a frail figure in baggy trousers, khaki shirt and a floppy sombrero steadied himself and subconsciously summoned the spirit of an ancient Hindu to celebrate a moment he feared he would never forget. The man scarcely breathed. He stared straight ahead toward the hills to his south, listening to the countdown near its nadir, waiting for the climax of an all but impossible undertaking he had helped conceive, then led through nearly three years of challenge and crisis.

His name was Robert Oppenheimer. Within nine short years he would become the storm center of the most controversial security case of our time.

Twenty-five yards away Kenneth Bainbridge, the scientist most directly responsible for the failure or success of the test, calmly faced the tension. Lying on an inch-thick foam sheet, he peered through darkened welder's goggles into the gloom, mentally checking the precautions he had ordered for this moment. One of them was that every soul on that desert would wear glare-proof glasses and face away from the detonation.

Bainbridge had come a long way from Cooperstown, New York, where he had been born the son of a wholesale stationer. He had taken over technical direction of the most complex, fateful scientific experiment in history.

Inside the South-10,000-yard shelter a twenty-four-year-old explosives expert who had written his college thesis on bombs fixed his gaze on four red lights on the panel in front of him and nervously fingered a "stop switch" that could halt the test at the last fraction of a second if necessary. Donald Hornig had been born in Milwaukee, gone East and married a Bryn Mawr girl. He had sold a lovely yawl, in which he had cruised New England waters, to buy a car and drive west to a landlocked sanctum in northern New Mexico where they made bombs. He had been the last man that night to leave the top of the tower.

Within eighteen years he would be the chief scientific adviser to the President of the United States.

At Base Camp, ten miles from the tower, a trio of America's highest-priced educational, military and technological talent lay side by side like dead men on the dampened desert.

The President of Harvard University scrunched his slender frame into the muck of a recently bulldozed slit trench. Dr. James Bryant Conant had long had doubts that the weapon in the tower would work. A skeptical chemist, he still wondered, as he lay there, whether the bomb would deliver the power expected of it. But as one of the half-dozen men in the United States most intimately involved in all development phases of the weapon, he felt obligated to witness its birth, however premature.

By Conant's side an Army officer with a hard-earned reputation and a promotion riding on the shot had stretched out his 200-pound bulk on the sand. Major General Leslie Groves wondered whether he would ever see a third star on his shoulder if the countdown reached Zero and nothing happened. The general was a supreme optimist, egotist and administrator, not necessarily in that order. He had had to be, to run the boldest, most dramatic scientific venture ever—the Manhattan Project.

If the bomb worked, Groves could perhaps take more credit for its success than any other man on that desert. He had enormous faith in himself. He was also the son of a Presbyterian minister and knew how to pray.

Prostrate beside Groves was the most influential scientific-technological figure in the U.S. Government: Vannevar Bush, a lean Yankee with a salty tongue and an empire of 30,000 workers under him. As head of the Office of Scientific Research and Development in Washington, he had masterminded the nation's effort to match its technical prowess to its military war machine. More than any other man, he had helped harness the talents of the scientists and engineers to the blueprints of the generals and admirals. It had been an organizational tour de force.

Right now, as the seconds swept by, Bush hoped to God he would have something worthwhile to pass on to the War Department and to the President in Potsdam.

On Compania Hill, a volcanic outcropping twenty miles northwest of the shot tower, a young Army sergeant shivered in his fatigues and swapped guesses with two pals on whether any of them would come out of the test alive. The chill air on that slope was charged with speculation that the bomb would either incinerate the atmosphere or tilt the earth off its axis.

Some of this was the beer talk of excited GI's, some of it the earnest concern of many of the hundred or so unofficial observers who had driven down from a laboratory retreat in the north to witness the shot.

The sergeant, T/5 Leo Mathew Jercinovic, son of a Yugoslav stonemason, had been a member of the high-explosive assembly team that worked on the bomb. Three days earlier he had helped put together the deadly jigsaw puzzle that now crowned the tower. Jercinovic knew every part of the bomb except the secret of its innermost nuclear core.

When he worried whether he would live to see another dawn, it was not entirely idle fear. He pulled his poncho closer to him and squinted through his goggles toward the southeast. One of the good things about working on the bomb, Jercinovic reflected, was the chance it gave a lousy enlisted man to rub shoulders with the big names of science.

They were there on the hill with him: Sir James Chadwick, discoverer of neutrons and head of the British atomic mission in the United States; Ernest O. Lawrence, inventor of the cyclotron; and a haughty Hungarian with beetled brows who had offered sun-tan lotion to everyone as protection against the bomb's anticipated ultraviolet rays.

The Hungarian had been rather unpopular with his colleagues. They thought him indifferent to their efforts to build the atomic bomb. He had worked apart from them, absorbed in his own lonely endeavor, thinking and talking of an era a league beyond the one they aspired to. Edward Teller was already siring an even deadlier weapon of war, the hydrogen bomb.

The countdown was passing Zero minus five seconds.

The scientists and GI's had gathered to observe the trial run of a weapon that had been built out of fear the Germans would build one first. That fear had been unjustified. This same weapon, however, might now abruptly foreclose the

7

holocaust raging through Japanese cities victimized by mass incendiary bombings. It might prevent the massacre that would inevitably follow invasion of Japan itself.

The answer lay in the hulking sphere on top of the tower: the answer to this war and, possibly, all wars; the solution to man's incessant wonder and conjecture about the universe down through the ages; the most fearful secret a nation at war ever sought to keep from its enemies *and* its allies.

Aloof from his associates on Compania Hill, one observer was ready to take the most intricate mental notes on the test. He huddled alone on a saddle between two hillocks and brooded at the lifting darkness to the east. Occasionally he ran a hand over the stubble sprouting from his chin. These last few days there had been no time for a harried physicist to shave.

It was difficult to make out the sliver of light that fixed the shot tower in the distance, especially for a man who wore thick-lensed glasses for his shortsightedness. He was a German refugee, born in a village in the industrial west, the son of a domineering Lutheran pastor who fervently believed men must act on what they think is right, despite the consequences. The son was doing just that. He believed the Soviet Union, as a wartime ally of the United States, should know the secrets of the atomic bomb. For three and a half years he had been supplying Soviet couriers with atomic data. The mental notes he would make of *this* event would be in Kremlin hands shortly.

He was a passionate waltzer and a flawless physicist. In years to come, when men discussed the world's most infamous traitors, Klaus Fuchs's name would lead all the rest.

Thirty thousand feet in the clouds, bearing down from the north, a B-29 Superfort groped through the murk. While the bomber followed a course fifteen miles to the east of the shot

8

tower, two explosives specialists, Dr. Luis Alvarez and Navy Captain William S. Parsons, leaned over the pilot's shoulder and peered out the cockpit's left window. The plane was approaching the detonation vicinity.

For most of those on the ground this test was the omega to three grueling years of work. For Alvarez and Parsons the test would be another milestone in an epic ending over Hiroshima.

Yet what happened to the bomb on the tower would have no direct effect on the fate of Hiroshima. Another weapon, far different in design and content, had been assigned that city. It was already crossing the Pacific to keep a rendezvous with history in three weeks.

Hiroshima's executioner was a bomb made from a rare nuclear metal called uranium. Although untested, enough was known of its explosive mechanism to make the scientists reasonably confident it would perform. Once it did, however, the United States had no more such uranium bombs to expend on Japan. It had taken nearly every gram of available uranium to build the Hiroshima bomb. The nation desperately needed a second bomb, made from more available nuclear material, to deliver the second part of a one-two punch that would bring Japan to her knees.

That was what the test bomb on the tower was all about.

Far from the test site in the Jornada basin there were others that dawn who could not hear the relentless countdown but who had a vital stake in its climax.

In Albuquerque, 110 miles to the north, Captain Thomas O. Jones dozed in a fourth-floor room of the Hilton Hotel. As local security chief for the bomb project, he had been on the phone all night with agents scattered throughout

9

a dozen towns along the perimeter of the test site. If radioactive fallout threatened disaster, Jones's men were to evacuate their towns swiftly and stealthily. But no one would be told the truth of *why* the evacuation was occurring.

While Jones dozed, two subordinates hovered by the single window with its southern exposure.

Elsewhere in Albuquerque, at an apartment at 209 North High Street, another Army man was preparing to end his weekend pass and catch a bus back to his job on a mesa outside Santa Fe. His wife was still asleep in the bedroom. At twenty-three, he was a corporal and shop machinist in the vital "X" Division which had fashioned a super-secret component of the bomb. Like the stubbled refugee on Compania Hill, he, too, had been giving information to the Russians. But not for the same reason.

David Greenglass enjoyed sleeping with his wife. As an enlisted man stationed in New Mexico, however, he would ordinarily have lacked the means to bring his wife out from New York and set her up in an apartment in Albuquerque. The only way he had been able to manage it had been through the beneficence of his brother-in-law, Julius Rosenberg.

Within seven years, Rosenberg, a convicted spy, would be dead in the electric chair at Sing Sing and Greenglass sentenced to a fifteen-year prison term as his accessory.

At No. 2 Kaiser Strasse in the Potsdam surburb of Babelsberg, it was already nearing one P.M. In the sitting room of his second-floor suite in the "Little White House," Harry Truman had just wound up a lengthy morning conference with Winston Churchill, British foreign minister Anthony Eden and Secretary of State James Byrnes. Truman, aware of the impending test in New Mexico, was anxiously awaiting word from Secretary of War Henry Stimson.

The outcome of the test would significantly influence the

attitude of the British and Americans as they sat down to parley with Stalin at Potsdam. It would also determine the tone of the surrender ultimatum being prepared for the Japanese Government.

Here and there along a pine-dotted mesa in New Mexico, far north of the test site, wives were watching and waiting on that pregnant dawn.

They were not supposed to know of the test. But a female grapevine is a wondrous thing. Their men, a few weeks before they had mysteriously disappeared from their homes on the mesa, had dropped hints that something besides a sunrise might occur that particular morn.

The bomb rested in its cradle.

It slept upon a steel-supported oakwood platform, inside a sheet-metal shack 103 feet above the ground: a bloated black squid girdled with cables and leechlike detonators, each tamped with enough explosive to spark simultaneously, within a millionth of a second, the final conflagration. Tentacles emerged from the squid in a harness of wires connecting the detonators to a shiny aluminum tank, the firing unit.

Stripped of its coils, the bomb weighed 10,000 pounds. Its teardrop dimensions were 4½ feet wide, 10½ feet long. Its guts contained two layers of wedge-shaped high-explosive blocks surrounding an inner core of precisely machined nuclear ingots that lay, as one scientist described them, like diamonds in an immense wad of cotton. These ingots were made from a metal called plutonium.

At the heart of the bomb, buried inside the layers of explosive and plutonium, lay the ultimate key to its success or failure, a metallic sphere no bigger than a ping-pong ball that even twenty years later would still be regarded a state secret: the initiator.

Within five seconds the initiator would trigger the sequence that hundreds of shadows had gathered to watch that dawn. The bomb would either fizzle to a premature death or shatteringly christen a new era on earth.

Weeks, months, years of toil had gone into it.

The nation's finest brains and leadership, the cream of its scientific and engineering force, plus two billion dollars from the taxpayers had built the squat monster on the tower for this very moment. Yet it had been no labor of love. There was not the mildest affection for it.

Other instruments of war bore dashing or maidenly names: Britain's "Spitfires"; the "Flying Tigers"; the "Gravel Gerties" and "Gypsy Rose Lees" that clanked across North Africa or blitzed bridgeheads on the Rhine; even the Germans' "Big Bertha" of World War I; and, soon, the Superfortress "Enola Gay" of Hiroshima, deliverer of an atomic bundle called "Little Boy."

The test bomb had no colorful nickname. One day its spawn would be known as "Fat Man" (after Churchill). But now its identity was cloaked in a welter of impersonal terms: "the thing," "the beast," "the device" and its Washington pseudonym, "S-1." The scientists, most of whom called it simply "the gadget," had handled it gently and daintily, like the baby it was—but out of respect, not fondness. One wrong jolt of the volatile melon inside its Duralumin frame could precipitate the collision of radioactive masses and a slow, agonizing death from radiation. Or instant vaporization.

The monster engendered the sort of fear that had caused one young scientist to break down the evening before and be escorted promptly from the site to a psychiatric ward; and another, far older and wiser, a Nobel Prize winner, to murmur, as he waited in his trench, "I'm scared witless, absolutely witless."

Alone in her house in the Taos Valley, 220 miles north of the tower, Peggy Pond Church had a premonition of disaster. Her husband had been headmaster of a boys' school in the Jemez Hills outside Santa Fe until the Army had dispossessed him one day and taken over his property with barely an explanation.

Now, with dawn breaking, Mrs. Church had, for the first time since she came to the valley, locked all her doors; then she sat down to record in her diary a dream she had had an hour before. She had not been able to sleep since then. She had dreamed of seeing "a strange and overwhelming wind . . . an invincible force that was about to destroy the earth."

At Base Camp a bandy-legged little dynamo they called "The Pope" pulled out his slide rule and balled a wad of paper scraps into one hand. No one, but no one, could beat "The Pope" when it came to originating bizarre experiments. He had performed the world's first successful experiment in man-made chain reaction. Now he would conduct a simpler experiment, his own personal measurement of the atomic bomb's power.

Enrico Fermi cocked an ear to the countdown.

The trills of the toads making glorious love near his foxhole almost drowned out the crescendo of numbers echoing across the desert.

5 . . . 4 . . . 3 . . . 2 . . . 1 . . .

II

Gathering the Wind

Who hath gathered the wind in his fists?
THE PROPHET AGUR, BOOK OF PROVERBS

THE COUNTDOWN had begun 2400 years earlier with the Golden Age of Greece.

Democritus, a Greek called the "Laughing Philosopher," conceived of the atom around 400 B.C. He taught that all matter consisted of tiny, indivisible particles made of the same material. These he called "atoms" after the Greek word *atomos* (indivisible). Rocks differed from trees, but only because of the different size and shape and weight of their atoms. It didn't occur to Democritus that the difference might lie ultimately in the composition of the atoms themselves. To him the atom was the smallest denominator.

His theory didn't become popular for two thousand years. During that time the atom was a source of heated discussion but little experiment.

It took Isaac Newton at the end of the seventeenth century to revive Democritus' doctrine. The great English scientist pronounced his agreement with it and others fell in line. For another hundred years most scientists accepted the principle that the atom was impenetrable.

Another Englishman upset the status quo in the early 1800's. Michael Faraday persuasively indicated that the atom contained particles of electricity—what later were called electrons. By the end of the century it was fairly certain that atoms had a structure of their own which could be penetrated. The rush was on to pry open the secret.

Scientists everywhere joined forces. They labored ceaselessly in tangential vineyards: Englishmen and Germans collaborated on X-ray studies; in France the Curies and Becquerel made startling discoveries about a lustrous white element called uranium; and a Dane, Niels Bohr, with a New Zealander, Ernest Rutherford, theorized and experimented with radioactive particles. In 1905 Einstein announced his theory of relativity.

So far atomic physics had been largely a European effort. America at the turn of the nineteenth century had no physicists of repute to match the top Europeans. Its university instruction, with few exceptions, was uninspiring. In the United States, physicists enjoyed no intellectual fraternity comparable to that on the Continent. Many of the more promising ones went abroad to complete their studies.

Three European centers dominated atomic study at the end of World War I: Copenhagen, where Niels Bohr reigned; Germany's University of Göttingen, a haven of ferment guided by Max Born and James Franck; and Cavendish Laboratory in Cambridge, England. To Cavendish in late 1925 came a gangling youth with a racking cough and the air of an apprentice mystic.

Julius Robert Oppenheimer had just conquered Harvard College after three lonely, driving years. He had started majoring in chemistry, switched to experimental physics, and finally arranged, though already carrying a load of seven undergraduate courses, to audit graduate lectures in theoretical physics. He had graduated summa cum laude that spring.

That Oppenheimer should have made Phi Beta Kappa at Harvard in his chosen field was not surprising. It was the youth's incredible range of knowledge *outside* his field that was startling.

As a child Oppenheimer had wanted at various times to be an architect, artist or poet. At five, when his grandfather gave him a box of minerals, Robert had sensed the genesis of a science career. By the age of twelve he had joined and read his first paper before the New York Mineralogical Club. The boy's racing brain was seldom turned off. One day he watched a classmate hurl a baseball out of a playground and draw the ire of a teacher. Oppenheimer calculated the force with which the ball had hit the sidewalk and demonstrated, to the teacher's bewilderment, that it couldn't have beaned anyone seriously.

By his senior year in school young Oppenheimer was regarded as a rather peculiar egg who preferred relaxing over Plato, Homer and Sophocles to playing mumblety-peg with his classmates. He also liked calculus and writing French sonnets. He preferred Baudelaire to baseball, Gibbon to girls. He once read all three thousand pages of *Decline and Fall of the Roman Empire* during a train trip from San Francisco to New York.

When he left Harvard, after three years of raiding the university's library stacks, Oppenheimer was already taking command of a Da Vincian range of interests from the arts and humanities to Oriental philosophy. He knew the sonnets of John Donne as well as the verses of Omar Khayyam. He could speak several other languages as fluently as his own. He was even dabbling in Sanskrit.

Such precociousness became evident at Cavendish to the visiting German physicist Max Born, who persuaded Oppenheimer to return with him to the University of Göttingen. At Göttingen it didn't take Oppenheimer long to impress—and antagonize—his companions. The school had its share of showboating scholars who reveled in the aura of giants like Born and the recent Nobel Prize winner Professor Franck. But Oppenheimer outdid them all. He improvised learned dissertations on the spur of the moment, monopolized classroom discussion with his dazzling eloquence and erudition. In his more modest moments, though, he made friends. He could talk quietly on philosophy or plumb the mysteries of Dante's "Inferno" with his colleagues as they walked the cobbled streets at twilight.

Something warm but unfathomable in this curious man drew others to him. He moved with a dancer's grace, all six feet of him. He radiated intensity from a pair of sapphire-blue eyes framing a delicately aquiline nose. He could be gentle, sympathetic and the very model of what one observer has defined as "politesse de coeur."

Thus, by the time he had received his doctorate, with distinction, from Göttingen and moved on to Holland's University of Leiden, Oppenheimer had widened his circle of friends considerably. Within six weeks of his arrival at Leiden he had extended the circle by giving a lecture in Dutch before the faculty and students. Affectionately they nicknamed him "Oppie."

By 1929 Oppenheimer had tired of Europe. He was homesick and impatient to return to the United States, where a tempting offer awaited him. For the next twelve years he would alternate as an assistant professor between the physics departments of the University of California at Berkeley and the California Institute of Technology in Pasadena.

The atomic cauldron began bubbling fiercely in the 1930's.

Experimentation so far had been intermittent and inconclusive. The massive uranium atom still remained intact. But in England, America and Italy a band of determined physicists prepared for the final assault.

The year 1932 was a vintage one for them.

James Chadwick, an Englishman, discovered the neutron, the key to unlocking the atom. An electrically neutral particle, the neutron would be used like a bullet to slice through the atom and penetrate the vaporous electron cloud surrounding the atom's nucleus. The ultimate result would be atomic fission, on which the bomb is premised.

In England and America scientists were constructing gargantuan Rube Goldberg contraptions for splitting the atom artificially. At Berkeley Ernest Lawrence was developing a 5000-ton cyclotron that could accelerate particles up to the astronomical speeds needed to pierce the atom. A pair of Englishmen, Cockcroft and Walton, were already operating the world's first particle accelerator.

The political cauldron was aboil that year too.

The neutron had been discovered in February 1932. Within the next twelve months Franklin D. Roosevelt was elected President of the United States and Germany's Weimar Republic collapsed.

Adolf Hitler assumed the reins of the Third Reich on January 30, 1933. Shortly afterward the Nazis staged a series of bully-boy rallies at certain universities.

In Kiel club-wielding Brown Shirts marched across the canal to the University one chill February day. Nazi students had called them in to help enforce a strike to lower tuition fees. The Brown Shirts strutted around the campus, shouting obscenities at the professors and cracking a few heads for good measure. Then they spotted Emil Julius Klaus Fuchs.

He was barely twenty-one and studying at Kiel for his physics degree. A Communist sympathizer, he was chairman of a student political group that had sought to infiltrate the campus Nazi organization. Some months back he had played a wrong card by gaining the Nazis' confidence, then informing on them after they had laid their plans for the strike. It was a Nazi student who pointed Fuchs out to the Brown Shirts. One of them struck him across the face, knocking his glasses off. They could have lynched him then and there, as they had others. Instead they pummeled Fuchs halfheartedly, then picked him up by his skinny hands and legs and heaved him into the icy Kiel Canal.

It was the humiliation that finally welded Klaus Fuchs to

21

Communism, militantly and irrevocably.

Some mornings later he rose early, took a train to Berlin and joined the Communist "underground." The Party advised him to leave the country and serve the cause from abroad. Seven months later Fuchs showed up in England, pale, famished, with a bundle of dirty laundry in a canvas bag.

Ever since Fuchs was born, the youngest child in a family of four, he had known a Spartan existence as the son of an itinerant Lutheran pastor who shuttled from one impoverished parish to another on the outskirts of Frankfurt. He grew up in a sheltered world of his father's making, his only boyhood friends his two older sisters and brother.

The fact that his father switched to Quakerism and became an outspoken pacifist in a land of militarists didn't help Fuchs enjoy a particularly happy childhood. Soldiers' sons razzed and taunted him. He was the anemic, studious type, always getting pushed around at school by the bigger boys. Life at home, under the hand of a righteous but uncompromising patriarch, was equally grim. It's doubtful that the timid Fuchs and his puritanical father ever enjoyed a really close relationship.

At eighteen, at the University of Leipzig, Fuchs joined a liberal organization opposed to the Nazis, who were already then, in 1930, a growing political force in Germany. He also made his first break with his father by joining the Reichsbanner, a semimilitary group designed to defend the liberals in case of violence by the Nazis. This was heresy for a boy reared in pacifism. But Fuchs had become disillusioned with pacifism. He did not think it was the answer to the abuses of the Brown Shirts. Since his earliest school days Fuchs had observed it was most often his Communist schoolmates who stood up to the young Nazi bullies. When his father moved the family to Kiel in 1931, Fuchs resumed his studies at the university there and offered himself as a speaker to the campus Communist Party.

From there the road led to his beating at the hands of the Brown Shirts, and to England.

In 1934 Europe's scientist of the year was Enrico Fermi. At his laboratory in the University of Rome the indefatigable farmer's grandson used Chadwick's powerful neutron to bombard and splinter a host of new radioactive elements from the nucleus of a uranium atom, then thought to be the most impregnable matter existing.

Fermi not only succeeded in his daring experiment; he had unwittingly split the atom and struck the first sparks of chain reaction. He had in effect created a sort of miniature atomic bomb.

Like Columbus, though, he failed to recognize the import of his achievement. The laws of physics and the most venerated scientists of the day had decreed that the uranium atom could not be split. Though Fermi had released valuable new radioactive components, he was unaware that he had fractured the atom. It would be almost another five years before those components had been isolated, identified and marked for eventual use in the first atomic bomb.

Though Fermi had dislodged valuable new radioactive elements from the atom's nucleus, it would be another five years before his experiment had been certified for what it was and the newly released elements isolated, identified and marked for eventual use in the first atomic weapon built by man.

The Nazi vise was crushing freedom throughout Germany and beyond by the mid-1930's. Scientists across the Continent began to feel its cruel clamp. In Italy, Mussolini's Black Shirts had begun pressuring individualists of every hue to lock-step with the Fascist state. Everywhere the Jews had become special targets.

Emilio Segrè, a wispy little physicist who had participated in the Fermi experiment, decided it was time to leave his beloved Palermo. Bruno Rossi, a Jewish physics professor at the University of Padua, sadly pulled up stakes. At the University of Munich a tousled genius named Hans Bethe realized he would be unable to retain his teaching post under the Nazis. Fermi and his wife, Laura, finally said good-by to Rome.

The United States, to its eternal good fortune, became the sanctuary for these and many more scientists from abroad.

One, a Hungarian named Leo Szilard, worried that the rash of new discoveries on the Continent might tempt evil minds. In Berlin, Otto Hahn and Fritz Strassman had refined Fermi's discovery and fired the uranium atom into two fragments liberating the combined energy of 200 million electron volts. Proportionately it was the greatest man-made explosion yet.

The atom had been conclusively split, atomic fission achieved. The scientists had tapped a source of energy 3 million times greater than that released by burning coal; an explosive force 20 million times greater than TNT.

Szilard feared what a Hitler in control of such power might do. Even as some scientists proclaimed that atomic energy could be released in great quantities, Szilard was cautioning his colleagues in Europe to impose self-censorship on the publication of their discoveries. At the same time, it was apparent to him that friendlier governments ought to be apprised of the new energy's military potential.

The United States seemed the logical nation to approach.

Although England was already investigating the possibilities of transforming atomic power to military use, the war that now threatened Europe would soon tax to the utmost England's industrial might.

Many European scientists had already fled to America.

Much to their disillusionment, they had encountered a curtain of complacency and indifference there. America was far from the war clouds, its scientists still more concerned with the abstract wonders of the atom than with its military potential.

Early in 1939, for example, Fermi got a mild reaction from the Navy Department. He had left his atom-smashing experiments at Columbia to go down to Washington and explain to the admirals the possibilities of using uranium as a powerful new explosive. Intriguing, nodded the admirals. Don't call us, we'll call you. That day Hitler's troops carved up Czechoslovakia into German protectorates. And within a week the Nazis had halted all further sales of ore from Europe's richest uranium source, Czechoslovakia's Joachimsthal mines.

Szilard knew it was time for direct action. He enlisted Albert Einstein's support in drafting a letter to President Roosevelt.

The letter, which Roosevelt finally saw a month after World War II had started, stated that chain reaction—the multiplying sequence of exploding atoms—could now almost certainly be induced artificially; that chain reaction could lead to the construction of an awesomely powerful bomb; and that the President should promptly assign some eminent personage to co-ordinate the requirements for such a weapon with the U.S. defense establishment.

Roosevelt moved swiftly. The immediate crisis was one of getting raw materials to build the bomb. Vital uranium sources were drying up all over the world as the war enveloped one nation after another. In all America in 1939 there was less than an ounce of metallic uranium.

F. D. R. appointed an advisory committee to contact the Belgians and see if the United States could lay claim to the rich uranium-ore deposits of Katanga Province in the Congo. Roosevelt himself, however, was preoccupied with

25

the international crisis and could not devote his personal attention to the uranium problem. Those around him lacked the scientific acumen to grasp the urgency of the situation. The advisory committee was allowed to move at an amble.

At year's end a beginning had been made. But it was a halting and uncertain one.

The pace quickened throughout 1940.

Two questions puzzled Washington and London: Could an atomic bomb be a decisive weapon in war? And what were the Germans doing in this field?

Exiles from Europe brought disquieting reports that the residue of physicists left in Germany were already at work on the bomb. There was feverish research activity at the Kaiser Wilhelm Institute in Berlin. The Germans were evincing interest in certain chemical plants in Norway and in uranium deposits in Portugal.

In America newly alerted physicists sought the key to chain reaction: a light uranium atom that would fission and explode more easily than the heavier atom known as uranium-238 (U-238).

They found the key at the University of Minnesota. There experiments isolated and determined that uranium-235 (U-235) was the rare atom that would, if correctly concentrated, produce a chain reaction. The energy released by exploding U-235 would, compared to that of TNT, be like an elephant's to an ant's. Clearly, enough of it in one weapon could make an atomic bomb decisive in war.

The only trouble was the scarcity of U-235. There wasn't enough around then to explode a hand grenade, much less a bomb. The stuff would have to be meticulously separated from the more available U-238, which itself had to be laboriously extracted from the precious uranium ore. At the moment, uranium ore was a devilishly elusive item.

26

Happily, the United States had a sagacious friend i director of Belgium's Union Minière du Haut Katanga, own ers of the vast Shinkolobwe uranium mine in the Congo. In August 1940, with the Germans overrunning his own country, Edgar Sengier instructed the mine to quietly ship to New York 1200 tons of high-grade ore under a cover name. The ore, packed in 2000 steel drums, left by freighter that October from Port Lobito in Portuguese Angola.

U.S. authorities were notified of the shipment, but somehow the notification records were mislaid. For two years the uranium lay undiscovered in a Staten Island warehouse.

Three events brightened the picture in 1941.

Chemists at Berkeley isolated an artificial element, plutonium, that would fission even better than U-235. The discovery meant that the United States might eventually be able to mass-produce the new element for an atomic weapon without relying on the tortuous process of gleaning bits of U-235 from raw uranium.

Next, Vannevar Bush, a spry Bostonian with a roguish twinkle, turned his talents as head of the Carnegie Institution to organizing American science for the challenge ahead. Impatient with the pace of Roosevelt's uranium advisory committee, he persuaded F. D. R. to appoint him the head of the new high-powered Office of Scientific Research and Development, with wide-ranging authority across the entire government spectrum. Bush immediately began jacking up the uranium project by improving the quality of scientific personnel involved and introducing first security measures. From now on, no scientific report on uranium research would be published in the U.S.

Late that summer Britain's prestigious M.A.U.D. Committee issued its long-awaited report. The M.A.U.D. Committee comprised the elite of Britain's scientists. Technically, its initials stood for Military Application of Uranium Detonation, but the more familiar name "Maud" derived from a message that Niels Bohr had sent months before from Denmark to a Miss Maud Ray, the Bohr family governess in Kent. The M.A.U.D. Committee had been trying since 1939 to determine whether an atomic bomb was possible. Their report's conclusion:

The bomb *was* possible. Indeed, it would be a decisive weapon. Construction should begin without further delay. Even if the war ended before the bomb was ready, the effort would not be wasted. No nation in the future could risk being caught without such a weapon.

Present at the top-secret M.A.U.D. Committee meeting which led to Britain's conclusion that the bomb could and should be built was a mild-mannered Harvard physics professor who would one day direct the world's first atomic bomb test.

Kenneth Tompkins Bainbridge stood at the back of the tiny room in London's Burlington House while the peers of British science sat around a large rectangular table and discussed the bomb in low, matter-of-fact tones. Bainbridge listened attentively. He was there on a secret mission from Washington, ostensibly to survey Britain's radar development, but also, with British co-operation, to gather information on their progress with atomic energy. Under his Back Bay tweeds he wore a special money belt for carrying his notes.

Within minutes Bainbridge was aware that the British already had a better than fair idea of how to make an atomic bomb. Unlike the Americans, they had honed their research to a point where they could talk credibly of the size, shape and method of assembling the bomb. They believed it was possible to build one within three years—but only with the most intense effort. Bainbridge detected a quaver of urgency as the scientists turned to him and quietly acknowledged that

Britain would probably be unable to undertake the effort herself. The nation was already fully mobilized for war and German bombing raids were wreaking havoc with her industry. The United States was in a far better position to launch the bomb project.

Bainbridge lingered after the meeting to jot down some notes. He tucked them into his money belt, then headed immediately for the American Embassy. There, in the Navy code room, he prepared a report on the British meeting for transmittal to Washington. Several days later Vannevar Bush and other U.S. leaders learned of Britain's decision on the bomb.

The news had a stirring effect in Washington, where Bush was striving to jolt the U.S. scientific community into recognizing the military significance of the bomb. But even Britain's optimism didn't completely cure some of the hesitancy Bush found in his own back yard.

His deputy, James Conant, was quite unconvinced that a crash effort on uranium research for a weapon not even on the drawing boards was in the best national interest. Conant, whose Harvard charges sometimes wondered whatever had become of their busy president, had argued with Bush that perhaps the project should be shelved for the duration of the war in favor of more immediately practical defense programs. Conant was finally brought around when scientific colleagues assured him that the idea of building a bomb was not only sound but essential if the Allies wanted to prevent Germany from getting the weapon first.

As 1941 drew to a close the progress report seemed discouraging: no chain reaction had been made; no appreciable amount of U-235 had been separated from U-238; only minute amounts of the new plutonium had been produced, and chemists feared it would take years to perfect a

29

method of producing it in bulk. Everything else was in the discussion stage.

Still, there had been obvious momentum. Men in high places had begun for the first time to scrutinize engineering problems, cost and time schedules. Most important, the bomb itself had been lifted from the depths of wishful thinking to the realm of practical consideration. Its construction was now possible. Was it *feasible?*

On Saturday morning, December 6, the nucleus of the project planners met in Bush's P Street headquarters in Washington. The President, they were told, had appointed them to a special "S-1" Committee to discover whether, and at what cost, the United States could make the bomb. S-1 was to report back to Roosevelt in six months.

The following day the United States was at war with Japan.

The scientists badly needed a Delphic Oracle in 1942.

The S-1 Committee reported back to Roosevelt on time. Their recommendation: a crash program, an all-out effort of staggering magnitude that would initially cost upward of $100 million and might produce a bomb by July 1944.

The recommendation was accepted, and the United States was at last engaged in the hideously complex exercise of determining the best way to build an atomic bomb. Now great uncertainty plagued the planners.

The business of gauging the fastest, most efficient way to build the bomb was like a game of blindman's buff played in the dark. The more the scientists worked to sophisticate their various methods for producing the bomb's nuclear material, the more perplexed they were as to the right method to use. The nagging question was: How much uranium or plutonium will the bomb require? Or, simply, how big do we build it?

Cyclotrons whirred at Berkeley. Nuclear reactors—

"piles"—mounted like pyramids at Chicago and Columbia. Cosmic equations and theoretical enigmas taxed the most inventive brains at Harvard, Princeton and other campuses. Bolstered by fresh research effort, estimates on the bomb's destructive power rose from an originally puny 600 tons to the equivalent of 2000 tons of TNT. That still didn't solve the questions of how much nuclear material would be needed and what the quickest way was to get it.

In September 1942, when Brigadier General Leslie Groves took over the newly designated "Manhattan Project," he was certain that never in history had so many embarked on so fateful an undertaking with so little certainty about how to proceed. The only solution seemed to be to charge ahead on a number of fronts and, by elimination, arrive at the production process that held the most promise.

Thus the Manhattan Project found that its immediate mission was to start the full-scale design and construction of three different types of separation plants, as well as at least one, and probably more, plutonium-producing reactors. The entire complex of separation plants eventually would be located at a spot called Oak Ridge in Tennessee. Here the elusive U-235 would be sifted from U-238 and processed for use in a nuclear weapon. At Hanford, Washington, the Manhattan engineers would appropriate a vast domain of acreage to construct a series of reactors that hopefully would produce the new element of plutonium in large quantities. Manpower—scores of thousands of technicians—would be needed to operate this sprawling empire.

That was quite an order for the Army Engineer Corps, into whose hands the Manhattan Project had been thrust. Its ultimate mission was to build a new weapon of war, the atomic bomb. In General Groves the Army thought it had rather a formidable weapon to start with.

* * *

He never would have been mistaken for a George Patton or a Douglas MacArthur. Not at first glance anyway.

Leslie Richard Groves was a paunchy, five-foot eleven-inch desk officer who had never led troops in battle, had worn lieutenant's bars for fifteen years before moving up the promotion ladder, and had been appointed to the provisional rank of colonel only since the outbreak of war. He sported a funny little mustache and had a handshake like a dead fish. At West Point he'd been nicknamed "Greasy."

His campaigns had been fought in Fort Benning, Georgia; Brownsville, Texas; Fort Leavenworth, Kansas; and in Delaware, Missouri, Hawaii and Nicaragua. In Nicaragua he'd been awarded a gold medal of merit from the president for repairing the waterworks of an earthquake-stricken village. Wiseacres called it Groves's "banana medal." He wore it proudly. Groves's entire career, in fact, ever since he graduated fourth in his class from "The Point," had been in the Engineer Corps. He was a bricks-and-mortar, rivers-and-harbors man. And the Manhattan Project, he was soon to discover, was far more than that.

Groves, however, had several qualities that were the stuff of MacArthurs and Pattons. He could be ruthlessly single-minded in accomplishing an objective. As deputy chief of construction for the Engineers, he had knocked heads and bulled through red tape to build the multimillion-dollar Pentagon in record time. He had had to meld "by-the-book" officers and clock-watching civilians into a smoothly functioning work force to do it. He had learned from the experience how to deal with stubborn contractors, sloppy designers, temperamental industrialists and carping politicians.

From his forebears Groves had inherited other leadership traits. His French ancestors (Le Gros) had bequeathed him a bit of noblesse and a sense of compassion which, however gruffly administered, could at the right time bolster a colleague or subordinate in distress. From his English ances-

32

tors, who had left the Isle of Jersey to settle in
Massachusetts, came an appropriate streak of pur
(Groves was a virtual teetotaler and rarely, i
smoked). His father, an Army chaplain who had served
parishes from Albany, New York, to Peking, China, combined the best of these characteristics, added a dollop of
barracks toughness, and passed the whole package on to his
son. Groves developed one other trait on his own. "He has,"
noted an admirer, "the most impressive ego since Napo-
leon."

Reluctantly Groves accepted command of the Manhattan
Project. He had already put in three years in Washington
and looked forward to troop duty overseas. Furthermore, he
was unimpressed by what he knew about the bomb project.
Within a month, however, he was riding the job with
gusto.

Mindful of possible espionage, Groves lowered a curtain
of secrecy over the project. No longer would atomic power
and the bomb be discussed openly. There would be no
repetition of the incident of a Senator innocently taking the
floor of Congress to discuss the economic perils of atomic
energy. The era of censorship and the code had arrived. The
next thing Groves did was to survey the critical uranium
situation. He dispatched scouts to scour the country for
whatever uranium could be found. A deputy located the
1200 tons of Union Minière ore in the Staten Island warehouse and arranged for its purchase on the spot.

As his first major personnel move, the General hired
Robert Oppenheimer to direct the laboratory that would
build the bomb.

As early as 1941, when he was first brought in contact
with the bomb project, Oppenheimer had been mulling over
the scatter-shot approach of the scientific community. It
seemed illogical for the Allies to undertake such a project

33

without co-ordinating the dozen or more laboratories operating throughout the United States, England and Canada. Confusion and duplication would result if they didn't.

Oppenheimer saw the answer in the establishment of one laboratory center under a single director where the bomb could be built collectively by theoretical and experimental physicists, mathematicians, ordnance experts, metallurgists, chemists, radiologists and all the other specialists needed for the task. The idea found support and was adopted. Oppenheimer seemed the logical man to head the new center.

He appeared to be temperamentally fitted for the job. If Los Alamos was to be under an Army chain of command and a general with a Napoleonic complex, it would need a technical director who understood the subtle temperaments and prejudices of the scientists, one who could act as a filter between them and the military. Such a man was Oppenheimer. He had matured from the precocious exhibitionist of Göttingen days into a more reflective and temperate human. Of all the physicists he seemed uniquely able to sympathize with the quirks, and ease the distresses of, the scientific ego.

There were liabilities. Oppenheimer was a theorist with no background in the experimental physics so important to the bomb project. Curiously, although he had always in his growing days been interested in all problems of the microcosm, the one subject that had never particularly captured his fancy had been nuclear fission. Also, Oppenheimer lacked administrative experience. Nor was he a Nobel laureate, an eminence jealously flaunted by those scientists who were. Finally, he had a bothersome record of Communist associations.

Shuttling between his teaching jobs at Berkeley and Pasadena in the early 1930's, Oppenheimer had quietly enhanced his stature within the community of scientists, artists and classicists on the West Coast. Oblivious to all but his

34

work and family, he had submerged himself in an orgy of self-culture. He mastered Sanskrit and added it to his roster of languages. At weekly poetry readings he familiarized himself with the Indian poets Kalidasa and Bhartrihari. He absorbed Hindu philosophy through the writings of the *Mahabharata.*

Oppenheimer lived detached from the contemporary scene. He spent his summers riding near the secluded family ranch in New Mexico. He showed no interest in politics or economics, never read a newspaper or current magazine, and owned no radio or telephone. Long after the event, he had learned of the stock-market crash. Though the Depression's impact on him personally was negligible—his father, a successful textile merchant, had seen to it that young Oppenheimer always had sufficient economic means—its demoralizing effect on Oppenheimer's students and friends left a sobering impression on the young intellectual. In 1936 Oppenheimer voted for the first time in a Presidential election. That year he took a closer look at the world around him. He was appalled by the treatment of Jews in Germany. He smoldered at reports of Nazi oppression and later helped arrange the exodus to the United States of various relatives living in Germany.

For the first time Oppenheimer began to understand how deeply political and economic events affect men's lives. He began to feel the need to shed his isolation and participate in civic and community affairs. It was not that easy an adjustment, however. Having no real framework of political conviction or experience to give him perspective, he became a political empiricist.

Oppenheimer grew close to a girl named Jean Tatlock, a member of the Communist Party. Through her Oppenheimer met other Communists and fellow travelers. He himself began traveling along the periphery of Communism: attending Communist study groups in Berkeley; becoming

35

red with Communist-infested labor unions and teach-
nions and various committees for "Democracy," "Intellectual Freedom," "Friends of the Chinese People," etc. He joined several Communist-supported causes, like the Spanish Loyalist movement, which were fashionable among the political dissidents he associated with in that period. For Oppenheimer the involvement was mostly one of sponsorship and financial contribution rather than of soulful dedication. It would prove a very transient but costly flirtation.

Oppenheimer never joined the Communist Party. Nor did he accept its dogma or theory, although he did not then regard it as a dangerous force. Indeed, he found some of the Communists' declared objectives desirable. But whatever relationship he had with the Party was a muddled one. For Oppenheimer in those days had no clearly formulated political views of his own. All he knew was that he hated tyranny in every form.

Oppenheimer got the nod from Groves because in the end his obvious assets outweighed the liabilities, and because no better scientist was available for the job. He proved the wiseness of Groves's choice in the way he handled his first test, persuading his colleagues to forsake their comfortable university jobs for the uncertainties of Los Alamos.

In 1940 he had left Jean Tatlock and married Katherine Pewning Harrison, an attractive dark-haired divorcée who also had a Communist background. He bought her a house on Eagle Hill in Berkeley and settled down to raise a family.

Meanwhile he was thoroughly exploring every theoretical facet of the bomb. He was already fashioning methods that would later be used in extracting uranium for the weapon. In the summer of 1942 he convened a top-flight study group at Berkeley. It discussed in detail every physical problem facing the bomb makers. The problem that especially fascinated Oppenheimer was how large a nuclear package would be needed to cause an atomic explosion.

That happened to be the chief problem then occupying the waking hours of Klaus Fuchs across the Atlantic.

Like Oppenheimer, Fuchs had developed an ingrown hatred of all types of repression. He was especially resentful of any sort of authority or regimentation. His prejudices had been shaped by his experiences with the Nazis and, curiously, with the British.

After the Jews, the Communists and socialists with their politically hostile tenets had become special targets of the Nazi movement. People like the Fuchses were considered potential enemies of the Nazi state and relentlessly persecuted. Fuchs's mother had committed suicide out of despair. His father had finally been arrested for his outspoken views and sent to a concentration camp. One sister, unhinged by fear that the Nazis had caught and tortured her Communist husband, had thrown herself in front of a train. Other relatives had been hounded out of Germany.

Fuchs arrived in Britain in 1934 at the age of twenty-one, and the only two pursuits that seemed to promise any future stability were his physics and Communism. For the next six years he lived the uneventful life of a research scholar. He immersed himself in studies at Bristol, then at Edinburgh University. Along the way he acquired several doctorate degrees and a reputation as a brilliant young physicist with a computer brain. Fuchs had also acquired a self-confidence that was already transforming itself into an arrogance capable of defying society and its accepted rules of conduct. Subconsciously, even then, he was striving to overcome the bonds of conformism and become an individual totally independent of the surrounding forces of society.

After the Nazis attacked France and the Low Countries in

May 1940, the British shipped Fuchs to an internment camp in Canada. Hitler's invasion of Britain loomed and Fuchs was still classified as an enemy alien, an irony heightened by the insults which he and other German refugees endured from a chauvinistic British officer en route to Canada. In the camp on the Heights of Abraham outside Quebec, Fuchs became second in command of a Communist cell. By the time he returned to England in early 1941 to accept a position with Professor Rudolf Peierls at Birmingham University, Fuchs's embitterment with the country which had sheltered him from Nazi persecution was total.

Fuchs began work with Dr. Peierls in May 1941. He concentrated on calculating the nuclear size of the bomb. He learned everything about the gaseous-diffusion process, a method of separation the Americans were studying. Within a month, he had contacted the Soviet Embassy in London and offered his services as a spy.

That was June, when the Nazis invaded Russia. Fuchs was obsessed with the notion that the Western Allies would deliberately allow Russia and Germany to fight each other to the death. He believed in the wisdom of Russia's policy and the holiness of its leaders. He was now ideologically a man without a country, a devoted Communist with no other allegiance. In August 1942 Fuchs became a naturalized British citizen. A dusty report in Scotland Yard files about his Communist days in Kiel was overlooked. Britain at war could not afford to pass up the services of so competent a young physicist. As a bona-fide citizen Fuchs would not be subject to the harassments of British security.

By the end of 1942 Fuchs had met four times with his Soviet contact in London and turned over to him reports of his work on atomic energy.

On a wintry day that same year Groves and Oppenheimer drove into the piney hills north of Santa Fe, New Mexico, to inspect a site for the laboratory Oppenheimer would soon head. One of Groves's deputies had carefully picked a spot near Jemez Springs, an isolated mountain village narrowly ringed with rugged canyons. But it was too constricting for the project Groves envisioned. The site was vetoed.

Instead the party drove eastward over nearly impassable roads toward a mesa named after the cottonwoods that covered it: Los Alamos. Suddenly Oppenheimer recalled a rustic boys' school he had often spied during pack trips from his family ranch nearby. They rounded a bend in the road and came upon a dozen boys playing soccer in the snow. Groves ordered the driver to circle the premises as inconspicuously as possible.

A month later, over the heartbroken protests of the headmaster, the Army took possession of the Los Alamos Ranch School and the 54,000 acres surrounding it. The land, it was explained, was needed for a "demolition range."

That December, all over the United States, scientists began to feel the first faint tugs toward the new laboratory aborning in the southwest.

In New York, physicists in their basement workrooms at Columbia were told to begin quietly packing their spectrographs and other equipment for transfer to a destination unknown. In Chicago, where Fermi had just gained fresh laurels (and the code name "Italian Navigator") for initiating the world's first man-made chain reaction, scientists summoned their colleagues from the outside, pledged them to secrecy and asked them in hushed tones to join a mysterious fraternity engaged on something known only as "the gadget."

In Berkeley, physicist Emilio Segrè, an enemy alien like Klaus Fuchs, sat down with his wife after dinner and brought out a map of the United States. As aliens, the Segrès obeyed a strict 6 P.M. curfew and stayed home every night. For some time they had feared they might even be interned. Half in jest Emilio asked his wife, "Where shall we hide?" He shut his eyes and dropped his finger on the map. It landed on New Mexico. "Let's go here," Segrè chuckled.

So it came to pass.

III

Los Alamos, 1943–44

THE WORLD had little to smile at as 1943 dawned. Britain had survived the blitz of 1940; the Germans had not invaded the isle. The Allies had successfully invaded North Africa and were giving Rommel a fight. But elsewhere the picture was still desperately grim. France had fallen; so had Corregidor. Europe was under the boot of the Hun. The Nazis were deep in Russia, their bombers still smashing at Britain.

The United States was at war with three nations on land and sea, with its naval forces not yet recovered from the disaster of Pearl Harbor. The Japanese had conquered the Philippines and threatened to overrun Southeast Asia. The Germans had barely begun to suffer the reverses that would turn the tide of war against them.

Their scientists had an eighteen-month head start on what was believed to be a concerted effort to build an atomic bomb. The race was on, and a nation kept in ignorance knew nothing of the question haunting its leaders: Could the U.S. beat Hitler to the Bomb?

The Germans had laid out a million and a half dollars for uranium research and supplies of special chemicals for plutonium-producing purposes. They had invested in cyclotrons and high-voltage apparatus. More than a score of their top scientists had been diverted to the program. Its code reference was 811-RFR-111.

The Nazis' activity had so alarmed Secretary of War

43

Stimson that he had voiced his fears to President Roosevelt early in February. Late that month the Allies moved to upset the Germans' time schedule.

Norwegian saboteurs in a daringly executed raid skied and snowshoed across the tundras of Telemark province to blow up 3000 pounds of heavy water at Norway's Norsk Hydro plant in Rjukan. The plant had been seized by the Nazis after Norway's fall in 1940. The Nazis, recognizing the possible value of heavy water to their atomic project, had increased its production. The saboteurs left it in ruins.

Other less violent rendezvous took place that same month in selected locations throughout the United States.

At the Underwater Explosives Research Laboratory in Woods Hole, Massachusetts, the director summoned to his office young Donald Hornig, a Harvard graduate student addicted to sailing and violin playing. The director escorted Hornig to a dingy attic in one of the labs and locked the door behind them.

"How would you like another job?" he asked the startled youth.

"What have I done wrong?"

"Nothing."

"What kind of a job?"

"Can't say."

"Well, where is it?"

"Can't say."

Hornig recalled that a lot of prominent scientists had disappeared from view lately. There was talk of a mysterious project somewhere west of the Mississippi. "East or West?" he asked.

The director shook his head. "Sorry, my lips are sealed," he said, and turned to leave. "Think it over and let me know in the morning."

Hornig didn't care for games. His answer was no. The following day his phone nearly jangled off the hook. James Conant called from Washington, asking Hornig what had gotten into him and didn't he know Uncle Sam needed his services. Other colleagues phoned to put on the pressure. That afternoon a long-distance call from George Kistiakowsky, an explosives expert, alerted Hornig to what was up. The call was from Albuquerque, New Mexico.

Suddenly things fell into place: the vanished scientists, the pressure from his colleagues, explosives, and Albuquerque. Hornig promptly changed his mind. Within two weeks he and his wife, Lilli, had sold their yawl and bought an ancient Ford with frayed tires. They loaded it with personal belongings and arranged for the rest of their household goods to be shipped after them. Then they pointed the Ford west and chugged off. Destination: Santa Fe.

In Rochester, New York, Dr. Stafford Warren, a shaggy-haired radiologist at the university, was invited to dine at a downtown club with a top Eastman Kodak official. Two Army officers joined them. After coffee the officers whisked Warren to a private room upstairs. While one of them locked the door and bolted the transom, the other checked the closet and bathroom and secured the window. For a full minute the officers said nothing, their ears cocked for eavesdroppers. Then the senior of the two, a one-star general, addressed Warren.

"Doctor," said General Groves, "we're asking you to come to work for the Government on a most important medical project." Groves vaguely outlined the "medical project" without once alluding to atomic matters. But Warren sensed the urgency of the General's mission. At the end of Groves's fifteen-minute exposition, Warren nodded. "When do I begin?" he asked.

Three weeks later Stafford Warren had become a consultant on radiation effects with the Manhattan Project. Shortly thereafter he and his wife entrained for New Mexico. Destination: Santa Fe.

In St. Louis, Los Angeles, Chicago and dozens of other cities, scientists received similar cloak-and-dagger approaches. Locked in attics, pinned down on park benches or trapped in empty rooms, they nodded consent one by one.

Kenneth Bainbridge got a mysterious call from Robert Oppenheimer to meet him at the National Academy of Sciences in Washington. Bainbridge flew down from Cambridge. As he and Oppenheimer strolled around the white-marbled Academy building on a crisp sunny day, Oppenheimer asked him bluntly if he would come and work at a new laboratory being formed in the Southwest.

Oppenheimer explained the urgency of the project, that the laboratory would be run from the top by an Army officer and that the scientists might even end up in uniform. Seeing Bainbridge's hesitancy, he whipped out a letter signed by General Groves and Dr. Conant attesting to the project's top priority. Bainbridge blinked and told Oppenheimer he wanted to think the matter over.

Some weeks later the professor packed his nine-year-old son into a 1939 Dodge sedan and headed west. His wife and two small daughters followed by train. The Bainbridges' destination: Santa Fe.

Once Oppie had told a friend: "My two great loves are physics and New Mexico. It's a pity they can't be combined."

Now, on a night in March 1943, aboard the New York-to-Chicago "Twentieth Century Limited," Oppenheimer found that facetious wish materializing. He was meeting with the busy Groves in the privacy of a Pullman compartment to plot the future of the new laboratory and of the bomb.

46

That night they hurtled through the inky darkness—general and scientist—toward a future neither could divine. The railroad tracks would lead them eventually beyond Chicago to Santa Fe.

The Royal City of the Holy Faith of Saint Francis could not have been a more improbable Mecca for the vanguard of the bomb builders.

Drowsed by four centuries of graceful, easy Spanish-Indian tradition, Santa Fe was a charming anachronism amid the war-boom fever of the rest of America. No neon signs cluttered its narrow streets. Its age and pace were mirrored in the seamed faces of Navajo grandmothers squatting amid their turquoise trinkets and cheap silver along the arcades of the old Governors' Palace.

But to Santa Fe in the spring of 1943 came the first of Oppenheimer's Army. They filtered in by twos and threes: bewildered, sleepless, irritated men who had sold their homes, deceived their friends and families, and deserted laboratories and students to sally forth to an unmentionable spot that might as well have been in the land of the yeti. They arrived in the old Spanish capital after hours and days of fighting crowded trains, missed planes and flat tires.

They found balm for their sagging spirits in the person of a sprightly, gray-haired matron named Dorothy McKibbin. Dorothy operated out of a cubbyhole command post in a senescent adobe dwelling marked by a single misplanned sign: U.S. ENG-RS (sic). Despite the modesty of her office, Dorothy functioned more grandly than any of the Spanish viceroys who used to inhabit the neighborhood. She was the Grover Whalen nonpareil of the Manhattan Project in Santa Fe, a one-woman American Express.

The new arrivals funneled through a wrought-iron gate, down a cobbled passageway overhung with carved beams and into a sunlit courtyard bordered by zinnias and squash

47

blossoms. At the far end, behind a blue-trimmed screen door, sat Dorothy. "You're expected," she would say with a smile. "Your driver is waiting." So would be mail, telegrams, phone calls, passes, furniture, laboratory equipment, lost relatives, pets or briefcases—just about anything a new arrival might be craving, including coffee and doughnuts—all carefully sorted and marked by Dorothy.

Her office at 109 East Palace would soon become a Shangri-la for every frustrated scientist and engineer who made his way to the strange new world of Los Alamos.

From Santa Fe the scientists were directed northward along a highway that sloped through sandy rolling country. The trucks with delicate laboratory equipment had to detour by a longer, smoother route via the sleepy junction of Espanola. But the most direct and picturesque passage to Los Alamos lay along the turnoff west from tiny Pojoaque.

It was a two-lane dirt job winding through a pastoral, almost Gallic setting—the road framed by poplars and willows, beyond them farmers tilling their fields with horse-drawn plows, and cows lazing in emerald pastures. Gallic, that is, except for the names on the post boxes: Trujillo, Montoya, Cristobal, etc. And the cow pastures backed against towering mesas streaked vermilion-gold in the late afternoon sun.

At the end of the road from Pojoaque lay Otowi and the Rio Grande, shriveled to a silty stream. Across the narrow railroad trestle spanning it rose the 7300-foot-high Parajito Plateau, site of Los Alamos. The final assault up its unpaved, boulder-strewn approach was a nightmare for all but the most iron-stomached. Bits of pumice clattered down the canyon walls and bounced off the sides of the sedans. The steep curves were barely navigable.

Only the vista from the summit rewarded the scientists who had reached their destination: rising westward, the

48

Jemez Mountains, richly forested with ponderosa pines that swept from sunny upland glades down to lush green basins with melodic names like Valle Grande and Valle Jaramillo; stretching southward from the Los Alamos Mesa to the Rio Grande far below, the huge fan of the Parajito Plateau, its rim scalloped by splendid canyons sliced in the soft yellow tuff by centuries of rain and melting snow; and beyond, to the east, the glistening peaks of the Sangre de Cristo range.

It should have been a paradise to build a bomb in. Initially it almost became a disaster area.

In mid-March, when Oppenheimer arrived with a handful of associates and their families at Los Alamos—code-named "Y" Site—laboratory buildings and temporary homes stood unfinished amid the slush of the winter's last snow. Families were forced to double up in Spartan log-cabin structures formerly used by the ranch-school boys. Many stayed in Santa Fe or were housed at nearby guest ranches. This necessitated transportation to and from the site. There weren't enough cars, and those available frequently broke down or had blowouts along the jagged trail up the Parajito.

Cooking and plumbing facilities were inadequate. Cafeteria service hadn't been installed at the working area, so box lunches were imported daily from Santa Fe. A wizened ham sandwich and a bowl of lukewarm chili during those first windy weeks on the mesa were gastronomical luxuries—when the car bringing them didn't collapse en route.

Telephone service was hopeless. Conversations between Los Alamos and Santa Fe were possible only over a Forest Service line. Even then, brief shouted instructions were about all one could get through. Lengthy discussions, even over such minor matters as procuring a special piece of equipment or medicine for a baby rash, required an eighty-mile round trip. Lilli Hornig took one look at the situation, and at the cheerless barracks that would be her first home on "The Hill," and burst into tears.

The scientists were impatient to get going and begin testing their equipment. The Army Engineers, however, were having trouble installing it. The construction contractor was beset with union headaches, unable to secure decent labor, and unwilling to allow the changes in building designs that some scientists sought to make on the spot. Frustrated, the scientists tried to take matters into their own hands and shear the military red tape. That only exacerbated feelings and heightened the confusion. The Army had its own way of doing things and no civilians would ever change it. It was the beginning of a long cold war between the "long-hairs" (Oppie's scientists) and the "plumbers" (Groves's engineers), as the two sides sneeringly called each other.

For a start, Los Alamos—top-secret "Y" Site of the Manhattan Project—hovered near chaos.

Only the urgency of the task ahead submerged the troubles that threatened to abort the new laboratory before its birth.

The very remoteness of Los Alamos—selected for its secrecy and distance from possible enemy air attack—was paramount to the scientists' purpose: to contemplate, without harassment, the nature of the new weapon; and to design its assembly and determine how to produce it—all in advance of receiving the vital nuclear components which would comprise its very soul. It was a horrendous undertaking, a bit like trying to manufacture a new automobile with no opportunity to test the engine beforehand.

Inside the heavily guarded military reservation, within a fenced enclosure called the "Technical Area," the scientists set to work on a multitude of mysteries, the most pressing of which was how to determine the "critical," or nuclear, size of the bomb: that precise point at which two nuclear masses, both "subcritical," could be joined to produce "criticality" —the chain reaction leading to atomic explosion.

It was about as easy as the first attempts to figure at what temperature water boils—only the Los Alamites were handling deadly material with no precedents to guide them. They must maneuver carefully enough to achieve the threshold they sought without inadvertently atomizing themselves in the process.

Controlling the atom-smashing neutrons was a thorny problem. Unless the two nuclear masses collided perfectly at the exact moment desired, they might dissolve each other prematurely in a shower of radioactive neutrons. Some way had to be found to shoot the two chunks together so fast there would be no time for them to predetonate.

The scientists hit first on the method of assembling the bomb like a gun. The object was to shoot one nuclear mass into another at a terrific speed, too fast to permit predetonation. It would not be easy to shoot the two projectiles on target. But the gun-assembly method seemed the most promising during those early days at Los Alamos.

While the assembly men attacked that problem, others began trying to gauge the damage an atomic bomb would cause. They studied the possible psychological and material effects of an atomic blast. For guidance they turned to the great explosions of history.

They pored over accounts of Krakatau, the volcanic isle off Java that blew itself into the sea in 1883, killing 36,000 persons. Its shock wave traveled halfway around the world and churned up a 50-foot-high tidal wave that rolled as far as Cape Horn. The blast was heard 3000 miles away. Four cubic miles of rock and pumice boiled into the atmosphere and brought on darkness for 16 hours. Three years later the volcanic ash was still circling the globe on wind currents, causing weird green suns and blood-red sunsets. Scientists estimated Krakatau's eruption was equal to a 10,000-megaton explosion.

In 1917 the munitions ship *Mont Blanc* had exploded in Halifax Harbor, Nova Scotia, killing 1100 persons and razing two square miles of the city. The shock was felt more than 150 miles away, windows were broken up to 60 miles away. The *Mont Blanc* carried 2600 tons of TNT and picric acid.

The Los Alamites, studying these and other explosive phenomena, realized that the atom bomb's force would fall somewhere between Krakatau and Halifax—hopefully a lot closer to Halifax, but just where they couldn't be sure.

By the summer of 1943 Groves's and Oppenheimer's original vision of Los Alamos as a neatly confined fortress for several-score bomb makers and their families had been shattered. The place was overrun with scientists.

They poured in from the Universities of California, Minnesota, Wisconsin, Chicago, Rochester, Illinois, from Stanford, Purdue, Princeton, Columbia, Harvard and M.I.T.; from the Bureau of Standards and the Carnegie Institution in Washington; from the Ballistics Research Laboratory in Aberdeen, Maryland; and from industrial firms and hospitals in New York, Delaware, St. Louis and points west.

Where once Los Alamos had rung to the shouts of asthmatic little scions with names like Lancelot Inglesby Pelly, it now reverberated with the guttural growls and animated babble of men with names like von Neumann, Teller, Fermi, Segrè, Ulam, Bethe and Rossi. They had come from Italy, Denmark, Hungary, Poland, Austria, Germany, and soon others would come from England.

To many of them, refugees from Fascist oppression, those early days at Site Y were a depressing reminder of concentration camps and stalags. The scientists lived in a world fenced off by barbed wire and guarded from the outside by pistol-packing Military Policemen. Their houses and laboratories were painted a dull uniform green. Everything they slept on or ate from bore the ugly stencil of "Government Issue." Most depressing of all were the security regulations.

Even as fellow physicists and their families were settling into Quonset huts at another atomic site clear across the country—a site code-named "X" and set in the oak-stippled hills of Tennessee—the rumors were beginning to fly.

The most natural question from an inquisitive public was: Why should all this talent and expensive equipment keep funneling into these two spots week after week, but nothing appear to come out? It must be another gigantic Government boondoggle, the citizens in each area reasoned, or else . . .

It was the "or else" syndrome that worried the security apparatus of the U.S. Government, which encouraged a smoke screen of phony stories to keep the public guessing. For a while the ruse was successful and quite a lot of fun.

People speculated that the scientists at Los Alamos and Oak Ridge were running: nudist colonies; homes for pregnant WAC's; Republican internment camps; or factories for producing, variously, windshield wipers for submarines, Roosevelt campaign buttons, wheels for miscarriages and the front ends of horses to be shipped to Washington for assembly. One nut showed up at Oak Ridge and said he understood the Vatican was being built there. He told the guards at the front gate he wanted to have a go at being the American Pope, and asked where could he apply for the job.

Such speculation was harmless. It was the more enlightened citizens—the ones who openly guessed that the scientists were building "something the size of a bushel basket

53

that could wipe out an entire city"—that scared Groves and the Counter Intelligence Corps agents under his jurisdiction. Such talk could spread.

Drastic steps were taken. Top scientists were assigned CIC agents (nicknamed "creeps") to shadow them whenever they left The Hill. The scientists were closely observed off and on the site. They were discouraged from maintaining social contacts with local people in Santa Fe or Albuquerque. Loose talk in a Santa Fe bar, or any other indiscretion, was promptly reported to the Los Alamos intelligence officer. Homes were "bugged" and more than one physicist was told to quit discussing his work with his wife.

Aliases were provided the better-known scientists. Enrico Fermi became "Eugene Farmer"; Niels Bohr arrived later as "Nicholas Baker"; Arthur Compton had two "covers," one for the East Coast, one for the West. The scientists got hopelessly mixed up and often forgot their aliases, much to the consternation of the CIC.

There were informal code names for the secret material and its processing: "top" for atom, "boat" for bomb, "topic boat" for atomic bomb, "urchin fashion" for uranium fission, "spinning" for smashing and "igloo of urchin" for isotope of uranium. The inner sanctums of the War Department and Los Alamos devised their own codes. Groves and Oppenheimer disguised proper names over the phone with a quadratic letter code that each man carried in his wallet.

All this had a mildly exciting James Bond flair compared to the chilling security laws that governed everyday life at Los Alamos.

There babies were born with no official homes, the only address on their birth certificates: "P.O. Box 1663, Santa Fe, New Mexico." Children were registered at school with no last names. Weddings occurred in a vacuum; the society pages in local papers carried not a line. Autos and trucks crashed in a vacuum; the accidents simply weren't recorded.

If a man went "psycho," it was safer to build him a special wing on the tiny hospital than to release him to the outside world. And men died in a vacuum; coroners were discouraged from filing detailed reports of the circumstances.

The most mundane aspects of life were tinged with secrecy. It was impossible to cash checks in nearby towns. Scientists were not allowed to maintain accounts in local banks. The work at Los Alamos was extra hazardous because of radiation danger, yet no one could take out new life-insurance policies. Nothing that would indicate the identities or whereabouts of the Los Alamites was permitted. Auto registrations, drivers' licenses, income-tax returns, insurance policies, food and gasoline rations—all were handled by a system of code numbers.

Certain words like "physicist" and "Los Alamos" were expunged from the scientists' vocabulary. They became nonwords, never to be spoken. Newspapers were cowed. When the *Albuquerque Journal* innocently reported that Los Alamos personnel had helped fight a forest fire in the Jemez hills, the editor was harshly reprimanded by security agents. Censorship was rigid. Telephone calls were monitored. Incoming letters were steamed open, examined and forwarded to their addressees. Outgoing letters were sent unsealed, and often they were blue-penciled and returned to their senders because of "objectionable" passages. Fermi, while on a trip, enclosed a strand of hair in a letter he wrote his wife at Los Alamos. When she opened it, the hair was gone.

Security was especially fearsome for the soldiers entrusted with Los Alamos' housekeeping chores. Retribution was swift for gabby GI's. It would come in the middle of the night in the barracks: a stabbing flashlight beam; a tap on the shoulder; the brusque order to dress and pack a duffel bag; a three-hour plane flight to an embarkation port near San Francisco; then banishment to any one of a dozen

Pacific atolls behind the front lines, where the misfit would spend the duration of the war. No mention of the man's violation ever appeared on his service record. But the effect of his empty bunk next morning on his barracks mates was profound.

Rarely was the security apparatus skirted. Once a GI became critically ill and his parents were summoned from the East to be by his side. The resident CIC chief balked and insisted that the boy's family be kept off the site. An Army chaplain intervened. "The word of Man usually guides us here," he told the officer. "This time, Major, we'll use the word of God. The boy's parents stay." And they did.

Outside Los Alamos the need for strict secrecy was equally urgent and in some respects more difficult to realize.

During that summer of 1943 Roosevelt fretted that the Nazis were pulling away from the United States in the race for the bomb. In Washington, Stimson was having the devil's own time keeping the security lid fastened. The Justice Department was threatening a lawsuit against the du Pont Company, which was then carrying a sizable burden of the bomb work. Labor leaders were talking of organizing some of the project's laboratories. Secretary of the Treasury Henry Morgenthau was raging because apparently no one thought him "fit to be trusted with the secret" of how a special deposit of $20 million in Treasury funds was to be spent.

Worse, a nosy Senator named Harry Truman wanted to inspect a 430,000-acre Government installation at Hanford, Washington, where some strange machines called "piles" were heating up the Columbia River. Stimson phoned the Senator. "It's part of a very important secret development," he explained.

"You won't have to say another word to me," replied Truman, and the inspection was dropped.

One potential but not too worrisome security problem appeared on the horizon that summer.

In mid-August, Roosevelt and Churchill signed a secret agreement at Quebec, pledging collaboration on the bomb project and an interchange of high-level American and British scientists. The agreement was an attempt to soften Britain's resentment at being gradually excluded from the project while the Americans, borrowing British theoretical know-how, produced the bomb on their own. British scientists at Los Alamos and Oak Ridge would soon become privy to the secrets of America's atomic bomb—"Projectile S-1-T." Among the scientists who would shortly arrive in the United States under the Quebec Agreement was Klaus Fuchs.

As fall approached Los Alamos swelled further.

The Army-style barracks, tar-papered dormitories, prefabs, hutments and trailers were bursting at the seams. Scores of new arrivals were shunted to a resort lodge at the bottom of a canyon fourteen miles away. In Santa Fe, Dorothy McKibbin fielded more than a hundred phone calls a day and dispatched daily to The Hill about sixty-five persons, two vanloads of furniture and at least one truck full of laboratory equipment. Harvard's mighty cyclotron, secretly disassembled and shipped west, arrived in Santa Fe. So did two Van de Graaff generators from Wisconsin and an accelerator from Illinois. From the Santa Fe railhead they were trucked to the top of the mesa. Temporary wooden lab buildings were hastily thrown up to house them.

The auto situation was still chaotic. Security agents embarked on a buying spree in local used-car lots. They rounded up every serviceable car and station wagon they could find. Each day the motley fleet dispersed—like the Paris taxicabs at the second battle of the Marne—to rescue scientists stranded at nearby ranches or to pick up equipment waiting in Santa Fe.

The influx showed no signs of abating. Scientists kept pouring into Los Alamos: detonator experts and explosives specialists; men like Marshall Holloway and young Louis Slotin, who would perform the deadly critical assembly chores; and a Navy captain named William "Deacon" Parsons, who would arm the first uranium bomb en route to Hiroshima. His wife showed up in a red convertible with two blonde daughters and a golden cocker spaniel named "Toby."

In the mélange of physicists, engineers, officers and GI's flooding the mesa, confusion became the great leveler. A benighted GI bumped into an elderly visitor wandering around the corridors of one of the laboratories. The scientist was lost and looking for the men's room. The GI led him to the right door, saluted and said, "Private Gray at your service, sir." The old gentleman smiled and shook hands. "Einstein," he murmured. "Thank you."

Meanwhile the vanguard of Oppie's army hammered out research schedules and held weighty conferences at Y Site. Though no significant amounts of plutonium were expected from the Hanford "piles" for at least a year, it was decided that Los Alamos would do the final purifying to make the plutonium suitable for weapons use. A purification plant would have to be built. Additionally, a host of physics experiments had to be performed to determine the bomb's design. The plant and the experiments required space. More timber was felled and new roads were bulldozed to the new sites.

Amid all this fever a letter arrived from Roosevelt to cheer the scientists on. It expressed the President's deep gratitude for their willingness to accept their task in the face of considerable danger and personal sacrifice. "Whatever

58

the enemy may be planning," wrote F.D.R., "American science will be equal to the challenge. With this thought in mind, I send this note of confidence and appreciation."

Two other items lifted spirits in October 1943. The first fragile bits of experimental plutonium arrived from Hanford, and Niels Bohr escaped the Germans.

The great Dane was the idol of many of the scientists at Los Alamos. He was known abroad as a warm and lively colleague, a masterful teacher imbued with oracular powers when it came to physics. Now, with the Nazis occupying his country and threatening his arrest, Bohr had fled Copenhagen to Sweden aboard a fishing smack. An infant granddaughter followed in a diplomat's shopping basket.

From Sweden the British flew Bohr to England. They put him in the bomb rack of an unarmed Mosquito, gave him flares and a parachute, and told him that if the plane was attacked, he would be promptly removed from the danger —the bomb rack would simply be opened and he'd be dumped into the North Sea. Bohr must have been relieved that this didn't happen. The Mosquito had to fly very high, and he had been given an oxygen mask and headgear with earphones for instructions. But the Royal Air Force hadn't reckoned with Bohr's enormous cranium. The gear wouldn't fit over his head and he never got any oxygen. He was unconscious when the plane reached England.

Niels Bohr was on his way to Los Alamos, however. He arrived there with the first members of the British mission in December.

Gun assembly had been the favored design for the bomb in 1943. The following year, though, the scientists began leaning toward a more revolutionary approach—*implosion.*

It wasn't that they distrusted the gun method of shooting

59

one subcritical nuclear chunk into another to produce an atomic explosion. That method involved ballistic principles with which the American scientists were familiar. A number of bombers, in fact, were already being modified to carry future weapons of this design. Though untested, the gun assembly was given a good chance of success as a combat performer.

Uranium-235 and plutonium were in woefully short supply, however, and the "gun" was an unwieldy design requiring wasteful amounts of nuclear material. It was not only inconvenient and time-consuming to have to modify B-29 bomb bays to fit the gun assembly's awkward cylindrical shape; it was also an extremely tricky business to fire nuclear projectiles at each other with the precision required for chain reaction. The threat of predetonation haunted the scientists. They turned to implosion in their uncertainty.

The idea of implosion was to take a subcritical nuclear hunk and surround it with explosive charges. The explosives would then be detonated *inward*—imploded—and would compress the hunk into a chain-reacting critical mass. A nuclear blast would occur because the shock waves from the explosives would converge inward, instead of dissipating outward, and concentrate their energy on the nuclear hunk. Thus, from the imploding explosives would come the nuclear explosion.

Although uranium from Oak Ridge would initially be more available than plutonium, the latter was considered a better nuclear material to use for implosion because it fissioned more readily than U-235. Plutonium would ensure a speedier reaction and less chance of predetonation. Its use would also require a smaller amount of nuclear material in the bomb. The spherical shape of the implosion design itself would enhance the bomb's explosive yield. From the viewpoint of economy and efficiency, implosion seemed the best bet.

What was needed now was a mechanism to focus the explosive shock wave on the nuclear hunk—an explosive lens that would act in principle like a glass lens. The scientists set about to manufacture some. By spring of 1944, when the first significant quantities of plutonium reached Los Alamos, implosion had replaced gun assembly as the preferred design for the bomb.

That June, hard on the heels of the Allied invading forces in Europe, a select band of Army intelligence agents and scientific consultants undertook a mission to learn the extent of Germany's progress on the bomb. Armed with Geiger counters and records of the whereabouts of all known German physicists and atomic research centers, the ALSOS mission rode into the Rhineland just behind the troops of Omar Bradley's First Army and the tanks of Patton's spearheading Third Army.

Even as the first implosion experiments rocked Los Alamos with their blasts, rumblings of a different sort swept the mesa. The cold war between the "long-hairs" and the "plumbers" had erupted anew.

Spring in the new community had brought little relief to home life. Nearly 5000 people had crowded onto the post and the baby population was soaring. The housing shortage was still acute. Fuel was a constant headache. There was no gas, and sooty coal had to be hauled in. Water was as scarce as ever. As the number of inhabitants went up, the level in the reservoirs went down. The faucets deposited almost more algae than water. Mothers howled over the mounting piles of unwashed diapers.

Bitterness smoldered against the lucky VIP scientists who had commandeered houses on "Bathtub Row" and who bathed in splendor, oblivious to the plight of the peons who lived in tubless abodes. Showers in the homes were no substitute and were, indeed, abominated by most wives.

Someone showed General Groves a scientific article which reported that men who take hot baths before bedtime became less fertile. If Groves would put bathtubs in all the houses, he'd make the wives happy, the men temporarily sterile—and solve the birth-rate problem.

Groves wasn't amused. The laboratory had grown like Topsy under him and it had been a disquieting experience. The general had foreseen a temporary wartime installation designed to build the atomic bomb, with no frills like bathtubs. A frugal man, he saw no point in constructing anything permanent—auditorium or church or officers' club. He didn't believe in coddling a bunch of civilians, no matter what their IQ's. They could lump it along with his officers and enlisted men.

Indeed, as boss of the Manhattan Project, Groves liked to think of the scientists under Oppenheimer as superior junior officers who belonged in their laboratories but who at the same time needed the discipline and benevolent authority of an Army chief. He found too many of them irritable, thrusting and impertinent. Things would have been a damn sight more manageable, he must have felt, had the original plan to commission all the scientists as officers gone through. Fortunately for the scientists, that idea had been scotched early in the project.

The scientists, scholars of independent thought and passionate conviction, considered Groves an insensitive Philistine. He was known only as "G.G.," a forbidding figure who popped up periodically on the mesa to raise hell with his subordinates and putter around the post in a private sedan. The scientists knew nothing of the pressures the general suffered in Washington and little of the scope of his worries. They scoffed at the fastidiousness he showed for every detail of post life.

Groves was forever poking into mess halls and inspecting

menus. Afflicted with personal diet problems, he disapproved of fatty foods for his personnel. But he kept a Hershey bar in his office safe. In his rich baritone he would dictate notes to an officer as he made his rounds: "Get rid of all horses not needed. . . . Tell enlisted men's wives living off-post they can't come to dances on-post for security reasons. . . . Advise the scientists' wives how lucky they are to be able to buy turkeys here. . . . Keep the 'Blue' and 'Brown' rooms at the guest house always available for me. . . . And keep an eye on Professor Brown, his wife has Communist tendencies."

Scientists were quite willing to believe that Groves disapproved of pregnancies and childbirth. They cheerfully hated him, rebelled at his tactlessness and made life miserable for his deputies. A number of these had already held the post of Los Alamos Commanding Officer and had left sadly disillusioned men.

When Colonel Gerald Tyler took charge in August 1944, things had reached an impossible state. The temperature on the mesa had hit a record 102 degrees, and tempers were even hotter. Many of the scientists had tired of the semimilitary regimen, waking up to a siren each morning and living under the magnifying glass of the CIC. Oppenheimer's own administrative assistant had left in a huff, and other scientists were in a rebellious mood. It had even become the fashion among some of their wives to stalk into the post commissary, grab a piece of hamburger that looked bad and hurl it on the CO's desk with the cry, "You expect us to eat that dogmeat?"

The scientists had gone so far as to form a Town Council that acted as a sort of Wailing Wall, Parliament and Supreme Court rolled into one. Through it they expected to channel their complaints to Colonel Tyler. The commanding officer attended just one Town Council meeting. He was presented with a list of demands. Tyler drew himself up and

63

barked: "Let's get something straight. I will consider requests, not demands. And the next person who throws a hamburger on my desk—be he man, woman or child—will go straight through my screen window."

The scientists, though, found Oppie a gentler and more understanding companion. Unlike Oak Ridge, where security had forced rigid compartmentalization among the various laboratories so that scientists were kept ignorant of each other's work, Los Alamos studiously maintained communication among its various technical divisions. This was done through the weekly "colloquium," where the division leaders discussed their work in round-table conferences.

The colloquium had been Oppenheimer's idea, and at first the security risks made it seem prohibitive. It was argued convincingly, however, that the cross-fertilization of ideas among the questing scientists was worth the risks involved.

That hurdle crossed, Oppenheimer had gone on to immerse himself in every aspect of the work at Los Alamos. In his unobtrusive way he got in on everything. His peers respected his ability to pick apart their brains and suggestions. The junior scientists marveled at his ability to soothe the elder prima donnas.

It was ironic, if inevitable, that there should have been a war between the two allied armies at the laboratory. Their generals were not bosom friends, but they harbored a more than tolerant respect for one another. Groves appreciated the value of Oppenheimer's popularity among the scientists. Oppenheimer welcomed the steel in Groves that could forge a measure of discipline among some of the chronic yelpers in his own ranks. They were an incongruous-looking pair— the burly, rumpled General striding through the summer mud of Los Alamos; the slender, round-shouldered Oppenheimer loping beside him in that odd flatfooted gait of his.

Still unknown to all but the top-ranking security officials of the Manhattan Project, Groves was keeping an especially sharp eye on Oppenheimer. He personally had expedited Oppenheimer's original appointment as director when Oppie's security clearance was being held up in Washington. Now, however, CIC officers had discovered, through a series of interrogations, that Oppenheimer bore a curious ambivalence toward his security obligations at Los Alamos. For the present, the matter was hushed.

As a matter of fact, the roots of treason had taken hold at Los Alamos from quite a different quarter.

On an afternoon in late August, Laura Fermi went on a picnic to Frijoles Canyon with some friends from the British mission. The car she was in was driven by a stranger, an uncommunicative type with a round pale face and round eyeglasses. He answered her questions sparingly, as if jealous of his words. And he drove very badly. He mumbled his name to Mrs. Fermi as they reached the picnic spot. It was Klaus Fuchs.

Fuchs had joined his British colleagues in America on December 7, 1943, the second anniversary of Pearl Harbor.

He had already turned over to the Russians everything he knew about the process of separating uranium for weapons use, including, presumably, the Americans' plan to build separation plants. He had suggested to the Russians how U-235 might be used in an atomic bomb. And he most certainly could have told them that the Allies now considered at least the uranium bomb a definite possibility.

Fuchs had come to the United States to help the Americans design a separation plant of their own. For four months he had attended secret meetings in New York's Woolworth Building with officials of the Kellex Corporation, which was

65

then involved in some of the design work. Sharing the table with Fuchs at these meetings had been General Groves and Dr. Conant.

With information from the Kellex and other meetings, Fuchs had met five times, from March through July 1944, with a pint-sized Soviet courier he knew only as "Raymond." At their first meeting on a Lower East Side street corner Fuchs had carried a tennis ball, as instructed, and his contact had worn green gloves and carried a book with green bindings. Thereafter Fuchs and Harry Gold had met on Madison Avenue; in Woodside, Queens; in Central Park; and in Brooklyn's Borough Hall Park. They had planned other rendezvous, but Fuchs never showed up. In August, Gold learned that Fuchs had "gone off somewheres to the southwest."

That same month a husky GI with unruly black eyebrows and black hair began work in a machine shop in Site Y's technical area. He was to help fabricate a new type of explosive lens for the bomb, and he was awfully inquisitive for a GI. His name was David Greenglass.

The advent of the implosion design at Los Alamos and the decision to perfect it encouraged Groves to advise the Joint Chiefs in August 1944 that several implosion bombs would be available between March and July 1945. Their explosive power would be the equivalent of "several thousand tons" of TNT. At the same time Los Alamos would continue its work on the gun bomb, which would be ready a year hence, in August 1945.

This new time schedule meant, in all probability, that the first atomic weapons would be used against Japan. The fact presaged a momentous political decision in the following year.

For by summer's end, with the war in Europe blazing

toward its climax, the U.S. Joint Chiefs of Staff had concluded that the unconditional surrender of Japan would necessitate an invasion of that country. At Quebec in September the British chiefs concurred and both Roosevelt and Churchill endorsed the plan. But no one looked forward to the blood-letting.

Unfortunately, the implosion effort at Los Alamos foundered in a sea of troubles. A new, unproven technique, it demanded new equipment and special personnel. Both turned out to be in drastically short supply.

It seemed impossible to recruit enough young physicists and skilled engineers. The physicists, those who hadn't been drafted, had heard of the grim living conditions at Los Alamos. The engineers shied away from what they had heard was a stuffy academic community in the wilds of New Mexico. Procurement problems threatened to sabotage everything. When Conant arrived from Washington in the late fall of 1944, the implosion program looked like a shambles. Recruitment and procurement difficulties were so serious that he feared not only the failure of the implosion effort but the wreck of the whole billion-dollar Manhattan Project.

The scientists at Los Alamos had conducted dozens of inconclusive tests on implosion. Time was running short. Conant thought the chances poor for an effective implosion weapon in 1945—a bomb possibly, but with a yield so piddling as to remove any claims of being a superweapon. Indeed, Conant and Groves were privately so discouraged that they gave up any idea of using the first uranium from Oak Ridge in an implosion weapon. The uranium would be assigned instead to the more certain gun bomb.

Back went Groves to his memo pad. The top-secret message he sent General George Marshall, Chief of Staff, reflected the gloom of the bomb builders. There would be another revision in plans: the military would have to use the gun bomb. Previous hopes for an implosion bomb by late spring of 1945 had been dissipated. That weapon would not be ready until late July. Its explosive wallop would equal no more than 500 tons of TNT.

One ironic note lightened the gloom somewhat, although the relief it brought was a passing thing. With the capture of Strasbourg by the Allies in November, ALSOS agents had recovered enemy documents indicating that Germany had been virtually out of the atomic bomb race from the start. The documents all but proved that the status of her bomb project now was just about where America's had been in 1942. The fears of a Nazi superbomb had been overblown all along.

The American atomic bomb would unquestionably figure in Japan's final humbling. But how?

If the United States dropped a single atomic bomb on Japan, the Japanese might think it a trial weapon, and our only one, and not expect a rain of similar bombs to follow. They would continue fighting. But if the United States followed up its first drop with a second bomb—the proverbial one-two punch—the Japanese might figure it had an arsenal of atomic weapons and would sue for peace.

U.S. military leaders thought that a logical premise for a plan of action.

The number-two punch, the knockout blow, would have to be an implosion bomb. The scientists knew there was not enough U-235 on hand to build another gun bomb in time. Implosion would use the more available plutonium. It would therefore be necessary to test an implosion device as soon as possible.

As far back as March 1944, Oppenheimer had told his

people there was no alternative to testing a full-scale implosion weapon. The immediate problems were: designing the instruments to measure the blast and nuclear effects of a possible explosion; how to recover the priceless nuclear material in case of failure; and where to test the bomb.

That was of first priority—locating a test site.

Throughout the spring Oppenheimer and Bainbridge had taken turns roaming the western part of the United States in search of a site that would meet the criteria of isolation, flatness and proximity to Los Alamos. They had searched by car, by plane and by map.

Eight sites had been considered: a desert training area near Rice, California; remote San Nicolas Island off Southern California; a strip of sand barriers in the Gulf of Texas south of Corpus Christi; a portion of the Mojave Desert which was being used to test Army tanks; the great sand dunes of Colorado's San Luis Valley; a uranium-mining area near Mesa Verde National Park; the mesa country of northwest New Mexico; and Jornada del Muerto.

Accurate, up-to-date maps were needed to tell the scientists precisely the type of terrain at each site: the elevations, contours and geological make-up so important to the experiments anticipated. Decent maps were so scarce, however, that General Groves had to put out a blanket order for all geodetic survey maps of the states involved, as well as pertinent coastal charts of the United States and most of the grazing service maps of New Mexico. Aerial mosaics and even old prospectors' charts were scrounged.

By summer they had narrowed their choice to New Mexico. The scientists had explored the region around the Air Force town of Alamogordo and the Jornada del Muerto in southern New Mexico. Bainbridge bounced by jeep over nearly every foot of the Alamogordo Range, dodging practice bombing runs by B-29's, before he found the right spot—an 18-mile wide, 24-mile long strip tucked in the northwest corner of the air base.

One day, shortly before the year ended, Bainbridge flew to Colorado Springs to see General Uzal Ent, the Air Force's commanding general for the New Mexico district. He asked the general's permission to have a section of the Alamogordo Bombing and Gunnery Range on the Jornada turned over to the Manhattan Project. The general took one look at Bainbridge's impressive credentials and okayed the request. And approval by Groves came swiftly.

Elated, Bainbridge phoned Oppenheimer the news that evening. Oppie was relaxing with a book of John Donne's poems. Bainbridge urged that they fix a code name for the new site without delay. Oppie turned to the opening lines of the holy sonnet he had just read:

Batter my heart, three-person'd God; for, you
As yet but knock, breathe, shine, and seek to mend . . .

"Trinity," said Oppenheimer softly. "We'll call it Trinity."

IV

Early 1945

TRINITY.

Its name evoked thoughts of Easter and visions of soaring cathedrals. It spoke of hymns, hushed vespers, children's choirs and pealing anthems from invisible organs—all the legend, ritual and mystery of the Christian Church.

Was it blasphemy to christen with such a name the birthplace of the atomic bomb?

Perhaps. And yet there was a hint of holiness about the vast silent valley that was Trinity—something in its history that touched the indomitability of man's questing spirit; something in its ageless and primitive beauty that suggested man's earliest temples of prayer.

The 432-square-mile patch of desert that Trinity encompassed had known violence since the beginning of time. Cupped between two jagged mountain ranges, 150 miles from the southern border of New Mexico, it was part of the Jornada del Muerto—Journey of Death—the residue of centuries of volcanic fury dating from the pre-Cambrian era. Its thrusting peaks and massive lava flows testified to that. It was a place of deadening heat and drought, interspersed with fierce winds and thunderstorms.

The Jornada had been named by the parched, perspiring Conquistadors who pushed across its wastes at the end of the sixteenth century in search of new lands for the King of Spain. Out of the shadows of the Oscura Hills, Apaches had swooped down to murder stragglers wilting under the sun's relentless rays. Later the Apaches preyed on early American pioneers who trekked across the Jornada. The arid stretch was the straightest route between thriving El Paso and the new trading post of Sante Fe to the north. The Apaches marauded unchecked through the region, setting the torch to wagon trains and pueblos alike.

In the 1840's the pioneers and Spanish-backed Mexican settlers brought the bad blood between them to a boil. The Americans mounted an expedition out of Santa Fe to beard the hated Spaniards in their den at El Paso. But the Jornada sucked their strength and made them easy victims for a well-armed Spanish force that intercepted them. The captive survivors were led back to El Paso on a blazing death march in which several Americans were shot and one had his ear sliced off.

Thirty years later civilization had brought grazing stock and stagecoach stops to the desolate Jornada route. The stages creaked across the desert, axle-deep in sand, leaving rut scars that would last decades. Then in 1869 the Jornada broke out again in a blood bath. The Apaches went on a vicious rampage, slaughtering settlers and copper miners in nearby villages. In the 1880's Billy the Kid terrorized the area. He headquartered in Las Cruces at the Jornada's southern tip and ranged north along the Rio Grande, pillaging banks and shooting up citizens until Sheriff Pat Garrett brought him down. For years afterward Garrett's reputation was so fearful that outlaws hid in isolated ranches along the Jornada to escape his guns.

Peace had finally come to the valley. Ranchers had moved in for good with their cattle, artesian wells had been poked in the gravelly soil, and the Jornada slumbered in tranquil seclusion.

Nature had preserved its own cathedral over the bones of Apache and Conquistador. Its spires were the ranges of Fra

Cristobal and Caballo to the west, the Oscuras and San Andres to the east: stark peaks with names like Salinas, Little Burro, Little San Pascual, Lady Bug and Skillet Nob. Its nave was the pink desert floor, vacant except for a ranch house or two, abandoned to the waterless stream beds that snaked down from the mountain valleys and wound across it, and to the yucca, sagebrush and Joshua trees that spotted its surface. Its only hymn was the sweeping sigh of the night wind and, occasionally, the crackling peal of thunder echoing off the mountains. The only sounds of day were the swish of the "sand devils" swirling tornado-like across the desert, the harsh "chack" of a swooping shrike or the lowing of a stray steer.

The Cathedral of the Jornada was a spot of overwhelming, utter loneliness.

It was the perfect place to test the bomb: isolated enough so that inquisitive citizens would disassociate any activity there from Los Alamos, but not so isolated that the scientists couldn't commute the 160 miles to The Hill with relative ease; flat enough so that vital instruments could focus unobstructed for miles in every direction and gauge the effects of the bomb; so uninhabitable that the nearest signs of civilization were a pair of abandoned coal-mining towns, Troy and Carthage, and a crossroads store and windmill called Bingham. If disaster occurred, few besides the scientists at Trinity would be victims.

Building contracts for Trinity were let and a twelve-man Military Police detachment moved down to open the camp and take up guard duties. There remained the problem of clearing out the few ranchers homesteading on the public grazing lands adjacent to Trinity.

The ranchers didn't go easily. In fact, the Army might have had an easier time evacuating Hopis and Navajos if the mesa site farther north had been chosen. But Secretary of the

75

Interior Harold Ickes had insisted that no Indians be displaced. So the MP's at Trinity took on ranchers instead.

The principal ones at Trinity were the McDonald family, owners of several thousand acres so arid that a single steer was allotted a square-mile grazing area. The Government paid them and their neighbors for their cattle and threw in a generous bonus. It came in one lump sum, though, and the ranchers took a severe tax bite. Some retaliated and refused to leave their homesteads.

The MP's waged a short war of attrition against the sullen ranchers. Water tanks for the ranchers' stock were found mysteriously punctured, and stray Herefords were accidentally riddled with buckshot. The ranchers took the hint and gradually disappeared. By the beginning of the new year Trinity was ready for operation.

January 1945 began poorly for the bomb builders.

Technical problems plagued them. There was trouble procuring vital molds needed to make the explosive lenses for the new weapon. At Hanford a crisis in producing the plutonium slugs had delayed shipment of critical nuclear supplies to Site Y. Salary disputes and living conditions had decimated the ranks of civilian machinists at Los Alamos. Of more than 200 recruited in the closing months of 1944, one third had left by the new year.

Morale was so precarious that Groves had summoned to his War Department office a dozen key aides, nicknamed the "Society of the Stupid," and warned them that if the bomb fizzled, "each of you can look forward to a lifetime of testifying before Congressional investigating committees."

The surging war in Europe and impending defeat of Germany had thrown a curious pall over many of the scientists, especially the foreign-born, who had embarked on the project primarily to win the race against the Reich and keep the bomb from Hitler. Now from some quarters came persistent questions about the purpose of maintaining the project's brutal pace and secrecy. The revelations of the ALSOS mission increased the unrest.

U.S. Intelligence had hinted right along that perhaps the Nazis' feared lead in atomic research was a bugaboo. No one knew for sure, however.

As late as August 1944 Groves had warned General Marshall: "If the enemy has made an active and uninterrupted effort it is a possibility that he could be ready in the near future to use the weapon on a limited scale." Even the Germans deceived themselves into thinking they were ahead. In December 1944 the head of their nuclear research project had confided to one of Hitler's top deputies that the Americans were still trailing.

In fact, when the captured documents from Strasbourg and other centers were analyzed, it turned out the Germans had been atomically impotent from the beginning. They hadn't even acquired the factories for mass-producing their nuclear supply. Their effort had been hopelessly mired in disorganization, misdirection and petty internal bickering.

The Germans had been initially handicapped by the exodus of so many of their best physicists. They had dragged their heels in organizing an atomic project geared to the war effort. Their government, overcommitted to a war on many fronts and cynical about the prospects of atomic weaponry, had stifled early efforts by the scientists to mount a program. There had also been insufficient technical equipment for so ambitious a project.

Once in motion, the German program had been directed by a succession of undistinguished physicists. Frustrated by an unsympathetic government, they wallowed in arguments and grudge fights with their subordinates. Some turned to drink. Groves, who never touched anything stronger than

77

sherry during the war, had a Nazi counterpart who used to boast he was never sober from dawn to dusk.

Klaus Fuchs spent the first week of the new year on a short holiday with his sister and her family in Cambridge, Massachusetts. Harry Gold caught up with him there.

After six months at Los Alamos, Fuchs was bursting with information. Gold learned for the first time the name of the laboratory; the progress that had been made on the plutonium bomb; and the theory of implosion. Fuchs's description of an implosion lens especially titillated Gold's superiors in Moscow. Before they parted, Gold arranged to meet Fuchs six months later in Albuquerque.

The new member of the British mission at Los Alamos had evoked mixed feelings among his colleagues. Nearly all of them praised his work. Quietly competent, Fuchs had become one of the stars of the laboratory's Theoretical Division. Within that division's implosion group, he worked closely under his mentor and fellow refugee from the Nazis, Dr. Peierls. He proved himself intellectually adroit and at seminars was quick to perceive and point out errors in a colleague's argument. He soon became second in command of the Peierls group.

Fuchs was extraordinarily conscientious. Usually the first to arrive in the morning, he worked till dark in his tiny ten-by-twelve-foot cubicle in the wooden building that housed the Theoretical Division. His office faced a pond outside, and Fuchs would while away his lunch hour feeding the ducks on it. He was lonely. He walked to work alone and walked alone to his meals. Elfriede Segrè, watching him shuffle by her cottage, dubbed him "Poverino"—Pitiful One.

Every Saturday night Fuchs attended a progress-report meeting of his group. He would discuss his week's work on implosion design and ask for questions. It was at the weekly meeting of the top-level Co-ordinating Council, however, that Fuchs could really show his mettle. This convocation of the Los Alamos elders reviewed the work in progress in each division. It was held every Friday at 4 P.M. and required a special white badge for admission.

Generally at these meetings Fuchs was a silent observer. Note-taking was forbidden, but some of Fuchs's colleagues were annoyed to see him furtively scribbling on occasion. Such deviations were forgiven, however, after Fuchs several times stood in for his superiors to brief the elders on the work of his group. His performances were flawless. He gave one series of lectures on hydrodynamics that his colleagues agreed was the most brilliant they'd ever heard. His platform manner was pleasingly precise, his dissertations coolly logical. He chalked his figures on the blackboard in a small neat hand. One superior could only marvel at Fuchs's work: "It's the most beautiful I've ever seen."

Not all his associates were so lavish in their praise. Fuchs could be singularly unresponsive in his relations with those around him. His good friend Mrs. Peierls found him excessively reticent. She took to calling him "Penny-in-the-Slot Fuchs," because in order to get a sentence out of him she had to drop one sentence in. "He's all ears and no mouth," grumbled a colleague. "You talk about your work to him, but you never feel he's giving you anything back."

David Greenglass, on the other hand, knew how to respond to proffers of friendship. He also had chosen the first week in January to go East on furlough. He'd barely gotten through New Year's Day before his brother-in-law, Julius Rosenberg, had dropped by his flat in Manhattan to inquire about Greenglass's work at Los Alamos.

Since he was fifteen, David had known Rosenberg and of Rosenberg's penchant for Communism. That was one reason Rosenberg had married David's domineering older sister,

Ethel. She'd been an active Stalinist before she was twenty. The two had shared their Communist sympathies and tried to indoctrinate young David on the side. Whenever Rosenberg visited Ethel in the Greenglasses' cold-water flat, he had left a pile of Soviet propaganda for David to read. Some of it must have caught hold. At the age of sixteen Greenglass had joined the Young Communist League. For the next few years, at Brooklyn Polytechnic and Pratt institutes, his technical studies had suffered while he cut classes to organize machinist shops for Communist-run unions. But he was always more precocious about his science than his Communism. By the time he married Ruth Printz, a blue-eyed wisp of a girl barely out of her teens, Greenglass had dropped most of his Party activities and was quietly earning his keep as a machinist in a Manhattan laboratory.

In late 1944 Rosenberg had given Ruth Greenglass $150 so she could go to Albuquerque and be with David on their second wedding anniversary. Rosenberg had already known from his Communist contacts that Greenglass was working on the atomic bomb in a laboratory somewhere near Albuquerque. Not until their fourth day together, during a walk along the Rio Grande, had Ruth mentioned to her husband that Rosenberg was giving information to the Russians and that he hoped David would pass along to him whatever he learned at Los Alamos.

Greenglass had balked at first. But he appreciated Rosenberg's favor to Ruth and was persuaded that his information would only be helping a wartime ally. When Rosenberg approached him in New York in January 1945, therefore, Greenglass willingly wrote down everything he remembered about explosive lenses. He even provided a sketch of a four-leaf-clover lens mold, hollow-centered, into which the explosive was poured. The explosive took the shape of the mold. When the mold was removed, an explosive lens remained.

Rosenberg was so pleased that he offered to finance Ruth

back to Albuquerque and set her and David up in a comfortable apartment there. He also wanted to arrange for the first meeting between David and his Soviet courier. At a dinner party in the Rosenbergs' Knickerbocker Village flat, Rosenberg gave Greenglass the torn half of a Jell-O box. His contact in Albuquerque would be carrying the other half.

In the first distressing days of the new year a Navy officer at Los Alamos had taken one look at the chaos about him and sorrowfully cracked: "It's too bad that with all this talent it couldn't be spent on something more useful to the war effort."

Suddenly, as January flew by, everyone was feeling a lot more useful. There was a fresh fever in the air and a feeling of new momentum in the laboratories. The scientists were now directing their energies toward perfecting the implosion assembly. At the same time they were readying for the inevitable test of the weapon. There was a flurry of administrative shifts and reassembling within Oppie's Army.

The mysterious lettered divisions that comprised the laboratory work force were changing hands, sprouting subdivisions or being replaced altogether by new ones. The letters "TR," for Trinity, began blossoming on secret organization charts. A new division—"G" for Gadget—was the busiest of all. Its staffers, headed by Robert Bacher, probed all the physics of the implosion bomb, and especially its nuclear size. On the theoretical level, many of the same problems were being tackled by members of the "F" (for Fermi) Division, who labored far into the nights trying to calculate the probable explosive yield of the bomb. Others theorized what the physical properties of the nuclear material would be like. Not enough had arrived yet from Hanford or Oak Ridge to be used for conclusive experiments, so the theorists were still operating largely in the dark.

The most dangerous work was undertaken by the nuclear

assembly experts of the Gadget Division. So secret and sensitive were their experiments that most were carried out at night in a remote recess of Los Alamos Canyon. The place was called "Omega" because critical assembly was supposedly the last step in the bomb project. There, near sinister-looking vaults where the first pieces of nuclear metal were stored, the assembly men played a deadly game. It was called "tickling the dragon's tail," and it would cost the life of more than one good man before the year was out. They rigged a machine called the "Guillotine." Louis Slotin, a fearless young Canadian, operated it. A uranium slug was dropped from the top of the Guillotine through the center of another slug. At the moment it passed through, the whole assembly went supercritical as a small chain reaction occurred. Invisible neutrons burst in sprays and the scientists measured the phenomenon.

The importance of the game at Omega was that it would tell the scientists the size of the nuclear package needed to precipitate a chain reaction in the bomb. The experiments would, of course, also indicate the amount of plutonium or U-235 that could safely be handled at Trinity or shipped across the Pacific for assembly in the Hiroshima bomb.

The first successful experiment came in mid-January. The needles on the scientists' delicate instruments danced crazily off-scale. The dragon had responded well.

Outside the laboratories, life for the scientists had become more tolerable. The work day at Los Alamos still began with the seven A.M. siren the scientists had sourly dubbed "Oppie's Whistle." Certain sights had become institutional: Fermi riding to work on his bicycle; Oppenheimer loping through the "Tech Area," trailed Pied Piper-like by several junior scientists; Niels Bohr jaywalking across the street, waving his arms as he declaimed on the healthful virtues of Los Alamos air.

Bohr had been a tonic to the harried men on the mesa. He took a keen and lively interest in all phases of the work and consoled the younger scientists in their blue moments. He was less appreciated by President Roosevelt and Winston Churchill, who found him annoyingly meddlesome when it came to political affairs. This characteristic of scientists would prove the bane of many a Washington official.

Bohr had been pressing Roosevelt and Churchill to confer with Stalin on the broad future implications of international control of the bomb. His ideas had been considered dangerously impractical. The two statesmen had drafted an aide-mémoire in late 1944, recommending that steps be taken to ensure that Bohr "is responsible for no leakage of information particularly to the Russians."

F. D. R. and Churchill insisted that utmost secrecy continue to shroud the bomb. In that same mémoire they had broached one other point: "When a bomb is finally available," they noted, "it might perhaps, after mature consideration, be used against the Japanese, who should be warned that this bombardment will be repeated until they surrender."

The scientists at Los Alamos, their waking hours consumed by work on the device, had for the most part given little thought to the prospect of the bomb being used against Japan. Some of their colleagues at Chicago, with more time on their hands to ruminate over the moral implications of the bomb, had given it deep thought, however. The Chicago scientists found it difficult to adjust to the idea that the bomb was no longer simply an anti-Nazi weapon. They also genuinely feared for the future peace of the world if the United States undertook to release atomic power in a destructive act of war.

The Los Alamos scientists seemed detached from all this. Absorbed in their labors, swept up in the invigorating atmosphere of the mesa, they lived remote from the problems of Washington and the world at large.

They found relief from the grueling pace of their special war effort in frequent skiing and hiking excursions among the Jemez hills; in pack trips and lively expeditions to abandoned mines; and in picnics and evening parties where the worries of the day dissolved in cocktails and high jinks. At one particularly festive costume party Klaus Fuchs came out of his shell long enough to lead a conga line through the post commissary, then retired sedately to a post behind the bar and passed out cold on the stroke of midnight. Fellow revelers covered him with a bed-sheet.

The laboratory had its share of intriguing characters. One fellow assembled a jazz band in his home every evening. Another performed explosive experiments in his living room. Edward Teller drove his neighbors wild by playing Hungarian rhapsodies on his piano at odd hours of the night. Teller had a monumental disdain for the regulations that governed everyone else at Los Alamos. He rose late, worked at home and spent his leisure in long lonely walks. Richard Feynman, a brilliant enfant terrible with a Brooklyn accent, played the bongos and occasionally wore socks. His idea of fun was to confound security officials by figuring out the combinations of safes containing classified documents, unlocking them and leaving notes that said, "Guess Who?" He defied the censors by writing to his ailing wife in Albuquerque, then shredding his letters into little pieces before putting them in an unsealed envelope. The purpose, he explained to the enraged censors, was to provide his wife with the therapy of reassembling the letters.

Radiation was one of the biggest hazards at Los Alamos. The arrival of plutonium had brought increased safety measures. A minor explosion had thrown several milligrams of plutonium in the face of a chemist, and officials worried that more serious accidents might lead to a security break. The most elaborate precautions were taken to prevent contamination of personnel handling the hot nuclear material. Workers wore smocks, coveralls, rubber gloves, caps, respirators, shoe covers and face shields. The items were worn only once and then laundered. In one month in the Metallurgy Division, 17,000 pieces of clothing were laundered and 9000 pairs of gloves decontaminated. Even then 60 per cent of the gloves had to be discarded.

All that, however, seemed a mild tempest compared to the dangers of automobile driving on the mesa. Accidents there were frequent and bizarre. A GI cracked up his car when a wild turkey flew in the window. Another ran down a cow and ended up in traction. One scientist, running back a little whisky from Albuquerque for his colleagues, hit a rock slide and drove into the Rio Grande. Sitting in the car, dazed, with water up to his shoulders, he heard an incredulous MP murmur, as he pulled him to safety, "Sir, you must have lived clean."

The Los Alamites still chafed under security regulations. The MP baseball team trained and played their opponents in a vacuum. Local sports pages were forced to ignore them. Security's tentacles stretched so far that the little boys who had once graduated from the old ranch school ceased to be graduates of Los Alamos. They bounded direct from "Public School Number 7" into Groton and Andover.

The "long-hairs" and "plumbers" continued to mix like oil and water, but there was far less combustion. It still irked General Groves to see a scientist standing dreamily in front of a window, chewing the end of a pencil and muttering equations to himself. Motion, not musing, Groves felt, ought to be the drill now. His deputy, Colonel Tyler, was still harassed occasionally by domestic traumas. The most celebrated involved the dormitory for single women at Los Alamos.

It was the habit of enlisted and civilian bachelors to visit the dormitory nightly and socialize over a friendly nip. The mothers of the mesa protested to Tyler that this was a shocking example of loose morals. They demanded action. Tyler wearily summoned the MP's and ordered them to throw all males out of the dormitory by midnight. The next ten days shook Los Alamos to its foundations. Young fillies accosted Tyler with cries of "Nazi!" and "Fascist!" The bachelors threatened to go to the White House for redress. And the Town Council hastily called a meeting to consider the crisis. The hall was jammed with irate men and women, many of whom hung over the balcony shouting, "Whaddya think we are, college kids?"

Tempers finally cooled, the MP's were withdrawn and the bachelors decided on a self-policing system. But Colonel Tyler was nearly a wreck.

In February Groves and Oppenheimer decided to "freeze" all further design methods at Los Alamos and concentrate wholly on the implosion bomb. A tight schedule was drawn up to meet the deadline of the Trinity test: detonators had to be on the assembly line by March 15; lens molds were to be delivered and ready for testing by April 2; plutonium spheres had to be fabricated and tested starting May 15; highest-quality lenses would have to be in production by June 4; fabrication of the bomb's sphere and assembly should begin by July 4.

At Yalta, Roosevelt and Stalin were debating another schedule: the date when Russia would enter the war against Japan. Stalin was already laying down his postwar demands in return for a pledge to open hostilities against Japan within three months of Germany's surrender. In the light of history, the timing and outcome of the first atomic bomb test would be ironically relevant to this fateful conference.

Work on the bomb accelerated on three fronts.

86

At Oak Ridge two mammoth plants, each operating a different separation process, were beginning to turn out in bulk precious kilograms of highly enriched U-235. The material was processed and forwarded to Los Alamos for the gun bomb that was being prepared for eventual use over Hiroshima. Pump troubles had faded and shakedown runs were almost at an end at Oak Ridge. New pumps and converters were being sought to match the expected soaring output. At Hanford all three plutonium piles were humming by mid-February, feeding enriched slugs of the chemical into greedy process vats. The plutonium would be separated from its radioactive matrix and forwarded to Los Alamos for final purifying into gold-plated ingots of bomb metal. These would comprise the guts of the first trial device to be tested at Trinity.

Once, in the caveman days of the early 1940's, scientists would have estimated that it would take 27 million years to produce a kilogram of U-235 and up to 20,000 years for a kilogram of plutonium. Now the plants were going at a rate that might supply the weaponeers with enough nuclear stuff to climax the war within weeks.

On the Great Salt Lake Desert of Utah a small group of American airmen were readying for that day. They roared their specially modified B-29's daily from Wendover Field, testing every phase and potential danger that might challenge the first atomic battle mission. They were members of the elite 509th Composite Group, which would carry the brunt of the first atomic bomb raids. Their B-29's had been stripped of all normal armaments except the tail gunner's slot. They carried dummy bombs called "pumpkins." The "pumpkins" were actually teardrop models of the implosion weapon, bulbous up front and tapered back to the fins. For battle use they were about 3000 pounds heavier than the Trinity device and contained similar explosive charges.

The airmen of the 509th ranged across the Utah-Nevada

87

border on simulated missions. They practiced dropping the "pumpkins" from their bomb bays and getting clear of the explosion fast. They made tight 158-degree turns and nosed their planes into shallow dives to gain getaway speed. Some of them thought the wings would rip from the fuselage. The bombers would need eight miles between them and the explosion in order to escape. They would have just forty-three seconds to make it.

At the height of the recruitment crisis at Los Alamos, the Army had set up a Special Engineer Detachment to channel technically trained enlisted men into the Manhattan Project. By early 1945 there were 1800 of these SED's on the mesa, more than one third of the entire scientific staff.

One of them was Sergeant Leo Jercinovic. He spent the quiet hours before dawn, from four to six A.M., firing off explosives experiments in Los Alamos Canyon. There was no wind to disrupt things at that hour, and Jerry didn't mind working so early. He'd spend the rest of the day getting ready for the next tests. It was tough, ticklish work shaping and assembling the heavy explosives that would be used for the bomb. But Jerry had known that kind of sweat since he was a kid.

He came from tough Yugoslav stock. His father, as a young stonemason on the Adriatic seacoast, had often swum a mile out to King Peter's island summer resort to raid the royal apple orchards for the family table. Later he had worked his way across the Atlantic to seek his fortune in the New World. Jerry's mother, while a young girl, had borrowed enough money to pay for her steerage passage to America in 1906. His parents had met in a small Illinois steel town, a melting pot for European immigrants.

Jerry hadn't learned English until he was seven. At vocational high school he had taken a shine to chemistry and after school hours had earned money as a pin boy at the local YMCA bowling alley. At the University of Illinois he had waited on tables and stoked furnaces until his father was killed in an industrial accident and Jerry had had to drop out. He had gone to work then in the explosives research section of a large chemical firm.

Drafted in 1942, Jerry had been sent back to college by the Army to get a degree in chemical engineering. Along the way he'd married a shapely brunette of good German stock who had found in him just the right sort of mate: smart, handy and full of nervous energy. He had arrived at Los Alamos in mid-1944 and been assigned to an SED barracks there. His bunkmate was a chunky machinist with a weak smile named David Greenglass.

Greenglass had reached the Special Engineering Detachment at Los Alamos through a procession of Army posts. He'd been trying to get into uniform even before he was married. The Navy had turned him down four times for color-blindness. The Army had finally taken him, put him through basic training at ordnance school and shifted him about the United States for a year before landing him in an explosives shop at Los Alamos.

When he returned from New York in January 1945, Greenglass recalled Rosenberg's parting words: "Watch yourself. Don't be obvious in seeking information. Don't draw attention to yourself by carrying on political conversations."

Greenglass obeyed the first part of the admonition to the letter. He would walk into a laboratory, casually pick up a piece of material and comment on how interestingly it was machined. Flattered, the scientist on hand would explain that the material was a neutron source and would go on to outline its uses. Greenglass would walk out with the information tucked securely in his head.

He was less discreet in his social conduct. He had taken to

89

boning up on history and government to supplement his technical bent, and loved spending evenings in the barracks talking politics with Jercinovic and others. In rambling bull sessions he drew quizzical looks from his mates by spouting off the names of key U.S. Congressmen and their voting records. Anyone who seemed as politically savvy as Greenglass was bound to be thought a queer duck in a barracks full of mathematicians.

By March the Trinity test had become priority number one at Los Alamos. July 4 was initially set as the target date.

A top-level council, the "Cowpuncher Committee," was appointed by Oppenheimer to "ride herd" on the implosion program. The laboratory's seven key divisions were mobilized from top to bottom for the critical months ahead.

Kenneth Bainbridge was placed in over-all charge of the test. He would be responsible for all phases of Trinity, from its operation to the safety of personnel. It was a responsibility which, for sheer complexity, magnitude and potential danger, was unmatched in scientific annals. Bainbridge's chief aide was a canny Canadian, John Williams, who had come from the University of Minnesota. Williams would oversee all services for the test—the nuts-and-bolts requirements of special equipment, transportation and technical personnel.

Trinity had assumed overwhelming importance to the bomb builders. It was an enormous step from theoretical guesswork and small-scale experiments to a practical test of this size. No one was content that the first trial of the gadget should be over enemy territory where failure would destroy the surprise element and might present the enemy with large amounts of recoverable nuclear material. Oppenheimer and his people were aware that none of them really knew whether an atomic explosion of the size envisioned could be produced. There were literally hundreds of mysteries that had to be, and could only be, answered through such a test. The chances of failure were frightening. The bomb would be the total of some 500 separate components, any one of which could ruin the test by a malfunction.

The stakes were fearsome. The information needed from Trinity was essential to the atomic-bombing strategy which could bring the war with Japan to a sudden end. As early as 1944 Oppenheimer had warned in a secret interlaboratory memorandum: "If we do *not* have accurate test data from Trinity, the planning of use of the gadget over enemy territory will have to be done substantially blindly."

The only thing that could finally resolve the technical doubts of the scientists was an experiment with full instrumentation. In those hesitant March days, as Trinity's plans took shape, the theorists at Los Alamos estimated that the test would yield an explosive force equivalent to that of 100 to 10,000 tons of TNT. The most probable figure: 4000 tons.

In Washington, government leaders had become acutely conscious of the hopes riding on Trinity. Stimson had just returned from a visit to Florida. At an Air Force redistribution center he had met and talked with men returning from Europe, en route to the war in the Pacific. Stimson had been profoundly shaken by the weariness he saw in their eyes. They would go to the Pacific and fight well again, he knew. But anyone with his responsibility owed it to these men to use whatever means were necessary to end the war quickly and decisively.

Vannevar Bush felt the same way. He had two sons in the war: one a pilot in the Pacific, the other an Army medic.

Leslie Groves, newly promoted to Major General, felt it perhaps the most keenly: the bomb must be completed, tested and used against the enemy as soon as possible. Too manpower, money and heartache had gone into it to its military effectiveness wasted.

Groves stood at attention one morning in General Marshall's office while Marshall, preoccupied, scribbled something at his desk. When Marshall looked up, Groves made a plea to extend the separation plant at Oak Ridge. He needed authorization for $200 million more. Marshall approved and apologized for keeping Groves waiting. He had a gentle explanation: "I was making out a check to my store," he said, "for $1.60 worth of grass seed."

Halfway around the world an atoll in the Mariana Islands of the Pacific was being transformed into a unique air base. At North Field on Tinian the first hangars were being readied for the B-29's of the 509th Composite Group. The airmen from Wendover Field, Utah, would be arriving soon to complete their special training. After that, everything would wait on the arrival of the first bomb—and on Trinity.

The bomb had not been built yet. But already events and their movers were rapidly transforming the nature of war—for then and forever after.

On March 9, massed B-29's conducted a raid on Tokyo. Their incendiary bombs killed 83,793 humans, injured half that number and destroyed more than a million buildings. Sixteen square miles of the capital were devastated; 1,500,000 persons left homeless. People died of suffocation, gasping for air, in open fields far from the fire. In Hamburg ten nights of conventional bombing wiped out 45,000 civilians. Rotterdam was obliterated by some ninety-four tons of incendiaries and blockbusters.

The fact that the atomic bomb was only a more economical way to achieve the same degree of holocaust did little to salve the consciences of the statesmen and scientists. Leo Szilard sent another letter through Einstein to the President, imploring an audience. This time Szilard, who had urged the bomb on Roosevelt in 1939 to stop the Nazis, was arguing that the bomb should not be used on Japan.

Stimson sadly realized at last that the horror of war was being escalated to a new dimension which the atomic bomb would simply refine. On March 15 he called at the White House to urge on Roosevelt thoughtful deliberation of how the United States might control that new dimension after the war. His pleas were not successful. The President seemed engrossed with the present and almost shrunken with exhaustion. It was the last time Stimson saw him.

Morale had ebbed in the tiny camp at Trinity.

Alone on the desert, forbidden to leave the site and ignorant of the purpose of their misery, the dozen MP's who had opened the camp had spent a barren Christmas together. Several WAC's from The Hill had come down Christmas Day to try to cheer them up.

As far as the MP's were concerned, they'd left the soup for the frying pan. At Los Alamos they had led a dog's life, pulling long chilling hours of guard duty around the post. As members of a mounted detachment, they had patrolled their beat on horses whose hair had been allowed to grow shaggy to keep the beasts from freezing at night. At Los Alamos, though, there had at least been furloughs and weekend passes—and people.

Just before Christmas the MP's had been hand-picked for the Trinity assignment. Most of them were hard-bitten ex-city cops and detectives skilled in police and security work. Groves had wanted only the cream for this job, and he'd gotten it by stripping the best men from other MP units around the country. These special GI's would become the outcasts of Trinity flat. They would guard the site with their lives. By the end of January their complement had grown to forty-five men.

Leader of the outcasts was a stocky, thirty-five-year-old first lieutenant who was crazy about polo. Howard Bush had reached Trinity via an accounting office and the National Guard. He had belonged to a cavalry troop in New York City for eight years and had finally been commissioned and gone on active duty at the end of 1942. A friendly bachelor, Bush was as popular with the WAC's on The Hill as he was with his men. He liked to wear a coonskin cap and mukluks when riding alone in the Jemez hills, but in more formal company he proudly showed off his serge breeches and the custom-made riding boots which he kept at a high gloss. He also sported one of the finest guardsman's mustaches extant. At Trinity, under the glare of a spring sun, Bush traded his coonskin for a wide-brimmed campaign hat, while his men wore rakish pith helmets. Led by a jaunty wire-haired terrier mascot named "Toff MacButin," he and his troops cut dashing figures as they cantered across the Trinity flats.

Only a barracks, a cookhouse and CO's quarters had greeted the MP's when they first reached Trinity. But with startling speed the camp expanded. The MP's watched in wonder as scores of workers and contractors, laboring under extreme pressure and secrecy, built a complete scientific laboratory on the desert within four months.

The construction task was immense: twenty miles of new blacktop road; a transportation fleet of more than a hundred vehicles; a complete communications network of telephone lines, public-address systems and FM radios; a stockroom to house tons of equipment to be shipped down from Los Alamos; and much more. Construction staffs at Los Alamos were raided for personnel. Every spare body not required on other projects was pressed into service.

Portable CCC structures were dismantled in Albuquerque, trucked 115 miles south and erected at Trinity. The camp would need at least three barracks; a service-and-supply building; a catch-all structure for offices, laboratories and officers' quarters; warehouses, repair shops, a quartermaster office, commissary, mess hall and kitchen. Not the least important requirement was a main latrine to accommodate 200 bladders.

Utility demands for this one-shot experiment were staggering: portable generators for lighting and electricity; thousands of dollars' worth of telephone connections to the nearest trunk line four miles distant; electrically driven pumps to provide twenty gallons of water a minute. The road work alone would cost $10,000: blading, scraping, surfacing and ditching improvements were needed on some ninety miles of road in the area. Special structures needed for the test included an explosives magazine that would hold five tons of TNT; six concrete chambers worth $36,000 to protect personnel and test-recording instruments; and an unloading platform for a railroad siding twenty-five miles away.

The transportation order would have delighted Henry Ford: 33 dump trucks; 8 jeeps; 11 carryalls; a pair of telephone trucks to lay 200 miles of phone wire; 4 vehicles to haul heavy explosives from the nearest main road thirty miles distant; a tank truck with a 700-gallon capacity for carrying drinking water from the nearest town; a gasoline-and oil-distributing truck; 12 panel trucks for installing and connecting instruments around the site; a couple of passenger buses for transporting technicians from Base Camp to the shot tower; a five-ton refrigerator truck; a snowplow, an ambulance, a fire truck and two bulldozers.

All this would shortly service a force of some 200 MP's, medics, cooks, mechanics, truck drivers, construction men, repair men, maintenance men, engineers, scientists and an occasional VIP. Total cost for this short-lived desert kingdom was $110,000.

As the camp grew, morale improved. There were no passes, but the MP's learned to amuse themselves. They fixed up a day room, went swimming in the old cattle cistern at the McDonald family's ranch house, and played volleyball and horseshoes. Bush organized a couple of polo teams. For mallets the men used brooms with the straw cut off.

The chow was good, if not Cordon Bleu. GI's, officers and visiting scientists cleaned their own trays after each meal. Even General Groves stood in line and washed his tray. His deputy, Brigadier General Farrell, who liked to dress GI-style, was refused breakfast one morning until he had shaved.

Lieutenant Bush did everything possible to ease the loneliness of his men. He bought them beer and arranged to have it shipped down from Los Alamos. He installed pool tables and imported movies. *Beau Geste* with Gary Cooper was socko. The Foreign Legion classic was a sardonic reminder to the MP's of their own plight.

The lieutenant appointed himself head gamekeeper. Antelope abounded at Trinity, and it was feared they might trample the delicate signal wires the scientists were stringing everywhere. Carbines were issued and safaris set off in jeeps and weapons carriers. Firing from behind yucca bushes and cactus, the GI's gradually decimated the antelope herds. It wasn't as easy to get rid of the rattlesnakes and tarantulas. The tarantulas crept into bunks and instrument holes. The rattlers were the bane of the bulldozer drivers. Each morning the drivers banged wrenches on their machines to rustle out any "diamondbacks" coiled inside.

Evenings were for poker. The Army, at great expense, had hired a well-digger from Texas to come to Trinity and keep the half-dozen wells on the site in working order. The wells were in better shape than had been expected and stayed unclogged. The well-digger spent his days admiring the scenery and dreaming of each evening's poker game and the pot he would win. The pot was never more than ten dollars, but for the well-digger it was more elusive than the one at Monte Carlo. The GI's and scientists developed a merry stratagem for bilking him. The conspiracy grew as the weeks went by. The Texan went home potless each night. The game got to be known as "Beating the Well-Digger."

On a cloudy April afternoon Lord Halifax and Felix Frankfurter walked together in Washington's Rock Creek Park. The British Ambassador and the Supreme Court Justice were deep in discussion of the broad issues of future control of atomic power which Niels Bohr had raised. They thought that perhaps Bohr's ideas deserved further exploration in Washington and London. As the two men ended their walk, the bells of the National Cathedral began slowly tolling. Other bells throughout the capital took up the dirge. It was April 12, 1945. Franklin Roosevelt was dead.

That evening, after he had been sworn in, Harry Truman concluded a brief Cabinet meeting at the White House. As the members filed from the Cabinet room, Stimson walked around the coffin-shaped table and gravely told the new President for the first time of the nation's efforts to harness the new power for war.

The next morning, at an eleven-o'clock meeting at the White House, military leaders advised Truman that Germany would not be beaten for another six months and that defeating Japan would take another year and a half. Shortly afterward Vannevar Bush was admitted to the Oval Office. In greater detail than Stimson had, he explained the new weapon that the scientists were preparing to test at Trinity.

Admiral William D. Leahy, at Truman's side, listened incredulously. "That is the biggest fool thing we've ever done," Leahy told his boss after Bush had left. "The bomb will never go off."

April was a good month at Los Alamos.

Scientists reported excellent progress in developing an electric detonator that would set off the bomb's high-explosive charges within a millionth of a second. The mysteries of the initiator—a key that could be turned on at the right moment to release atom-smashing neutrons—were being gradually unraveled. From Hanford came word that major shipments of plutonium to Los Alamos would begin in May.

Stafford Warren and a handful of other radiologists were already anticipating and worrying over the prospects of radioactive fallout. Warren estimated that one million curies of radioactive fission might be released by the Trinity explosion. All through April he pored over meteorological charts and traveled widely, analyzing cloud and wind patterns over the entire southwestern United States. There was really no way of gauging accurately, however, what the fallout effects of an atomic explosion would be. It was all speculative.

On April 25 a secret memorandum circulated in Los Alamos on the "strategic" possibilities of radioactive fallout. It was a frank discussion of how fallout could be made to work for the United States in a battle situation. The idea was to render an area of 100 square kilometers uninhabitable through fallout. This could be done, said the memo, if the explosion created a thunderstorm that would rain down fallout. "However," it added, "we do not expect to poison an area of more than a few square kilometers." The memo suggested that the scientists and military might seek weather conditions for delivering the bomb that would be favorable for inducing a thunderstorm. It concluded: "If you are interested in this possibility, we should try to work out more explicit details."

* * *

Another memorandum was being read that day at the White House in Washington.

It began: "Within four months we shall in all probability have completed the most terrible weapon ever known in human history, one bomb of which could destroy a whole city."

It was Henry Stimson's prescient warning to the new President and his policy makers that resolutions must now be made regarding the future control and sharing of the atomic bomb. Stimson noted that although the United States was now in sole control of the resources to build and use the bomb, it would not remain so indefinitely.

Stimson concluded: "Our leadership in the war and in the development of this weapon has placed a certain moral responsibility upon us which we cannot shirk without very serious responsibility for any disaster to civilization which it would further."

Stimson's words would carry special irony for the delegates meeting that very day in San Francisco for the founding of the United Nations. Not one among the members of the U.S. delegation knew of the impending test at Trinity or, indeed, of the Manhattan Project. They would be laying foundations for the future control of world armaments with no knowledge of the weapon that would change the whole armaments picture. In effect, they would be ratifying a pre-Atomic Age charter that would be obsolete before it became operative.

At Los Alamos and Trinity on April 27, the GI's received dismal news: All furloughs would be canceled until after July.

The tempo had jumped another notch.

V

May–June 1945

In the early hours of May 7 the German armies surrendered unconditionally to the Allies.

Shortly after dawn that same day the scientists at Trinity carried out a dress rehearsal of the big test. They detonated 100 tons of TNT explosive; for extra realism, in the TNT they inserted an amount of radioactive fission from a plutonium slug.

The dress rehearsal gave the scientists a chance to calibrate the instruments they would use to measure the effects of the Trinity shot. It told them something about the type of protection they would need for a nuclear blast. It helped camouflage the real purpose of the Trinity preparations. And it served to tighten the organization, timing and teamwork of the test crew.

The rehearsal still didn't remove the uncertainty as to how lethal the Trinity explosion might be.

On May 9 in Washington the President's Interim Committee met for the first time. This was the top council of eight senior advisers Truman had established to conceive and set in motion proposals for wartime use and future international control of the bomb. It was chaired by Stimson and included, most prominently, Bush, Conant, Truman's respected adviser James Byrnes, and George Harrison, a special consultant to Stimson and president of the New York Life Insurance Company. The meeting took place at the Pentagon.

The Interim Committee's immediate problem was how to break the news of the Trinity test to the nation. Another question that arose was: How long would it take the Soviet Union to produce an atomic weapon? Byrnes thought the answer would be of considerable importance in determining how the United States would try to deal with the subject of atomic armaments in relation to Russia. The answer might tell American leaders whether the United States should try at an early stage to collaborate with the Russians or whether it should try to outdistance them in building an atomic arsenal. Bush and Conant estimated it would take the Soviet Union between three and four years to produce an atomic weapon. General Groves's estimate was twenty years. The three became locked in a vehement argument.

Before the meeting broke up, the Committee probed one more problem. In a number of scientific enclaves, specifically at the Chicago Metallurgical Project, unease over the bomb project was mounting in the wake of Germany's surrender. With the pressure of the race between America and Germany for the bomb no longer in force, some soul-searching was being done about the objectives of the Manhattan Project and the necessity of using the bomb against Japan. Should the United States abandon secrecy and advise its other allies—France, China and Russia—of the project? Would America's image and interest be well served by the use of the bomb against a nation already doomed to defeat?

Time was running out for the doubters. Later that same day, in another conference room at the Pentagon, General Groves met with his Target Committee to discuss the most suitable type of city to be the first victim of the bomb.

In New Mexico the locus of activity was shifting from Los Alamos to Trinity.

There were still serious problems to be resolved on The

Hill before a guarantee of the test's success could be given. But already a selected group of scientists were preparing the intricate experiments needed to gauge the full power of the blast that might occur at Trinity. They would have to measure the bomb's violent air blast and the shock wave along the ground; the phenomenon of the explosion itself and how fast it would build up; the speed at which the fireball ascended—a matter of life or death to the B-29's carrying the bomb; and, finally, the distribution of deadly radioactive fallout.

By far the most important experiments were those diagnosing how the implosion assembly worked and those measuring the speed of the explosion itself. The Venetian Bruno Rossi directed this chore. His task defied comprehension. He would have to determine the velocity at which the energy of the blast multiplied in intensity. The faster it intensified, the more powerful would be the explosion. The problem was how to measure this prodigy: It all took place within 1/100 of a millionth of a second.

Other scientists faced almost equally complex experiments. Before long the yuccas and rattlers at Trinity would find themselves in company along the desert with a profusion of weird instruments with impossible names like geophones, galvanometers and oscilloscopes. Some scientists tried to simplify things by naming their instruments after characters in *Winnie-the-Pooh*. By the second week in May four "Heffalumps" and a shipment of "Eeyores" had arrived at Trinity. So had "Jumbo."

Jumbo was the 215-ton brainchild of a pair of Berkeley physicists. They had responded to Oppenheimer's plea to build a container that would preserve the precious nuclear material in case the bomb test fizzled. Recovery of the nuclear core had been one of Oppenheimer's most perplexing problems. If the nuclear material failed to detonate, but the conventional explosive around it did, the TNT could scatter the nuclear metal clear across the Jornada. And there wasn't enough of the stuff to squander.

A lot of bizarre and expensive ideas were suggested, but General Groves finally settled for Jumbo—a monstrous onyx-black jug that could withstand enormous blast pressure and probably save nearly all the nuclear material. After a model, "Jumbino," was tested at Los Alamos, the real thing was built by a firm in Barberton, Ohio. It measured 25 feet long, 10 feet wide and had a 14-inch-thick shell of solid steel. The bomb would be slipped through a plug at one end which in itself weighed a couple of tons.

A special flatbed railroad car carried Jumbo from Ohio to New Mexico. The huge vessel, cloaked in a canvas tarpaulin, followed a secret route avoiding narrow tunnels and low overhangs. The tortuous 1500-mile journey ended at Pope, New Mexico, a decrepit, one-shack railroad siding twenty-five miles west of Trinity. An unloading platform had been installed there especially for Jumbo. The container was transferred to what must have been the world's largest trailer truck (sixty-four tires, each the size of a man) and hauled by two tractors across the desert to a spot near the detonation area.

It all seemed a palpable waste of effort. Two months before, Oppenheimer had made up his mind to use Jumbo only as a desperate last resort. Nonetheless, the big jug was insurance.

The Interim Committee met on May 14 to discuss plans for releasing the news of Trinity to the world. They selected William L. Laurence, an accomplished science reporter, to compose the press release. Laurence had already left his job at *The New York Times* to become a consultant for the Manhattan Project. He would be the only newspaperman privy to perhaps the biggest story of the century. A native of

Lithuania, he had come to America in 1905, landing in New York virtually penniless. He had gone to college and worked his way through Harvard Law School by tutoring rich boys. He was a pugnacious-looking little man who had won a Pulitzer Prize in the course of his journalistic campaigns.

General Groves summoned Laurence to his office at the War Department. Standing before a map of New Mexico, with the Trinity area circled in grease-pencil black, Groves told the reporter of the coming test. He asked Laurence to get ready to write the descriptive account of the test. He also instructed him to prepare press releases that would cover four eventualities, which would begin approximately like this:

1. "A loud explosion was reported today. There was no property damage or loss of life."

2. "An extraordinarily loud explosion was reported today. There was some property damage but no loss of life."

3. "A violent explosion occurred today, resulting in considerable property damage and some loss of life."

4. "A mammoth explosion today resulted in widespread destruction of property and great loss of life."

There was, of course, no need to prepare a cover story for the possibility of a complete fizzle.

Laurence carried out Groves's instructions and shortly paid a visit to Los Alamos. His unannounced appearance there threw the scientists into a minor panic. Aghast that a newspaperman should have breached their hermitage, they calmed down only when Laurence explained his special role in the coming test.

Before May ended, there were fresh crises at Trinity and Los Alamos.

Two accidental bombing "raids" by Alamogordo-based B-29's disrupted the Base Camp temporarily. The airmen

107

had been flying 1500-mile practice sorties in preparation for overseas missions. They had long used lighted targets near Trinity for their night exercises. Their bombs were 200-pound "dummies," each carrying about five pounds of high explosive. On two separate nights the B-29's mistook the Base Camp lights for their targets. They managed to set fire to the Trinity carpentry shop, blow up part of the riding stables and scare hell out of the MP's.

At Los Alamos more technical troubles cropped up. It was the old bogey of predetonation. The scientists were bedeviled by faulty detonators. So precise did the timing have to be, so vital to the test was perfect detonation, that the scientists couldn't be satisfied with detonators that failed only one per cent of the time. They needed mechanisms that would fail only once in 10,000 tries and, if possible, less. The search for a reliable detonator became a holy crusade. There were problems with firing circuits and the molds for casting the explosive lenses. Supplies of firing circuits fell way behind and delayed testing. The circuits were produced outside the laboratory and badly needed improvements in their dependability. The molds were in short supply too. Without them, improvement of the lens design and vital testing of the bomb's high-explosive assembly could not proceed on schedule.

It was a dark month on the mesa.

In Washington, Stimson urged a delaying game. The pressure was on for the Big Three to meet at the beginning of July and thrash out the issues raised by Stalin's heavy-handed demands at Yalta. A postponement of the meeting until after the Trinity test might give Truman the trump he needed to bargain more decisively with the Russians.

Event piled swiftly on event in the capital.

On May 25 the Joint Chiefs set November as the target

date for the invasion of Japan. Three days later Stalin informed Washington that the Red Army would be ready to strike Japan by August 8. Truman, apprised of the latest estimates on the Trinity test, suggested the Big Three meet on July 15. He had been informed, meanwhile, that the Japanese might fight to the last man. The United States should consider any steps, no matter how drastic, that might permit Japan to surrender honorably and easily without forcing further loss of life on both sides.

On May 31 Stimson chaired a crucial meeting of the Interim Committee. The meeting at the Pentagon ran from 8:30 A.M. to 4:15 P.M., with discussions carried on through lunch. The Committee's scientific advisory panel, which included Oppenheimer, Fermi, Arthur Compton and Ernest Lawrence, also attended. Groves, Conant, Bush, General Marshall and the new Secretary of State, James Byrnes, were there.

Stimson used the occasion to express his philosophy on the bomb. His remarks were addressed primarily to the scientists. He told them he did not regard the atomic bomb as a new weapon principally, but rather as a revolutionary change affecting the relations of man to the universe. He said the nation's leaders wanted to take advantage of this. In measured language the Secretary speculated that the bomb might mean the doom of civilization, or its perfection; it might be a Frankenstein monster that would destroy its creators or it might be the salvation through which world peace would be secured.

At the end of that session the Interim Committee agreed that the bomb would have to be used as soon as possible against Japan, and without prior warning. The most effective target would be a dual one—a military installation or vital war plant surrounded by buildings highly susceptible to damage. It would help if the war plant employed a large number of workers who would be the sacrificial examples in this all-important military "demonstration."

In reaching its decision the Committee carefully considered the alternatives of warning the Japanese in advance or demonstrating the bomb in some uninhabited area. Both alternatives were considered impractical and too risky. Nothing could have injured more seriously the Allies' efforts to persuade Japan to surrender than a warning or demonstration followed by a dud. Even the Trinity test would not prove that a bomb dropped from an airplane was certain to explode. Trinity would be a static test, one that could not resolve the uncertainty of whether an atomic bomb, dropped from a moving plane over an enemy city, would explode at a predetermined height. Finally, the Committee realized all too well that the United States had no atomic bombs to waste on harmless demonstrations. After Trinity it would have to utilize its one or two remaining bombs in the most convincing way possible.

Stimson was quite sure, as the May 31 meeting closed, that he and the Washington policy makers had impressed the scientists with their arguments on the decision to use the bomb. He was anxious that these spokesmen for the scientific and intellectual community should feel that the politicians and generals were approaching the fateful decision as statesmen and not merely as soldiers eager to win the war at any cost. The Secretary turned to Dr. Oppenheimer. How many people did Oppenheimer think would die in an atomic-bomb attack? Twenty thousand, Oppenheimer answered. Stimson had one more question. What would be the yield of the weapon at the Trinity test? Oppenheimer thought for a minute and answered, "About two thousand tons, Mr. Secretary."

That same day at Los Alamos the Cowpuncher Committee set July 20 for the Trinity test. The following day, June

1, the Interim Committee's recommendations on the use of the bomb were presented to President Truman.

Shortly after four P.M. on June 2 a battered secondhand Buick moved slowly down Alameda Street toward the Castillo Bridge on the outskirts of Santa Fe. It stopped to pick up a solitary figure waiting at one end of the bridge. The Castillo spans the tawny Santa Fe River, and it was here that Klaus Fuchs and Harry Gold held their seventh meeting.

Fuchs's Buick had terrible tires and was a few minutes late because he had had to get one of them patched. He had also thoughtfully given a lift to several Los Alamos colleagues and had dropped them off at the La Fonda Hotel bar, where the bartender happened to be an FBI agent. When Gold climbed into the car, he observed that Fuchs looked a lot better for his sojourn in the Southwest. Fuchs was wearing his customary brown leather jacket with the collar open and the tortoise-shell glasses that made him look at once owlish and aesthetic. His normally sallow complexion was ruddier, and he'd added a bit to his 5-foot, 9-inch frame. He weighed about 150 pounds now and seemed broader in the shoulders. His dark hair was receding ever so slightly over his bulging forehead.

The two men drove around for perhaps twenty minutes. Fuchs reported that tremendous progress had been made on the bomb and that a test was planned for the following month on a desert site to the south. He indicated that he would be there to watch it. Fuchs then turned over to Gold a sheaf of documents on his implosion work at Los Alamos, including a description of the proposed nuclear and explosives assembly. The meeting ended and Gold caught a bus to Albuquerque to keep an appointment with another Los Alamite, David Greenglass, whom he had never met. Fuchs drove back to Los Alamos.

In his monastic quarters in Bachelor Dormitory Number

102, Fuchs pondered his day's activities. There was a knock on the door and his nearest neighbor, physicist Richard Feynman, walked in. Feynman, whose wife was deathly ill in an Albuquerque sanitarium, had recently moved into the dormitory. The two men sat on Fuchs's metal-spring GI bed and sipped orange juice as they talked. Fuchs chain-smoked and nervously shifted his legs. Feynman, as usual, tried to keep the conversation on a light plane. He kidded Fuchs for not taking more interest in social affairs. "Klaus, you're missing a lot of fun in life," he joked. Fuchs frowned and turned the conversation to more serious matters. They had talked before of the unusual rapport between the American and British scientists at Los Alamos. "Don't you think the Russians should be told what we're doing?" Fuchs suddenly asked. Feynman nodded absently. It was a fair enough question in those days. "Then why don't we send them information?" persisted Fuchs. Something in the way Fuchs emphasized the word "we" disturbed Feynman. He told Fuchs it wasn't for individuals like themselves to assume such responsibility. The two chatted aimlessly awhile longer, but Fuchs seemed lost in his thoughts. Finally Feynman rose to leave. Fuchs never looked up as his colleague shut the door behind him.

It was one of the few times Fuchs came close to revealing the other side of his tortured personality.

Feynman was Fuchs's closest companion, but not even he could suspect the schizophrenic nature of the man in the room next to him. For Fuchs, as he would one day reveal, had, in his arrogance and sickness, undergone a complete inner deterioration. He had used his Communist beliefs to conceal his thoughts in two separate and controlled compartments. One compartment housed the personality Fuchs wanted to be: free and easy with his fellow men. The other, dark and muddled, was where he harbored his treasons. His colleagues, except for that fleeting instance with Feynman, were given no hints of Fuchs's dark side. They saw only the retiring physicist who tried to enter inconspicuously into the community life in self-conscious spurts of sociability.

Fuchs thrived in the clear mountain air of Los Alamos. On days off he went mountain climbing, picnicking or skiing with a few choice friends. He liked to swim and bask in the sun. The Peierls family always included him in weekend hikes, or "marches" as Mrs. Peierls liked to call them, and once he accompanied them on a holiday trip to Mexico. At occasional evening parties Fuchs enjoyed playing "murder" or charades. No matter what the music, he insisted on dancing Viennese waltzes with his partners. The tempo might be Western-hillbilly or Latin tango, but Fuchs would turn it into a lively three-step.

He continued to impress his colleagues with his work, if not with his camaraderie, and was unusually co-operative in reporting his work on implosion to his seniors. Each Friday afternoon, a few minutes before four, two or three fellow workers in the Theoretical Division would drop by Fuchs's office and tell him it was time for the Co-ordinating Council meeting. "Ja," Fuchs would reply curtly and join them. They would walk down the hall together, Fuchs trailing behind, never opening his mouth. He was, however, sufficiently respected to have been made a member of the joint U.S.-British Declassification Board. He seemed extraordinarily conscientious about security details. But at the same time his colleagues noted that Fuchs was one of the more tenacious members in trying to get secret atomic material declassified.

In all, Fuchs seemed to merit the trust of almost everyone at Los Alamos. Among the boisterous bachelor types on The Hill he was regarded as a comparatively virtuous soul. Mothers delighted in having him around their children. Fuchs understood children, treated them as a big brother might and felt at ease in their company—so much so that he was in

113

constant demand as a baby-sitter. If you wanted someone really dependable to look after the kids on a Saturday night, your best bet was to call Klaus Fuchs in the bachelor dormitory. The only thing he insisted on was that your home have either a phonograph or an encyclopedia. He was a model baby-sitter.

At 8:30 Sunday morning, June 3, Harry Gold reached the top of a steep flight of stairs in an Albuquerque walk-up and knocked on the door of the first apartment. Puffing and pouting from his exertion, he was irritated by the smiling stranger in bathrobe and slippers who casually greeted him.

"Mr. Greenglass?" Gold inquired. The man nodded and Gold brushed by him impatiently. "I come from Julius," he announced. He flashed the torn section of a Jell-O box. David Greenglass fished the matching section from his wife's purse and held it aloft with a mock flourish. Gold introduced himself as "Dave from Pittsburgh" and asked what information Greenglass had ready for him.

The Army corporal had just finished breakfast, and he asked Gold for a few hours to prepare some material. Gold left, and Greenglass shut himself in the living room for the next six hours to work on his report. On a dozen sheets of 8-by-10-inch ruled white paper Greenglass laboriously drew a series of sketches of the explosive lens he was helping to fabricate at Los Alamos. In his spidery handwriting he described how the lens molds were used and provided a detailed explanation of the experiments themselves. When Gold returned at 2:30 P.M., the two men exchanged envelopes. Gold took the one containing the lens-mold sketches; Greenglass took one from Gold containing $500 in cash. "Will it be enough?" asked Gold. "Plenty for now," said Greenglass. The two men parted after the briefest amenities.

It had taken less than five minutes for David Greenglass

to sell one of the most sensitive secrets of the entire U.S. atomic-bomb project to the Soviet Union.

Like Fuchs, Greenglass had impressed his superiors. In the "E" shop where he worked, he demonstrated such an interest in the details of implosion design that he was soon elevated to assistant shop foreman over the heads of a dozen other loyal but duller SED's. Like Fuchs, too, Greenglass seemed punctilious about security regulations. When required occasionally to fabricate a complete lens mold, he would copy from a blueprint kept in the shop. But never would Greenglass try to smuggle out a blueprint and run the risk of being caught by guards with such incriminating data. He relied always on what he could carry out of the laboratory in his head.

Where Greenglass differed from Fuchs was in his attitude toward his espionage duties. Fuchs felt he was spying for righteous moral reasons on behalf of all humanity. Greenglass came to regard his betrayal as an intriguing and remunerative adventure. Fuchs loftily disdained offers of money from Gold, specifically a $1500 token of appreciation. Greenglass, with two mouths to feed on an enlisted man's pay, willingly accepted his brother-in-law's financial aid and Harry Gold's $500. He intended to use the money to cover the medical expenses of his wife's recent miscarriage. But Ruth Greenglass saw his acceptance of the money in a different light. In a burst of girlish naïveté, she had sobbed when she saw the money in the envelope from Gold. The venality of the exchange had ruined her dreams of pretense that what the Greenglasses were doing was simply in the interests of scientific enlightenment.

On June 6, less than four days after Harry Gold had met with Fuchs and Greenglass, Stimson told the President that the Interim Committee had decided the bomb project should not be revealed to the Russians until after the first bomb had been used successfully against Japan.

The President and his Secretary of War spent the better part of an hour at the White House discussing how to handle the ticklish possibility of the Soviets' raising the subject of the bomb at the Potsdam Conference in mid-July. They decided that if the Russians asked to be taken on as atomic partners, Truman would have to stall them off as best he could. The two leaders agonized over how the secret could be kept longer from the Russians, a problem that would be magnified if the Trinity test proved resoundingly successful. They apparently did not consider the possibility that the Soviets might already know of S-1 and the secrets of the bomb.

June was a happier month for the scientists struggling to solve the riddles of implosion before the fateful test.

Molds for the explosive lenses began arriving in quantity. Late deliveries had already delayed the Trinity test by a fortnight. The problem of detonator reliability had been all but solved, and the scientists were about to perfect a technique for making the key to successful detonation, the initiator. Only the firing circuits were still in desperately short supply.

In remote Sandia Canyon a proving ground was built for the ultra-secret experiments on the initiator. This was to be the tiny sphere, less than an inch in diameter and code-named "urchin," that would sit in the center of the bomb's plutonium core and release the neutrons at a predesignated moment. It would have to function so perfectly that no neutrons would be released ahead of time to cause predetonation. The project was placed in the hands of Hans Bethe, one of the most revered of the German refugee scientists.

There was, however, absolutely no way to guarantee the

reliability of the initiator. That mechanism, more than any other part of the bomb, represented the truly unknown. It could be partially tested, as one tests an automobile engine by sparking it instead of turning it over. But no one could foretell how the initiator would perform until its acid test within the bomb at Trinity. This was the signal reason, technically, why the most knowledgeable scientists in the project rejected the idea of a harmless demonstration of the bomb for the benefit of the Japanese. If any one component could have wrecked such a demonstration, it was the initiator.

Equally vital to the success of the bomb were the multiple external detonators that would be used to set off the high explosive around the nuclear core. These, at least, could be tested for almost total reliability. Still, the labor at Los Alamos to achieve that reliability was back-breaking. So great was the urgency to get a dependable detonator system that every available scientist in the Explosives Division was assigned to the project. As a result, other experimental programs suffered from lack of manpower.

The single most important requirement for a reliable detonating system was a device that would fire all the detonators simultaneously within a fraction of a millionth of a second. The scores of electronic detonators, clustered around the shell of the bomb, would then detonate with equal pressure on the high-explosive and nuclear material inside. If one detonator fizzled or went off even a millionth of a second too early or too late, it could ruin the symmetry of the bomb's nuclear guts and cause a misfire. The scientists spent June testing literally tens of thousands of detonators, trying to decrease the chances of failure. And in a cubicle at the laboratory Donald Hornig labored to perfect a special switch that would provide a split-second simultaneity in firing the detonators.

The busiest, most undermanned and most crisis-beset spot

at Los Alamos was S Site, where the all-important testing of the explosives charges for the bomb took place. The test firings culminated the work on the vital lens molds. Out of the molds had finally come the tapered circular lenses of high explosive that would be used to compress subcritical hunks of plutonium with stunning swiftness into a seething critical mass.

Overseeing this hectic operation was a hawk-faced Russian named George Bogdan Kistiakowsky. Kisty had been born in Kiev and had fought against the Bolsheviks in 1919 as a sergeant in the White Russian cavalry. Tough as a Cossack's boot, he created legends with his temper—once he hurled a red leather book across a room because it reminded him of the Communist colors. But he coddled a beautiful gray stallion in the MP stables at Los Alamos.

Kisty had been brought kicking and screaming to Los Alamos—he had wanted to go overseas on the ALSOS intelligence mission—and his "pound of flesh" had been that the authorities allow his daughter back East to visit him each summer at the laboratory. The daughter told her friends at college she was summering with her father at a "dude ranch," and that led to the assumption in some circles that Dr. Kistiakowsky was helping the war effort as a gentleman cowboy.

In fact, Kistiakowsky had built the "X" (for Explosives) Division at Los Alamos into a fertile fiefdom of some 600 scientists and technicians, and had been spurring on the implosion program since its inception. There were never enough technicians, though, to keep up with the burgeoning activities at S Site. By the time a new batch of recruits had been briefed on the mysteries of mold design and taught how to handle high explosives, new experiments requiring new shops and technicians demanded further recruits. The labor supply kept dwindling. Kisty's colleagues marveled at his energy and Slavic fury. He badly needed both to weather the crises—delay of materials and shortage of manpower—that plagued his project to the end. One day, like Donald Hornig, he too would sit in the White House as the President's prime minister of science.

Even as Kisty raged at the frustrations of S Site and Hornig labored sleeplessly over his detonators, the most deadly work of all continued unabated at Omega Site at the bottom of Los Alamos Canyon. There, in an oblong, white-walled room, a thirty-three-year-old physicist from Winnipeg, Canada, defied radioactive death by manipulating, with an ordinary screwdriver, two silvery-gray hemispheres of plutonium metal. Louis Slotin had been chosen to test the criticality of the world's first atomic bomb. He was tickling the tail of the Trinity dragon.

Since his first successful critical assembly five months before, in January, Slotin had conducted numerous other assemblies and christened them all with whimsical names like Jezebel, Godiva, Honeycomb, Scripto, Little Eva, Pot and Topsy. These had been uranium assemblies, however. Now Slotin was experimenting with plutonium, the guts of the Trinity bomb. He hovered over the single metal desk in the center of the room. The light from two powerful lamps played on the silver buckle of his gaudy Mexican belt. Only the clicking of a Geiger counter broke the silence. From time to time Slotin glanced at another instrument, which recorded on a roll of paper, in a quivering thin red line, the radiation emitted by the plutonium lumps. As he prodded the lumps closer to each other, the Geiger counter clicked faster and the red line jumped across the paper.

On June 12, for the first time, Slotin tested two full-scale plutonium hemispheres for criticality. The results of his experiments would tell the scientists shortly how much plutonium they needed in the bomb to create an atomic explosion.

* * *

That same day the Interim Committee in Washington ived a petition from seven scientists engaged in the Chicago end of the bomb project. The group was headed by Dr. James Franck, the Nobel laureate from Göttingen, Germany, and included such illustrious names as Leo Szilard and Glenn Seaborg, discoverer of plutonium.

The Franck Report, as it became known, argued against the advisability of a surprise atomic attack on Japan. It urged, instead, a demonstration of the new weapon on a barren island before representatives of the United Nations. If the United States were to be the first to release this new means of indiscriminate destruction upon mankind, warned the report, it would lose moral support the world over, engender an atomic arms race and jeopardize chances for future international control of the bomb.

The Franck Report was turned over to the Interim Committee's scientific panel. At least half the members of that panel—Oppenheimer and Fermi—were personally engaged night and day in completing the first atomic weapon to be tested at Trinity. The nightmare they lived with was not whether the bomb should be used on Japan, but whether the bomb would work.

With each click of the Geiger counters at Omega and with each explosion at S Site, the chances of success at Trinity grew. The site itself had become transformed.

Armies of construction men had moved in with the scientists to change the barren flats into a jungle of wire, shacks and intersecting roadways. Scores of electronics experts had been shunted down from Los Alamos. All available SED's had been pulled off The Hill to work on the test. Nearly 300 scientists, engineers, GI's, consultants, Army and Navy officers, weather specialists and other technicians had now been assigned full time to Trinity. To meet the crush, Bainbridge had ordered eighty-five vehicles of every size and shape. Three new barracks had been erected, an extra latrine added, and hospital and mess hall space increased. Even so, the Base Camp was crowded beyond capacity.

As June progressed, the adobe roads crumbled under the flood of people and traffic. More than twenty-five miles of new blacktop road were laid. The new roads linked the detonation area with the key instrument and personnel shelters to the north, west and south. Each of these main shelters was marked off 10,000 yards from the detonation point and given a code name. South-10,000 was Baker; North-10,000, Able; and West-10,000, Pittsburgh. By the end of the first week in June, final space assignments for the shelters had been made.

An elaborate telephone hookup connected the shelters and key offices at Trinity. South-10,000, where Oppenheimer and other VIP's would watch the test, had its own telephone switchboard. The phones were crude and operated by cranking a generator. Phone lines were laid between Trinity and Los Alamos, and transcripts of all conversations were relayed to the chief Intelligence officer. A teletype was also installed at Base Camp so that messages could be sent directly between the two sites.

Two special outside radio frequencies were needed: one so that the scientists could communicate among themselves in the field and with the MP guards patrolling the site; and the other for transmission between the ground and the B–29 bomber that was expected to observe the test. The frequencies were to be on separate wave lengths that could not be monitored by outsiders. Communication hitches developed almost immediately.

About twenty vehicles for key scientists were equipped with FM Motorola sets. After months of finagling with Washington for the proper frequency, the scientists discovered that their wave length was identical with one for a freight yard in San Antonio, Texas. Though the yard was some 600 miles from Trinity, the scientists could plainly hear the railroadmen shifting their freight cars. Worse, the control tower at the Socorro airport listened in on their conversations.

In mid-June, when the B-29 crews began their practice runs over the detonation area, they found to their horror that the plane-to-ground frequency was the same as that for the Voice of America. Anyone tuning in to the government broadcasting network could overhear the conversations between Base Camp and the B-29's. That security fumble was never rectified in time for the test, although the FM frequency for the scientists and MP's was finally changed.

With no place to go and nothing to dispel the monotonous regularity of the heat and loneliness, the men at Trinity found their biggest diversion in work, ten to eighteen hours of it a day. There never seemed to be enough bodies on hand to master the staggering work load. Everyone, from mess attendants to division leaders, worked at fever pitch.

The scientists and GI's rose at five A.M. and were at work on the flats by six. They broke for lunch at noon. The mess hall featured a crude air conditioner, and the men had an hour to cool off and sample the chow which had been trucked down from Albuquerque. It was always a struggle to return to the desert. The hours right after noon were the most unbearable. The sun scorched the sand flats with temperatures above 100 degrees. Its broiling rays steamed men's clothes to their bodies. Most of the workers wore GI shorts, shoes, woolen socks and visored green fatigue caps. They eschewed shirts whenever possible. Swirling "sand devils" blew grit in their eyes and choked their lungs and nostrils. Alkali dust coated and clogged their instruments. Many of them took to wearing protective goggles or handkerchiefs across their faces. At the end of the day the tops of men's bodies were literally white from the alkali dust. When they returned to their barracks, the scientists and GI's found their bunks covered with a sheen of the stuff. There was no escaping it.

Once on the desert, a man never quite became clean again. The dust, the dirt, the overpowering heat and dryness left a scaly layer of filth on his body. Everything caked up: his clothes, his shoes, his skin. The cold showers at Base Camp—there were no hot ones—did little good. The water was so "hard" that men often emerged with a pale crust of magnesium oxide on their torsos. The first thing a man did when he left Trinity was to stop off at the Hilton Hotel in Albuquerque and "shower down" for an hour.

In the midday heat men who were burying measuring devices in the sand or opening terminal boxes to fix broken wires constantly tensed against rattlers or toads that might spring out at them. Tarantulas and scorpions were underfoot everywhere. Lizards and the poisonous orange-black Gila monsters slithered out from under rocks that the scientists moved for their instruments. A man laying wire through the sagebrush might feel the savage sting of a fire ant or the excruciating bite of a desert centipede.

Early in the game, dinner at five P.M. had signaled the end of work and a chance to play poker or walk into the desert to watch a spectacular sunset. But as the tempo quickened, the scientists found themselves back on the desert after dinner, absorbed in their work till midnight and beyond. It was during these hours of darkness that accidents occurred to frustrate them further. Men digging holes sometimes sliced through carefully laid coaxial cables. Jeeps would swerve off the roads and demolish lines of low-slung communication wires.

There was danger as well as inconvenience to one's health at Trinity. A B–29 lumbered lazily over the test site one afternoon. The tail gunner suddenly spotted some antelope and began stitching up the desert with .50-caliber machine-gun slugs. A dozen scientists, directly under the plane and out of the gunner's line of vision, dropped their instruments and hugged the ground in terror as the bullets thudded about them. They threatened to quit the project right afterward.

Sanitary conditions brought equal cries of outrage. Drinking water was hauled by truck from nearby towns. But the water used for bathing, washing silverware and brushing teeth came from local wells. It was brackish, steely hard and full of alkali and gypsum. The alkali had corrosive properties that could affect a man's skin. The gypsum acted like a laxative. The camp dispensary was flooded with cases of skin disease and diarrhea. Some of the GI's discovered, when they washed their hair in the water, that the strands turned stiff as cement stalks.

Toward the end of June a harsh security clamp-down went into effect. All recreational trips to nearby towns were forbidden. Petty distractions like laundry, dry cleaning and mail all had to be cleared through security. Travel instructions were issued for the 200-mile commute between Los Alamos and Trinity, and they were more involved than those for a trip to Outer Mongolia. Scientists were discouraged from stopping for gas or food along the southward route to Trinity. They were forbidden to stop in any town south of, and including, Socorro, which was forty miles from the site. Special courtesy cards were issued for emergency use at designated service stations in Albuquerque and the town of Belen. Finally, much to the disappointment of the dust-caked desert workers, all stopovers in local hotels between the two sites were prohibited.

A rigid pass system was inaugurated. All Trinity-bound personnel had to secure a pink War Department pass, stamped with a large "T," which was presented to guards at the border of the Trinity site and exchanged for a badge that had to be worn at all times on the site. Another exchange had to be made when personnel left Trinity. Despite security, more than one GI challenged the system and won. The soldiers would drive out on the test site at night, obtensibly to fix a piece of equipment; then, dousing the headlights on their jeeps and using moonlight they would cut across country to avoid the MP's at the main gates. Usually the GI's made a beeline to Las Cruces, the nearest town south. The liquor in Las Cruces was still as lethal as it had been in the days when Billy the Kid took his red-eye neat in the local bar.

In June the final organization charts for Trinity were drawn up.

It was an impressive cast, headed by Kenneth Bainbridge and his alternate, John Williams. Enrico Fermi was to be the chief consultant on all nuclear physics experiments. For these some 300 gauges of every type were being installed at instrument stations around the site.

In charge of assembling the bomb at Trinity was Navy Commander Norris Bradbury, George Kistiakowsky and Robert Bacher. Bradbury, a slim, brusque explosives specialist, had had strong moral reservations about coming to work on the bomb project. His colleagues had finally persuaded him that it was his patriotic duty, but he had been a reluctant arrival at Los Alamos. He was to be responsible for all problems involving the assembly of the bomb.

The assembly operation would be divided into two segments: nuclear and high-explosives. Bacher, the Cornell professor who had taken over command of the Gadget Division at Los Alamos, would oversee the assembly of the plutonium core. Kistiakowsky, head of the laboratory's Explosives Division, would manage the assembly of the high-explosive lenses. One of the Special Engineers working under him would be Leo Jercinovic.

Donald Hornig was to head a three-man detonator unit known as "X-5." Joseph McKibben, a tall, shuffling Missou-

125

rian, would run a group responsible for arming all timing and remote-control signals. A genial University of Wisconsin physicist, Julian Mack, had charge of the platoon of experts taking photographic measurements of the test. John Manley, a blue-eyed Irishman from the University of Michigan, would boss a fifty-man force measuring air blast and earth shock. All physics experiments were under the control of Robert Wilson, a thirty-one-year-old Princeton graduate who had run the Research Division at Los Alamos. He had a company of seventy-five men under him.

There were other assignments involving procurement, transportation, radio communications, searchlight plotting of the radioactive cloud and the launching of a number of balloons to obtain shock-wave velocity and other data from the explosion, if there was one. And preparations were made for an operation which everyone prayed would be unnecessary: evacuation missions in the event of fallout.

Ever since the first grams of plutonium had arrived at Los Alamos, the medical division had been studying the toxic properties of the deadly metal. Its metabolism was similar to that of radium: enough of it in the human body would eat through vital tissues, disintegrate kidneys and cause fatal bone cancer. No cure had yet been found for the agonies that could result from overexposure to radiation and fallout. The best the scientists could do was to devise protective measures against the danger.

The Trinity site had been chosen partly because its location favored such neighboring towns to the northwest as Socorro and San Antonio. The prevailing winds blew northeast, and the nearest town in that direction was Carrizozo with less than 1400 inhabitants. Furthermore, it was hoped that the Oscura Mountains to the east would deflect some of the fallout, as well as cushion much of the blast and shock wave. Immediately following analyses of the high-explosive dress rehearsal shot in May, however, it became apparent that if the atomic fireball rose higher than 10,000 feet, the contamination might be widespread. It appeared to the radiologists that Carrizozo and several tinier hamlets on the eastern rim of Trinity could well have been inundated with fallout if the May shot had contained a bomb-size nuclear core.

One of those concerned was Captain James Nolan of the Army Medical Corps, who had been in charge of the post hospital at Los Alamos. Nolan and the chief radiologist, Stafford Warren, drew up a set of proposed evacuation plans, and Nolan flew to Oak Ridge to deliver them personally to General Groves. Groves had been preoccupied with many matters, but the prospect of fallout had apparently not been high on his priority list. Now he snorted at the suggestion that troops and trucks be assembled outside Trinity for evacuation purposes.

"What are you, a Hearst propagandist?" he asked Nolan.

Groves meant that if he had to compromise security by sending an evacuation force into nearby towns, the secret of the test might end up headlined in the next day's newspapers. To Nolan the General seemed genuinely annoyed that the possibility of evacuation due to fallout had even been raised.

Nevertheless, Groves acted with dispatch. Working closely with the governor of New Mexico, he received authorization to declare martial law throughout the southwestern part of the state if necessary. He also made secret arrangements with the governor to carry out massive evacuations if fallout became a serious menace.

At least twenty security officers were to be stationed in towns and cities as far as a hundred miles away. Some of these would take charge of evacuation missions in the event of severe fallout. Almost all were armed with barographs to record blast and shock effects accurately in case local citizens complained of window shatterings or tried to sue the government for larger damages. A total of 125 men under Lieutenant Bush's command were to guard the Trinity site during the test. They would block off all exits, prevent any civilian from accidentally straying into the test area and ensure that all personnel were clear of the detonation area before firing time. Another force of 160 enlisted men, under Major Thomas Palmer, was to take up posts north of Trinity, with enough trucks to be able to evacuate ranches and towns at the last moment if fallout threatened.

Preparations were made to halt all air traffic between Albuquerque and El Paso on the day of the test. Trinity personnel not needed for the test were to be evacuated beforehand from the site. When the shot went off, all remaining personnel would be at least six miles from the detonation, observing it from reinforced bunkers. As an extra precaution, additional doctors were brought down from Los Alamos to handle any emergencies.

Even after the evacuation force was arranged for, the radiologists voiced concern. Warren, who had surveyed the entire region in a low-flying plane, worried for the safety of some 200 Apache Indians living on an unmarked reservation to the east of Trinity on the other side of the Sierra Oscura. He also estimated there were still some 1000 cattle and sheep ranchers, scattered about the vicinity on remote mesas, who might be endangered in the event of a sudden wind shift. The radiologists were equally concerned over the safety of the Trinity people. Although it was assumed the winds would blow any fallout away from the site, there was always the chance that a shift might carry the fallout cloud back over the site and dump radioactive dust and dirt on the camp.

One of the reasons the bomb would be detonated from a high tower was to lessen the chances of the fireball's sucking up an inordinate amount of earth that could be radioactively poisoned and spewed back over the area. Even so, it was obvious that a lot of debris would go up with the fireball. Radiologists recommended in June that the ground beneath the tower be coated with asphalt for a radius of 300 yards. They even considered borrowing a portable airstrip from a Naval base on the West Coast and spreading it over the test site to diminish the danger. The recommendations came too late to be acted upon.

But Bainbridge and several advisers set out by jeep to survey every possible escape route from Base Camp in case the unexpected happened. They found only three exits: an almost impassable trail that wound through Mockingbird Gap to the south; a worn road in poor condition that ran southwestward toward Elephant Butte; and a single new blacktop road that ran northward by way of the South-10,000 shelter.

It was not the sort of discovery to reassure the faint-hearted.

The GI's and scientists at Trinity had long discussed among themselves what might happen if all calculations proved wrong and the bomb turned out to be infinitely more powerful than anyone had imagined.

Leo Jercinovic and his fellow SED's sat around in the camp PX at night and talked about it over beers. They hid their fears in jokes and banter about how the explosion might tilt the earth off its axis or affect its solar course. They joshed about the possibility of a runaway explosion igniting the atmosphere and encircling the globe in a sea of fire. In their hearts many of them were profoundly scared of what the test might bring. Eavesdropping MP's, who knew next to nothing about the bomb, relayed the fears to their mates in camp.

The scientists, who knew more than anybody else of the bomb's destructive power, worried about the same things.

One of them, Edward Teller, was assigned to make a final review of all such possibilities. Teller considered every area where the scientists might have miscalculated the bomb's potential. He spent hours conjecturing science-fiction fantasies and situations that an atomic bomb might produce if undiscovered laws of nature were suddenly activated by its explosion. Always there was the haunting thought that the test blast might introduce some violent phenomenon beyond the ken of the scientists.

Unknown to the scientists and GI's, military authorities had alerted and were holding in readiness a number of psychiatrists at Oak Ridge. They would be rushed to Trinity in case an epidemic of fear swept the camp at the last moment before the test. Improbable as that seemed, there were rumors that some of the MP's had become "rock-happy" from too many months in isolation and might crack under the strain of fear of what the bomb would do. The psychiatrists might also be needed to soothe those scientists, already afflicted with pre-test jitters, who might suffer severe bouts of manic depression if the test failed.

By mid-June the steel tower for the Trinity bomb was rising girder by girder over the detonation circle—a pinpoint of sagebrush and sand that would be code-named Zero. The tower would be slightly over 100 feet high, with a steel stairway and platform stations every 25 feet up. At its top a special wooden platform with a removable section in the center was built to support the bomb. Sheaves mounted at the tower's pinnacle would hoist equipment through the center of the platform. The removable section would have to be strong enough to support a five-ton load when in place.

The scientists had decided to test the world's first atomic bomb from the top of a tower for several compelling reasons besides lessening the fallout factor. A static test of this sort would allow them far more leeway in gauging the effects of the bomb. Their instruments could be perfectly placed and calibrated. It was infinitely safer, also, than firing the device from a cannon or dropping it from a plane, where a ballistic error might cost lives and create havoc. Finally the scientists wanted to confirm a vital theory that would affect the bomb's use over enemy territory.

The military had contemplated exploding the bomb at such a height that damage from air blast, rather than from ground shock, would be the overwhelming destructive factor. They were proceeding, however, on the basis of evidence gathered from small-scale experiments only. The Trinity shot, close to the ground, would determine once and for all whether air blast or ground shock caused the most destructive results.

On June 16 the Interim Committee's scientific panel issued a report that would have telling impact on the President and his advisers. The panel had spent several days studying the proposals in the Franck Report, which advised against using the bomb in a surprise attack on Japan. The panel's conclusion read: "We can propose no technical demonstration likely to bring an end to the war; we see no acceptable alternative to direct military use." Thus, the scientific panel had upheld the decision to bring the bomb to bear against Japan as swiftly and destructively as possible.

On June 18 a secret meeting involving the fate of ten million fighting men was held at the White House. It was a tumultuous day in Washington. Dwight Eisenhower, the hero of Normandy, had returned home to be greeted by roaring crowds along the capital's Pennsylvania Avenue. Stimson developed a migraine headache in the course of the day and barely dragged himself to the meeting in Truman's office at 3:30 P.M. Present were the Joint Chiefs of Staff, Secretary of the Navy James Forrestal and Assistant Secretary of War John J. McCloy.

131

The military leaders outlined their strategic plans for ending the war with Japan: a two-phase invasion of the enemy's homeland, code-named "Downfall." The first phase, "Olympic," envisioned an amphibious landing November 1 on Kyushu, the southernmost of the Japanese islands. This would be followed four months later by a second great invasion, "Coronet," of Honshu, the island heart of Japan. The plans had been prepared without reliance upon the atomic bomb, which had not yet been tested.

The Japanese were estimated to have some 5,000,000 soldiers and 5000 suicide "Kamikaze" aircraft to throw against the U.S. invading force of 5,000,000 men. General Marshall told Truman that it would take until late fall of 1946 to bring Japan to her knees and that half a million American lives might be lost. Stimson advised the President that the Japanese would mount a ferocious defense of their homeland. The vision of vast land armies clashing in a final slaughter was brutally sobering to everyone in that room.

The prospects were so horrendous, in fact, that the meeting seemed about to break up on a note of total gloom when the President suddenly asked John McCloy for his opinion. Stimson's deputy had maintained a discreet silence throughout the meeting. What he said now brought wintry stares from the military chiefs, most of whom were only vaguely aware of the Manhattan Project and inclined to skepticism about the bomb's power. It was as if a dirty phrase, unmentionable and unthinkable, had been dropped at a church meeting. Why not use the atomic bomb, McCloy suggested, as a club over the Japanese in demanding their surrender? Japan should be informed that the United States had the bomb and was prepared to use it. The result might avoid the costly invasion proposed by the Joint Chiefs.

Truman found the suggestion intriguing. He had already decided that an ultimatum should be given Japan following agreement among the Allies at the Potsdam Conference. By then he would know if the Trinity test had succeeded. If it had, Truman wanted to give Japan a clear opportunity to end the fighting before the United States made use of the new weapon. Mention of the bomb and of America's readiness to use it would give the ultimatum extra teeth. There was only one hitch to McCloy's proposal: there was no assurance—even if Trinity was successful—that the first bomb dropped over Japan would explode. The proposal was sidetracked.

That day, June 18, at a meeting in the Gamma Building at Los Alamos, Robert Oppenheimer estimated that the chances of firing the Trinity bomb before July 20 were only fifty-fifty. Delays in the delivery of lens molds, and the consequent delay in producing explosive lenses, had put a crimp in the scientists' efforts to meet the tight schedule. Plutonium was arriving in increasing quantities from Hanford, but there still wasn't enough to meet the needs of the countless experiments that had to be run off before the test. Yet Oppenheimer was being heavily pressured from Washington to have the bomb ready for testing before the Potsdam Conference began. It was imperative that the test be held as soon as possible after the first Big Three meeting on July 15 so that, if it was successful, Truman would have some badly needed bargaining leverage to exert on Stalin.

The pressures had taken their toll on Oppie. From an already spare frame he had dropped thirty pounds. In his worn blue jeans and garishly checked shirts he resembled a scarecrow. The poetic face was sunburned but drawn. The eyes, blue as gentians, wore a perpetually harried look. Oppenheimer knew the names of most of the Mexican-Indian laborers, as well as the scientists, at Los Alamos. But when they nodded good-morning to him these days and murmured "señor," Oppie seemed barely to notice them.

He was worried. He was absorbed. Still, he was never unconscious of the role he and his colleagues were playing in the drama. Early one morning, walking to work, he turned to a younger scientist and blurted, "Aren't these the most exciting times?"

Except for the terrible pressure, they were also, by and large, happy times for Oppenheimer. His unpleasantness with the security people, their probing interrogations of his Communist past, seemed to be over and forgotten. His wife, Kitty, was at Los Alamos with him, helping out in the laboratory's health division. Their children, Peter and Katherine, were also there and the family had spent many a weekend riding horseback through the canyons and hills. Until recently, when all leisure time had disappeared, Oppenheimer had reveled in the outings with his family and colleagues. The clean air of the mesa had had a tonic effect on his tubercular condition. Only an annoying dose of chickenpox in recent weeks had marred his health. But now frayed nerves and lack of sleep were sapping his energies.

It was paradoxical that this man, who drove his army of scientists as relentlessly as a drill sergeant, should be so frail a physical specimen. The men under Oppenheimer compared him to a football coach because he had had the ability to organize them as a team and make them play their hearts out. Yet he had done it without the sergeant's brute force or the coach's bravado. He had moved them with spirit, logic and the quiet strength of his own example. In his inimitable way this fragile philosopher had done at Los Alamos what no robust Titan could have done.

Along the way Oppenheimer had changed his attitude toward the bomb. At the beginning of the project he and other physicists had been engrossed in the bomb's physical mysteries. They had looked upon it as merely a gadget, a technological artifact that would exploit scientific principles long known. Now, as they unraveled the enigmas of its

134

physiognomy and speculated on its awful power, the scientists began to appreciate the broader military and, finally, political implications of the bomb. Some expressed doubt that the bomb should be used as a weapon to end the war. Others, mindful of the original purpose in building the monster, accepted the military and political leaders' decision to use it against the enemy. They believed, however, that the circumstances of military use imposed certain obligations on America. For that reason Oppenheimer was one of those who strongly urged in the last weeks in June that the United States, before using the weapon, advise its chief allies of the progress that had been made on the atomic bomb and suggest future controls for world peace. The Soviet Union especially should be consulted.

On the evening of June 19, on a train platform in the New York suburb of Flushing, Harry Gold met with his Soviet superior, Anatoli Yakovlev, and recounted in detail his meetings two weeks earlier with David Greenglass and Klaus Fuchs in New Mexico. Gold turned over the lens implosion and other documents given him by the two spies. Yakovlev listened intently as Gold described the startling progress made on the atomic bomb and passed along the information from Fuchs that the first full-scale test would probably take place in July.

In Los Alamos, Klaus Fuchs turned over the keys to his Buick to his colleague, Richard Feynman.

Feynman's wife had died in Albuquerque, and the young physicist needed a car to go down and take care of the funeral arrangements. On the way there, the Buick's tires gave out and Feynman had to leave the car and hitchhike the last thirty miles to Albuquerque. When he got back to Los Alamos that evening, he was weary and sad. Fuchs poured Feynman a glass of orange juice and quietly asked him

135

about the funeral. Then he saw that Feynman didn't want to talk about it and depress himself further. It was obvious that his colleague needed distraction. For the next few nights Fuchs made it a point to have Feynman invited to the homes of his various friends. Fuchs took care of the arrangements. The camaraderie of candlelit dinners and lively shop-talk far into the night proved a comforting therapy.

The final week of June rushed by.

In Washington, Stimson and Harry Truman prepared to leave for the Potsdam Conference. Stimson spent the week in huddles with British Embassy officials and the Interim Committee, at which the bomb was the principal topic. The Interim Committee examined the news releases prepared by reporter Laurence and agreed that the commander of the Alamogordo Air Base should issue a "cover" story, if Trinity was successful, explaining that a remote ammunition dump had exploded. If it became necessary to evacuate the area, the populace should be told it was because poisonous "gas shells" had exploded.

The status of the bomb's use remained tangled for the present: the Chicago scientists feared that dropping it on Japan might impair future chances for effective international control; the Interim Committee's scientific panel could see no acceptable alternative; the Committee itself was for dropping the bomb, but favored the panel's suggestion that the Russians be apprised of the project beforehand. Vannevar Bush and James Conant especially urged that the Russians be notified. They had opposed from the start any policy that would needlessly risk prejudicing U.S. relations with Russia. In the last two months both men had become convinced that the United States should seek Russian co-operation before dropping the bomb.

The Committee finally agreed that it would be wise for Truman to advise Stalin at the coming conference that the

United States had been working on the bomb and expected to use it against Japan. Truman might also suggest to Stalin that the two nations hold future talks on the bomb's postwar role. If Stalin pressed for further details, Truman could say the United States was not ready to divulge them yet.

At Los Alamos it hadn't rained for weeks. The parched river bed of the Rio Grande had been baked a terra-cotta brown. In the Jemez hills, where the aspens splashed gold across the dark green slopes, the yellow chamisa and Mariposa lilies sagged for want of moisture. A dry hot wind blew over Site Y, fanning a number of small forest fires close to the laboratories. The grass withered in the tiny plots behind the scientists' homes, and foliage and pine needles dried up on the trees. General Groves, on one of his periodic tours, worried that sparks from the fires might be blown onto the wooden laboratory and office buildings. He made a note to Colonel Tyler to have the Fire Patrol increased. As usual, a water shortage was on, and Coca-Cola was used for brushing teeth.

In the Frijoles Canyon, fourteen miles south of Los Alamos, Mrs. Evelyn Frey awoke each day in her lodge to "the thunder" of the experimenters. Everyone who lived near the laboratory on the mesa and heard the explosions that summer referred to them as such. Mrs. Frey's picturesque lodge had been jammed for months with GI's and technicians who had been unable to find lodgings on The Hill. She put them up on cots and double-decker bunks and fed them local dishes and hamburgers by the thousands. The Army paid her for her troubles. That last week in June, as the test date loomed nearer, fewer and fewer scientists had dropped down from The Hill to visit Mrs. Frey and sample her enchilladas and tortillas. Once Klaus Fuchs wandered in at dusk to pay his respects. The old lady found him pleasant but strange. He liked to sit in her kitchen and watch the cooks make dinner.

137

In the "Tech Area" at Los Alamos the news was cheering. The dragon ticklers at Omega had succeeded in measuring the first critical assembly of plutonium. On June 24 the scientists, on the basis of this experiment, definitely established the size of Trinity's nuclear package. The mysteries of the initiator had also been solved and the first complete unit had been produced. The scientists were so excited that one of them dropped the unit on the floor and nearly lost it down an open sewer pipe.

On June 27 a shipment of brand-new detonators arrived. The du Pont Company had been working overtime to develop the most rugged and reliable mechanism possible. The new detonators, three quarters of an inch in diameter, would reduce the scientists' chances of misfire from 1 in 300 to 1 in 30,000. Elated, Oppenheimer made final plans to fix the date for the test. On June 30 the Cowpuncher Committee reviewed all schedules of the various divisions working on the test.

At Trinity that evening the scientists and GI's got the word. The test would be fired on the morning of July 16 at four o'clock. That was the earliest possible date. Even if all parts functioned perfectly, the bomb would yield no more than an estimated force equivalent to that of 5000 tons of TNT.

VI

July 1–14, 1945

UNDAUNTED by puny predictions of the bomb's performance, the men of Trinity girded for the test. Those final two weeks on the desert they sweltered unceasingly over their instruments. They worked twenty-hour days, sometimes more, and consumed gallons of orange pop and coffee. Oppenheimer's cough worsened. The GI's developed painful raw spots on their backs from bumping against jeep seats as they jounced about the site. The heat and dust were so bad that the scientists pleaded with their wives at Los Alamos to send down fresh underwear by the gross.

The Jornada was ablaze with yellow cactus and mesquite. The sharp-tipped swords of the yuccas thrust high as a horse's head. Science, however, had intruded on the landscape. The desert was bound like some sleeping Gulliver with a lattice of cords and cables. Nearly 500 miles of them connected strategic instruments with observation and control stations. Hundreds of heavily insulated wires bordered both sides of the roads and were draped along poles no higher than fence posts. When poles weren't available, the scientists strung the wires over yucca bushes.

Bainbridge fussed and fidgeted over every detail of planning. More than any other man, he knew that the test *had* to work and that as much information as possible must be obtained from it. The time, the effort, the expenditures of human talent and technical materials could not be repeated.

141

Only one test could be made of the bomb, and Trinity was it.

By July 1 all proposals for new experiments had been halted. Bainbridge and his key staffers spent the last fortnight checking with project leaders on the status of their experiments and the readiness of their equipment. There were nightly meetings to hear progress reports and to plan assignments for the following day. Liaison and esprit had improved tremendously. The grumbling and griping had been replaced by an almost Good Samaritan atmosphere. A scientist needing help on one of his experiments would suddenly find four colleagues at his side ready to assist. From Bainbridge down to the lowliest SED an awareness gripped all at Trinity that they were approaching a historic and momentous event.

All major administrative and technical decisions were referred to a top council which included, principally, Bainbridge; his alternate, John Williams; and Frank Oppenheimer, chief administrative aide to Bainbridge. Oppenheimer, a tall nervous man, was the younger brother of Robert. He had been assigned to Trinity with special responsibility for the physical safety of the personnel there. He had done a commendable job in helping start the Oak Ridge separation plant; he also had a Communist past and had headed a Communist cell in the late 1930's at Stanford. He had since resigned from the Party and come to work on the bomb project under his brother's direction. He was Bainbridge's "man Friday."

After technical uncertainties, weather was the biggest question mark at Trinity. Since June 25, a fourteen-man group at Base Camp, headed by meteorologist Jack Hubbard, had been receiving weather reports at hourly intervals. Hubbard could draw on a wealth of information sources, including the Army Air Force weather stations at Alamogordo and Kirtland Field, Albuquerque; the local Civil

Aeronautics Administration office; and the Army's weather division in Washington, D.C. He even had access to international weather reports. Armed with data from these sources, the weathermen at the beginning of the month predicted nearly ideal conditions for the days surrounding the test date. The forecast for July 16, however, was dubious at best.

In her Santa Fe office, Dorothy McKibbin marked the upbeat in the tempo of activity. Though no one had told her the date, she knew intuitively that the day of the test was at hand.

Voices on the telephone were taut with strain. An unusual number of requests for hotel accommodations flooded her office. They came all at once from VIP's in New York and Washington, from CIC bigwigs and Pentagon brass. Not all could be handled. One general who wanted a suite at the La Fonda Hotel ended up in a boardinghouse, sharing a double bed with a sergeant. Over Mrs. McKibbin's desk streamed messages for special automotive parts to be delivered promptly to trucks waiting outside town. The trucks were carrying equipment to Trinity, and the drivers had been ordered by security men to stay out of Santa Fe, regardless of breakdowns. Mrs. McKibbin found herself running an emergency spare-parts service.

There were other curious incidents. One Los Alamos wife kept badgering her to do something about the local watch shop which was dallying on a repair job on her husband's timepiece. Mrs. McKibbin couldn't understand the urgency in the woman's pleas. The wife was Mrs. Samuel Allison, whose husband had just been ordered to Trinity to conduct the official countdown of the test. A sentimentalist, he wanted his own watch for the occasion.

* * *

143

On The Hill a strange air of skepticism mingled with the scientists' general relief and exhilaration that two years of unremitting toil was nearing an end. In a few days they would know whether their theories and calculations had been right or wrong.

To many of them Trinity was not only a means toward ending the war. It represented the climax of an intriguing intellectual match between the scientists and the cosmos. The prospect of solving the bomb's cosmic mysteries, of having their calculations proved correct, seemed far more fascinating and important to the scientists than the prospect of their opening an era obsessed by fear and devoted to control of those very mysteries. They were unbottling the atomic genie, but others would have to worry about its care and feeding. The scientists at Los Alamos felt they had every right to celebrate the end of a long endeavor and to toast their hopes for success at Trinity.

Those hopes, however, were tempered by a perverse skepticism over how the bomb would perform. The scientists refused to believe what their own calculations told them. The bomb had a blackboard potential of nearly 20,000 tons, or 20 kilotons, of TNT. But no one thought for a minute that such a yield would be achieved. The manifold uncertainties of the weapon—the fact that implosion and plutonium had never been tested on such large scale—frightened the scientists into a "fizzle" syndrome. The most prominent among them actually wagered against the very beast they had spent years nurturing and training for this test.

They did so in an informal betting pool that took place the first week of July. The entry fee was $1. The bets on the explosive yield of the Trinity bomb ranged from 45,000 tons to zero. Edward Teller alone scoffed at his colleagues' pessimism and picked 45 kilotons. Hans Bethe figured on 8 kilotons at most. George Kistiakowsky thought his guess of 1400 tons was highly optimistic. Oppenheimer bet the yield would be all of 300 tons. Louis Slotin bet 2 tons. John Williams ventured 200 pounds. And Norman Ramsey, a Harvard physicist, made what he thought was the most intelligent bet in the pool. He took zero.

Two weeks before the test date the war in the Pacific was entering its final stage and the Japanese knew defeat was inevitable. They were without allies. Their navy was nearly destroyed, their island vulnerable to a blockade that could deplete its industry and virtually starve its populace. Japanese cities were bleeding sores from the relentless bombing raids of the B-29's. The Japanese High Command faced the massed armies of America and Britain, the rising forces of China and the ominously threatening divisions of Soviet Russia. Yet Japan was expected to wage a fanatical defense of its homeland if invaded.

Stimson was in the President's office early on Monday, July 2. With him he had a draft of the ultimatum that would be issued Japan following the Potsdam Conference. It set forth the terms Japan must accept to avoid complete destruction of her homeland: demilitarization, surrender of all conquered territories and punishment of her war criminals. The warning demanded that those in authority proclaim at once the unconditional surrender of Japan's armed forces. No mention of the atomic bomb was contained in the draft.

The Secretary of War was back the next day to continue his discussions of the bomb with Truman. Uppermost in both men's minds was not the consideration of whether Japan's surrender could be achieved without using the bomb, but whether *any* military or diplomatic course could hasten Japan's capitulation. Already, in a fenced-off property on Long Island, New York, black cinder-block structures were being erected. The buildings at Brookhaven Laboratory would house the first thousands of shell-shocked casualties from the invasion of Japan. Other rehabilitation centers throughout the United States were being planned for the wounded and emotionally shattered survivors of that event.

On July 3 Leo Szilard composed a petition at the Chicago Metallurgical Laboratory. It was for the President's eyes, and it concluded: "We, the undersigned, respectfully petition that you exercise your power as commander-in-chief to rule that the United States shall not, in the present phase of the war, resort to the use of atomic bombs." General Groves, who considered Szilard somewhat of a pain, allowed the petition limited circulation and saw to it that scientists at Oak Ridge and elsewhere got the word they could organize counter-petitions if they desired. Even Szilard's Chicago colleagues found his petition too extreme for their liking. The modified petition, which seventy of them finally signed, urged Truman not to use the bomb unless the Japanese had been fully notified of the surrender terms and had still refused to capitulate. Truman never saw the petition. Security officials deemed it a superfluous document in light of the decisions then being made at highest levels.

British and American policy makers met on July 4 at the Pentagon, and the British, led by Lord Halifax and Sir James Chadwick, concurred in the U.S. decision to use the bomb against Japan. One reservation bothered everyone: If Truman at the Potsdam Conference said nothing of the bomb to the Russians and then used it against Japan a few weeks later, Stalin might feel affronted and relations among the Big Three would suffer. It was agreed that Truman must watch for the right moment at Potsdam to broach the subject of the bomb to Stalin.

From July 2 to July 4 the telephone wires burned between Washington and Los Alamos. A new and serious crisis had hit the laboratory and Oppenheimer was pleading for a postponement of the test date.

The crisis erupted in Kistiakowsky's Explosives Division. Just when the lens-mold bottleneck seemed to be easing, the scientists discovered that scores of the molds were arriving in faulty condition. They bore cracks and bubbles that made them unfit for the delicate tolerances required in the bomb's explosives assembly. Kisty was frantic. Tension and grief threatened to demoralize his entire shop. Desperate, he charged into the fabrication plant at S Site to take personal command of the repair efforts. Using ordinary dental tools, tweezers and scrapers, Kisty and the explosives men struggled around the clock to have the defective molds ready before the test date.

Oppenheimer, meanwhile, fought a losing battle with Groves on the phone. He was sure that the test could not be held successfully on the 16th. Besides the molds crisis, he was also having wiring troubles at Trinity. He had dispatched all but a few of the remaining electricians at Los Alamos to help in the emergency. The responsibility of risking failure on the 16th through too hasty preparations, however, was one which Oppenheimer did not want and which he thought the military should not undertake. Oppenheimer wanted no alibis if the test fizzled. A few extra days would give him time to settle the molds and wiring crises and have everything in proper shape for the test.

Groves refused to bend. The test must go as scheduled. The general had talked with Conant and the "upper crust" in Washington, and they wanted the test held as soon as possible. Indeed, Stimson and others were urging July 14 as the most desirable date. That was now out of the question, but Groves was under pressure from above to honor the July 16 date. Stimson and Truman simply had to have an early test to strengthen their hand at Potsdam.

The general was bearing up with remarkable fortitude. Only his waistline was suffering. He no longer had time to play tennis, but candy helped recharge him with quick energy. Hence the chocolates in his safe. He worked a seventeen-hour day at his office in Foggy Bottom and managed to run the Manhattan Project through one overworked phone and a long-suffering secretary.

On a typical day Groves was at his desk by 8:30 A.M. and stayed there until 1:30 the next morning. He would meet with at least a half-dozen officials and make some thirty or more phone calls around the country. His secretary—indeed, the closest thing he had to an adjutant general—was a thirty-two-year-old widow who wore her brown hair in a crown-like braid. Mrs. Jean O'Leary had won her job by rebuking Groves once for cowing other stenographers with his brusque, non-stop dictation. She ran the Manhattan Project command post when Groves was away on business, and she rightly earned her soubriquet, "Colonel O'Leary."

Groves simply didn't believe in large staffs. He attended to everything personally, refused to read or write down anything, and relied almost completely on the telephone. Fascinated by the individual projects of certain of the bomb makers, he would huddle with them at Los Alamos and Hanford. Or, waiting for train connections in Chicago, he would phone them at the Metallurgical Laboratory and have them come down to the station. There, on a bench in the waiting room, he listened to their whispered progress reports. Always, security occupied his thoughts. On train trips out of Washington, Groves slipped his secret papers between the mattress and bed sheet and slept on top of them.

On July 4 the general placed a long-distance call to the commanding officer at Hanford. There had been concern over the lagging rate of plutonium shipments from Hanford to Los Alamos. The huge plant on the Columbia River was doing its utmost to accelerate production of the valuable slugs for the bomb's nuclear core. Now Groves ordered the plant to increase its shipments further for the following week.

The struggle to obtain enough nuclear material to make the bomb had been waged behind the scenes ever since the first shipment of uranium slipped surreptitiously into the country in 1940. With the discovery of plutonium, the raw materials project had surged ahead on two fronts. Confident of the uranium gun-assembly method, the scientists had relegated all their U-235 to the Hiroshima bomb, perhaps the most outrageously expensive and wasteful weapon ever built for one combat mission. The artificially produced plutonium had been assigned to the Trinity bomb. The clandestine delivery of the two nuclear elements to the Hiroshima and Trinity weapons was one of the great undercover stories of the war. The terminal point was always Los Alamos.

The U-235 drama began in the vast Shinkolobwe mine of Katanga Province, Belgian Congo. Shinkolobwe alone supplied three quarters of the uranium for the Hiroshima bomb. Armies of workers extricated the uranium ore and put it through massive crushers before shipping it to America. Each month several hundred tons of ore were placed in drums aboard 16-knot vessels and sent racing across the U-boat-infested waters of the South Atlantic. The U-boats sent at least two of the cargoes to the bottom. But by the end of 1944 some 3700 tons of raw uranium had reached America.

From New York Harbor the ore was transferred in railroad cars to an Army warehouse in Middlesex, New Jersey. So toxic was the stuff that the drums and freight cars carrying it had to be opened with utmost caution using special monitoring devices. From Middlesex the uranium ore, a grayish gravel substance, traveled secretly to Tonawanda, New York, where a Union Carbide plant refined it into a chemical compound called uranium tetrachloride. From Tonawanda the uranium was dispersed to three more refineries, which processed it further and shipped it to Oak Ridge for final separation. Under heavy guard the material was trucked in special containers to the secret site in Tennessee.

The uranium's final trip from Oak Ridge to Los Alamos could have been used for an Alfred Hitchcock script. Airplane was the early mode of travel. But the risks of losing the material in a crash or having it exploded by sudden turbulence persuaded the Army to move the U-235 by train and car.

At 10:30 A.M. on specified days two CIC couriers in civilian clothes showed up at Y-12, one of Oak Ridge's production areas. The agents wore snub-nosed Smith & Wesson revolvers under their armpits. They carried out the enriched uranium in a pair of plain-looking suitcases, each weighing about ten pounds, and gingerly deposited them in the back seat of an unmarked Chevrolet sedan. The sedan, followed by an escort car bristling with tommy guns, set off for Knoxville.

At Knoxville the couriers boarded the Louisville & Nashville train bound for Cincinnati. In their private compartment they bolted the doors and placed the suitcases gently on the floor. Two hours later in Cincinnati their special car was switched to the Pennsylvania Railroad's Chicago-bound "Southland." The couriers took turns guarding the suitcases at night aboard the sleeper. Next morning plain-clothes agents from the Chicago Manhattan Project office met the train. The couriers and the U-235 were escorted to Chicago's Dearborn Station. There, at 12:01 P.M., they boarded the Santa Fe "Chief" for what appeared to be a trip to Los Angeles. Shortly after two o'clock the following afternoon, though, the "Chief" made an unscheduled stop at tiny Lamy, New Mexico. The couriers were met by Los Alamos security men and driven the last miles to the laboratory, where the U-235 was turned over to the post commander.

The plutonium's delivery was a Wild West saga of less devious but more rugged proportions. Despite the booming Hanford operation, no significant amounts of plutonium had reached Los Alamos before the late spring of 1945. At that time they came by train and the couriers were handcuffed to the containers. Shipments steadily increased, but the first grams of the precious stuff were eagerly snapped up by the scientists, who wanted to use them for various preliminary experiments, and by the metallurgists, who wanted to probe the plutonium's active properties. At the beginning of July there was not enough plutonium at Los Alamos to build the Trinity bomb.

Hours after Groves's July 4 order, though, Colonel Franklin Matthias, Hanford's commanding officer, put the plant on a breakneck production-delivery schedule. Shipments had been leaving for Los Alamos twice a week; now they covered the route nearly every day. It was door-to-door delivery made by automobile over a thousand miles of some of the roughest terrain in America. The motor convoy roared with its treasured cargo down a winding, treacherous southeastward route that crossed six states—a brutal two-day round trip. The GI's and security officers who ran it were hand-picked for nervelessness and driving skill. They knew that the material they carried was priceless and invaluable to the war effort. They were expected to be pistol experts as well as master mechanics. Once a month they underwent blood checks for radiation exposure.

The plutonium went to Los Alamos in the form of a nitrate or as a plain slug immersed in chemically treated water. The slugs were shielded by lead coats and placed in special cans. Each unit weighed twenty pounds. The stuff was transported in converted Army ambulances that had been outfitted with struts and braces to hold the material

151

steady. An eight-man security detachment, armed with .45's and submachine guns, set out every other day on the ten-hour, 500-mile drive from Hanford to Salt Lake City, Utah. A CIC agent rode the lead escort sedan, followed by a truck carrying spare parts, the ambulance with the plutonium and a rear escort car with another security man. The agents communicated with each other over short-wave radio as the convoy barreled down Route 80 through Oregon and Idaho, at speeds up to sixty miles an hour.

At Fort Douglas, an Army post on the fringe of Salt Lake City, the convoy changed security officers and drivers for the second leg of the trip. This was the hairiest hitch—a fourteen-hour haul over 450 miles of winding, precipitous and often unpaved road. From Monticello, Utah, to Cortez, Colorado, the road sliced through purple sagebrush country. From Cortez to Pagosa Springs, Colorado, it zigzagged between 7000-foot peaks where rock slides and washouts threatened. The spare-parts truck overturned one night at Durango, nearly killing its occupants. The last stretch over the Continental Divide was a nightmare of twisting turns and roller-coaster runs where a faulty brake meant instant disaster. It was always a relief to hit Tierra Amarilla on the other side, to coast through the little adobe village and along the rest of the way down to Espanola, gateway to Los Alamos.

The principal security officers on the Hanford-to-Los Alamos route were First Lieutenants William Riley and Nicholas Dazzo. A routing officer, making out slips for the Riley-Dazzo run one day, forgot Riley's name and decided to christen the whole operation the "Razzle-Dazzle Express."

Another emergency hit Los Alamos just as the plutonium deliveries picked up. The demand for experiments on the scarce material had grown so that hourly allotments were given the scientists to perform their various magic on the incoming slugs. The slugs were so radioactive, however, that they had to be plated first with protective nickel at the laboratory's purification plant. When the slugs were assembled for the Trinity test, they were shaped into two tightly fitting plutonium hemispheres that would make up the core. In the first week of July a blister rash broke out on the hemispheres' surface and threatened to undo all the work on the nuclear assembly.

The blisters—tiny pinholes caused by a defect in the plating—appeared on the undersides of the hemispheres where the two parts would meet. The blisters were infinitesimal but large enough to cause a fatal misfit between the hemispheres. The scientists feared they would have to remake the entire nuclear core, an effort that would take them nearly three weeks and effectively erase the July 16 test date.

The Gadget Division was thrown into turmoil. Every effort was made to eradicate the blisters. Failing that, the scientists sought some way to fill in the spaces between the hemispheres, which had been caused by the blisters. Someone had the brainstorm that loosely packed gold might be the solution. Oppenheimer was contacted and spent a day frantically searching the laboratory before some gold foil was finally located in an office safe. Several ounces were requisitioned and the scientists fought against time to plug the core with gold.

Trinity's procurement battles in the final weeks sorely tested the security apparatus of the bomb project and the administrative genius of its officers.

The fight for the nuclear material had ranged from the Congo across the Atlantic to Oak Ridge and Hanford. The struggle to procure myriad parts and equipment for the Trinity test encompassed all parts of the globe. The idea of supplying a large research laboratory like Los Alamos was challenging enough. Supplying it secretly, in wartime, with the equipment needed for a test no one had ever made before—at a test site 1200 miles from the nearest large market and more than 100 miles from the nearest rail and air terminal—seemed a preposterous pipe dream. But the project set up a secret network of purchasing offices, warehouses and phony shipment addresses. And, amazingly, the plan worked.

The main purchasing point was an Army Engineers office at Eighth and Hill streets in Los Angeles. Agents there received from Los Alamos coded teletype requests for everything from test mice to weather balloons. The Engineers turned the requests over to University of California officials located on the floor below. The University, as scientific overseer of the Los Alamos laboratory, issued the supply orders in its own name to appropriate branch purchasers in Los Angeles, Chicago and New York. The branch offices then went to work contacting suppliers in their areas.

Everything purchased for Trinity east of the Mississippi River was shipped to a Chicago warehouse near Lake Shore Drive. Everything purchased west of the Mississippi went to a Los Angeles warehouse. The warehouses belonged to the mythical "Calexico Engineering Company" and were nothing more than security cover points where the shipments were unwrapped, checked and relabeled. The original labels were removed to throw snoopers off the scent of the supplies' ultimate destination. The new labels were addressed to a "Mr. J. E. Burke" of the University of New Mexico's Department of Physics—only the supplies never reached Burke. They were diverted instead to a railroad siding on the outskirts of Albuquerque. There, at a collection point run by the Army Engineers, the items were picked up by trucks and hauled directly to the Trinity site.

The operation didn't always work smoothly. Entire railroad cars sometimes disappeared for days with their vital materials. One routing mistake, and a carload of steel containers could end up in Altoona, Pennsylvania, instead of Albuquerque, New Mexico.

The problem of priorities was awkward. By early July, Trinity carried the highest procurement priority in the nation—"XX." This was a super-urgency rating that could be used to obtain parts whose lack would seriously jeopardize the test schedule; but Trinity officials were loathe to use it. It often meant interfering with other important war projects. Requests at Trinity for a special oxide used in electric lighting might deprive certain war plants of fluorescent lamps needed for night work. A special drafting device sought by the Trinity planners might delay the same item from reaching PT-boat navigators in the South Pacific. The XX priority was used sparingly.

Throughout the first week of July the traffic in supplies to Trinity multiplied astoundingly. Money was no object. The scientists spent $40,000 in one short period on miscellaneous objects like radio tubes and canvas water bags. Seismographs, too delicate to be stored in a baggage car, rode out by train from Boston to Albuquerque on soft Pullman berths. The crane that would hoist the Trinity bomb to the top of the tower cost $20,000. And the tower, which took weeks to build for a possible one-night stand, cost nearly six figures. The war had depleted supply stocks, and many of the items had to be scrounged secondhand. Condensers were in short supply. High-quality cameras for recording the test were almost impossible to obtain. There was head-scratching over how to buy thousands of dollars' worth of high-speed film without raising suspicions. Lenses for some cameras were not on the market at all and had to be ground to order.

The procurement men ranged far afield for their needs. Tourmaline, a mineral used in making special gauges to measure the explosion, was secured on a top-priority order from European and South American mines. Coaxial cables had to come all the way from Britain. The Manhattan Project literally cornered the world supply of lead glass in Belgium so that the scientists could fashion a lens through which cameras could photograph the test without harm from gamma radiation. And in one instance the government's diplomatic resources were tapped to recover a dozen special barographs from Argentina. The instruments were needed at Trinity, but the only U.S. firm that made them had just sold its last lot to the Argentine government. An emergency directive from Washington annulled the transaction and returned the barographs to the United States.

Two of the most harassed men at Trinity were Robert Van Gemert and Harry Allen. They were charged with supplying and transporting the mountains of equipment to the test site. The commercial trucking situation was chaotic. So Allen and Van Gemert organized their own transportation fleet. Their forty-five drivers and fifteen trucks constituted the "largest undercover truck line" in New Mexico. The trucks, loaded with tons of batteries, cables, transistors and gauges, left Los Alamos each evening for Trinity. Other trucks from Albuquerque and Santa Fe swelled the fleet along the way. The truckers drove all night, slept during the day at the site, then returned under cover of darkness to pick up fresh supplies from The Hill. Allen was constantly awakened in the dead of night by frantic calls from drivers stranded with flat tires or stalled engines. Somehow, though, the supplies got through.

They poured into a special stockroom at Trinity at the rate of eight tons a day. By July 5 the stockroom was a snarled and bursting thicket of weird instruments and testing gear. The scientists took to calling it Fubar: Fouled Up Beyond All Repair.

*   *   *

The situation on the desert was only slightly less chaotic. Heat waves rolled across the flats and drenched the scientists as they knelt by their equipment. Sand and dust storms bunged up many of the instruments and caused a rash of eye infections. The most feverish work was devoted to perfecting the timing circuits that would have to work with infinite precision. These devices would activate hundreds of recording instruments split seconds before detonation. If they failed, the scientists would have no decent records of the test.

Exasperating troubles occurred with the British-imported coaxial cables. These connected the measuring gauges with recording devices buried thousands of yards from the shot tower. To the scientists the cables seemed made of old chewing gum. Their insulation melted under the fierce heat and caused short circuits. Out went an SOS to the procurement people to locate four miles of ordinary garden hose through which the cables could be strung.

The B-29 flew over Trinity daily, buzzing the shot tower in preparation for its role in the test. Led by Luis Alvarez and Deac Parsons, the bomber group plotted its intricate operation: how the plane would approach the tower seconds before detonation, drop its instruments to measure the speed and pressure of the blast, then swerve away in time to avoid the spiraling fireball. The B-29 would use Trinity as its "dry run" for the first atomic combat mission. The force of the Trinity explosion would, hopefully, tell Alvarez and Parsons at what height to detonate the bomb over Japan.

Enrico Fermi and a fellow Chicagoan, Herbert Anderson, planned another daring experiment. They wanted to race in, minutes after the shot, and recover radioactive dirt samples from the detonation area. They had been frustrated in their plans at first. The idea had been to use Navy helicopters to hover over the area and scoop up debris in a bucket. Trinity lay nearly 5000 feet above sea level, however, too high an altitude for helicopters. Anderson hit on the idea of using Army tanks to invade the fallout area. A pair of surplus Sherman tanks were located and shipped to Los Alamos for a complete face-lifting. Each was lined with two-inch-thick lead walls, weighing twelve tons, to protect the occupants from radiation. The tanks would be sealed, with oxygen pumped in from the outside. A device on the tanks' bottoms would fire into the fallout area a rocket carrying a small scoop at one end. A cable attached to the rocket would ensure recovery.

Little if any planning was done to test the bomb's lethal effect on humans and human habitation. The purpose of the test was to see if the gadget worked, and few of the scientists and military seemed interested in what it might do to buildings or live "guinea pigs." General Groves vetoed the idea of erecting test buildings with "dummy" humans on the site. He felt it would stretch security and take too much time and manpower. A few simulated parts of buildings were finally scattered about the site just before the test, but it was a piddling experiment.

The medical people worked furiously and were treated like interlopers. Worried that the explosion's glare might burn the retinas of eyes, the medics issued welder's dark goggles for the test. They also set a radiation exposure limit of 5 roentgens for all personnel. It was dangerously high, compared to safety tolerances today. But the scientists had been badgering the doctors to allow them a liberal dosage standard. They were by now so emotionally involved in their experiments that they resented interference from any quarter. They wanted to be able to roam the test site freely after the shot to check their recording instruments. Some of them actually demanded reckless exposure limits of 25 to 50 roentgens.

Chief radiologist Stafford Warren slept particularly poorly. Every time the winds shifted he found himself changing evacuation and monitoring plans. He had already decided to evacuate any area outside Trinity that received over 50 roentgens' exposure in one week. He was also doubling as camp psychologist and kept in constant touch with his team of psychiatrists at Oak Ridge. Several younger scientists were talking wildly of failure and possible disaster on July 16. Their fears were threatening to infect the rest of the camp. Warren quietly called in the doom-sayers, ordered them to pack their bags and go back to Los Alamos.

The weathermen had become the cynosures of Trinity, treated more deferentially than the gods of Mount Olympus. The scientists hung on their hourly reports and predictions for the test date. Only the forecasters could determine whether a rehearsal of the timing circuits would have to be canceled because of thunderstorms; whether the winds of July 16 would blow in such a way as to endanger Trinity and outlying areas with radioactive fallout; or whether conditions on that fateful day would even permit the firing of the bomb.

It was known that the weather on the morning of July 16 would be a serious handicap. The call went out the first week in July for additional forecasters who could pinpoint on-the-spot weather changes even more unerringly than Jack Hubbard and his crew. Two Army officers were dispatched to Trinity, one of them the chief weather forecaster for the Normandy invasion. Working from computer cards in Washington, the officers determined which day in the last forty years had been most nearly comparable to the conditions expected on July 16, 1945. Their choice was July 28, 1900, and the forecasters then pored over all available weather maps for the 1900 date.

Telephone conferences with Army headquarters in Washington were held daily. Radar balloons floated up every few hours over the site. An instrument-crammed Beechcraft flew each dawn over the Sierra Oscura to the northeast, testing wind patterns. Frank Oppenheimer lugged smoke pots to the top of Oscura Peak to try to fix the direction the fallout cloud might take. With each prediction of the wind flow for July 16, security agents scurried off to survey the affected areas for possible evacuation. In the final days the forecasters switched their predictions so often that the security men chased themselves dizzy and almost collapsed from exhaustion.

Nothing was left to chance. A full-scale rehearsal, timed to the minute, was held for the bomb's nuclear assembly. On July 2 a mock-up plutonium assembly was driven over Los Alamos mesa to see how it could take the bumps. On July 3 and 4 the mock-up was driven to Trinity, unloaded at the tower, reassembled and hoisted to the top. It was "wired," lowered and disassembled the next day. The unit was returned to Los Alamos in good condition July 6.

That night Kenneth Bainbridge held an urgent meeting at Base Camp. The test director pulled out the handmade chart on which he had mapped the progress of the preparations. He called it "The Universal Anticipator." It told him that things were lagging, especially the work on the shot tower. Days before, the professional riggers who had originally built the tower had been banished from the site because they were not cleared for the sensitive security work involved in the final preparations. As a result, there was no one to build the shack at the tower's top to house the bomb; or the dustproof shelter at the tower's base for the final assembly of the gadget. Someone would have to rig the hoisting pulleys on the tower and the maze of cables needed to connect the bomb with ground devices. Bainbridge asked for volunteers immediately.

A number of scientists offered their services. It was tricky work and the volunteers were unsure of themselves. One hundred feet up, with gale winds whistling about them and swaying the top of the tower, they picked their way around the flimsy scaffolding, clinging for dear life to the girders. Occasionally bolts, wrenches and other tools slipped from their grasp and hurtled to the ground. Bainbridge stood below chewing on a pipe stem, anxiously watching the work, wondering if it would be finished in time.

At eleven o'clock the night of July 6 a special train pulled out of Union Station in Washington. It was bound for Newport News, Virginia, and it carried the President of the United States and his Secretary of State. The heavy cruiser *Augusta,* lying in its berth at Newport News, had been stocked and fueled for the long trans-Atlantic voyage. Its destination was Antwerp, Belgium. Harry Truman and James Byrnes would board it the next day for the first leg of their trip to Potsdam and the conference code-named "Terminal."

Four thousand miles away the finishing touches were being put on the three-story stucco residence at Number 2 Kaiser Strasse in Babelsberg, where the President would establish his "Little White House." Babelsberg was a Russian-occupied suburb of Berlin, lying in a woodsy area between the capital and Potsdam. The residence being readied for Truman had once been owned by a German movie director who had become a Nazi gauleiter and was now doing time in a labor battalion somewhere in Russia. The Russians had thoughtfully redecorated the house. They had even put roses in Truman's bedroom.

It was fitting that the President should hear the results of the world's first atomic bomb test in Potsdam. There, not so many years before, a gentle physics professor had opened hundreds of congratulatory letters on his fiftieth birthday. Absent-mindedly, he had sorted them into vegetable baskets. Three years later Albert Einstein had been forced to flee Germany for America.

The mantle of secrecy tightened over every aspect of the project as the test date neared. Security was on Groves's and Oppenheimer's minds constantly. The project had come too far; too many man-hours, too much grief and worry, had been expended for the secret to be allowed to leak out accidentally in these final days. Every precaution was taken to prevent that.

When Oppenheimer called Groves on July 7 to discuss final arrangements for transporting the U-235 across the Pacific for the Hiroshima bomb, Groves insisted on ordering *two* transport planes to carry the tiny unit from Oak Ridge to San Francisco. The second plane, the empty C-54, would trail the one carrying the material and would report its position if it crashed. The U-235 could not be permitted to fall into unauthorized hands. Secret arrangements were made meanwhile for two couriers to escort the U-235 from Los Alamos to Tinian. Groves chose Captain James Nolan and Major Robert Furman, one of his Engineer aides, for the job. The Navy ordered its heavy cruiser *Indianapolis* to stand by to transport the two officers and their cargo across the ocean. The U-235 mission was code-named "Bowery."

It was absolutely essential that the uranium reach Tinian intact. No similar amount of U-235 would be available for months. Furman's and Nolan's orders were explicit: they were to save their cargo before any human life. If the *Indianapolis* sank, the first life raft would go to the U-235.

Despite precautions, the secret of the bomb project and the impending test threatened to leak out through a succession of seemingly trivial incidents.

The press, exercising voluntary censorship, had been

prone to slip-ups recently. The letter columns in some newspapers raised goose pimples on security officers. One letter to the editor of the *Toledo Blade* blatantly suggested that the atomic bomb be used to ensure victory. A Cleveland paper printed a story on Los Alamos, entitled "The Forbidden City," suggesting all kinds of fantastic goings-on there. It shouldn't have come as any surprise to the Counter Intelligence Corps that a reporter could have located the laboratory. Anyone with two good eyes could have found Los Alamos just by following the trail of beer cans from Santa Fe.

At Trinity the CIC took extreme measures the fortnight before the test. An Army Engineer was allowed to attend special church services one Saturday in Socorro. A CIC agent spotted him chatting in a bar there. Within hours the officer had been hustled back to Los Alamos and reassigned to a housekeeping detachment in the South Pacific. It was impossible, of course, to catch everybody. In Los Alamos, hunched over his drawing board, Klaus Fuchs drew a graceful curve of the estimated yield of the first atomic bomb. He could smile to himself, knowing it was a good calculation. It would not vary much from the final result.

The bomb's high-explosive assembly was ready for its "dry run." Again the scientists put a mock-up unit through its paces. The explosives went through a trial assembly at Trinity on July 8. The next day the unit was driven eight hours over a rock-strewn course to see how the actual assembly might withstand the trip from Los Alamos. The mock-up was returned to the laboratory on July 10 and each of its explosive castings was carefully inspected. The assembly passed the test with flying colors. All castings were in perfect condition.

On that day Oppenheimer wired two colleagues, Ernest Lawrence and Arthur Compton, the following message:

"Any time after the 15th would be good for our fishing trip. Because we are not certain of the weather, we may be delayed several days. We do not have enough sleeping bags to go around, so we ask you please not to bring anyone with you." Lawrence accepted the invitation. Compton, fearing his absence from the Chicago Laboratory would arouse suspicions, declined.

Enrico Fermi and Samuel Allison drove down to Trinity together the evening of July 10 in an old jalopy. They were fast friends, having worked together on the Chicago end of the project. Allison, who had headed the Cowpuncher scheduling committee at Los Alamos, had just been chosen to make the countdown for the test. He was delighted, but still grousing about not having his own watch for the occasion. Fermi worried aloud about the radioactive fallout and the possibility of the bomb's exploding with far greater force than anyone had imagined. He turned to Allison and cracked, "If we make it down okay in this heap, we'll come out of Trinity alive."

At Base Camp, George Weil had just turned in after a hard day of testing the rockets he would use to retrieve radioactive samples after the test. Weil had assisted Fermi in the historic chain-reaction experiment in Chicago three years before. He would be with the Italian Navigator once again in one of the lead-lined tanks assigned to the recovery operation. He was half asleep when Fermi bounced into the barracks and demanded to see a demonstration of the rockets. "Now?" Weil muttered groggily. Now, Fermi insisted.

The two men drove into the desert, about a half-mile from camp, and shortly before midnight fired off one of the rockets. It performed beautifully and Fermi was ecstatic. Not so the camp commandant, Lieutenant Bush. The explosion had wakened him and he'd watched horrified as the rocket carved a telltale swath across the sky. The next thing Weil and Fermi knew, a swarm of jeeps was buzzing angrily out from camp. "What the hell's going on!" Bush roared when he reached the scientists. Fermi tried to explain in his broken English, but the lieutenant wasn't appeased. He dressed down the Nobel laureate in his choicest barracks billingsgate, ordered the rockets confiscated and warned the owners not to conduct any more midnight experiments on the desert without his approval.

The journal of the next four days tells this story:

WEDNESDAY, JULY 11 At eight A.M. General Groves and Vannevar Bush left Bolling Field in Washington for a four-day inspection trip of West Coast atomic plants and engineering facilities. They would be joined later by Dr. Conant. The general and Bush had Trinity very much on their minds. The test was now virtually in the scientists' hands, however, and the two officials wanted to be sure that all arrangements were ready for shipment of the U-235 to Tinian.

On that pile of Pacific coral, 7000 miles from Trinity, the long wait was beginning to tell on the men of the 509th Composite Group. Tired of killing time over poker games, PX beer and comic books, they felt bored and isolated from the war that was gearing for its climax. Over the horizon from Tinian, troopships plied the ocean, mustering for an invasion fleet that would carry six infantry divisions to the shores of Japan. Battleships, aircraft carriers and destroyers steamed through the Tinian waters to assembly points throughout the Western Pacific. In Pearl Harbor, Guam and Manila, men were on the move and ships were slipping out of port in the small hours of darkness. All the conventional power of a mighty nation was being massed for "Downfall."

No one on Tinian had yet told Major Charles Sweeney of

165

Lowell, Massachusetts, that he would fly the first combat mission with a plutonium bomb. Sweeney, a friendly twenty-four-year-old Army pilot, had spent months at Wendover, diving his B-29 in peculiar patterns and dropping those strange black "pumpkins." If Trinity succeeded, the bomb he would later drop on Japan would dwarf much of the firepower crisscrossing the waters of the Pacific that day.

At Los Alamos, Kenneth Greisen, a Cornell explosives expert who talked softly and carried dynamite sticks, packed nearly 200 new detonators in the trunk of his car and set out for Trinity. There were enough of the mechanisms for the entire bomb, plus a full set of spares. The detonators were tamped with explosive. Just south of Albuquerque a state trooper stopped Greisen for speeding. The cop ambled around the back of the car to check Greisen's license plate. For one awful moment Greisen feared he might open the trunk and find the detonators. It would take Greisen a week in the pokey, he knew, to explain that one to the police. Luckily, all he got was a ticket.

Robert Oppenheimer, a gaunt 115 pounds, riffled through a stack of papers in his laboratory office that afternoon and gave some final instructions to his secretary, Anne Wilson. She suspected he was leaving on an important mission, but the director was too distracted to answer her questions with more than a perfunctory yes or no. A little before seven o'clock Oppenheimer pulled an extra carton of cigarettes from his desk. Then he walked home to say good-by to his wife and children. He looked in on his sleeping baby daughter, Toni, and gave three-year-old Peter a hug. Kitty waited for him at the door with a good-luck token she had found in their back yard: a tiny four-leaf clover. "Remember our code," she told her husband as they parted. The Oppenheimers had planned a small party if the test was a success. Oppie would let her know if the party was on by sending a five-word message, an obscure line from a sonnet by Baudelaire: "You can change the sheets."

Late that night a sedan drove down Los Alamos Canyon toward Omega Site, honked its horn to warn the sentries and pulled up beside the nuclear-materials vault. A quarter-moon bathed the building in an eerie blue light. Physicists Robert Bacher, Marshall Holloway, Louis Slotin and Philip Morrison stepped into the vault to make the final adjustments on the plutonium ingots that would go into the bomb's nuclear core. The ingots, smoothly honed and gleaming in the lamplight, were stacked and ready for the trip to Trinity.

Bacher looked up at one point and saw an MP guard sitting against the wall, rifle across his knee, reading to himself. Odd, he thought. The soldier has so little idea of the drama taking place before him that he has to turn to a science-fiction magazine.

THURSDAY, JULY 12 Gray gusts of spume battered the *Augusta* as the cruiser sped northeastward through choppy seas. Below decks that drizzly morning Truman, Byrnes and Admiral Leahy reviewed the outline of the President's principal aims at the forthcoming parley: a swift end to the Pacific war and establishing the foundation for a durable peace. The weather cleared in the afternoon, and the President played shuffleboard, strolled with Byrnes on the forward deck and during a ship's tour ran into his third cousin, Fire Controlman 2/C Lawrence Truman of Owensboro, Kentucky.

Just before three P.M., Philip Morrison, accompanied by a guard and a radiation specialist, removed the nuclear core from its vault at Omega. The core had been separated, for safety reasons, into several subcritical pieces. Morrison carried them in a pair of sealed valises equipped with ther-

167

mometers to measure the plutonium's radioactivity. Carefully he laid the valises next to him in the back seat of an Army sedan. Then, led by an escort car filled with security men and trailed by another with members of the nuclear assembly team, the core departed for Trinity.

Five hours later Morrison's car turned off a dirt road at the site and stopped before an abandoned ranch house ringed with carbine-carrying MP's. A makeshift laboratory had been set up in the four-room adobe building that had once belonged to the McDonald family. The assembly room, facing the shot tower a mile west, had been vacuumed and its windows carefully sealed against dust with black masking tape. Morrison laid the valises on a table against the wall and retired for the night. The final critical assembly of the core would begin the next morning.

At Trinity it had showered that afternoon and an unexpected snag had ruined a dress rehearsal of the test. The scientists were trying out the bomb's firing circuits and using a chunk of high explosive to simulate the bomb. No explosion occurred, not even a puff of smoke. During the thundershower a lightning bolt had prematurely discharged the device for signaling the bomb's detonation. All hands realized that had it been the real thing, the Trinity test would have ended in failure.

The explosive assembly, meanwhile, was getting its final check inside a large air-conditioned building at Los Alamos. Two explosive assemblies had been made that day, one for Trinity and one for a final dress rehearsal that was to gauge, in particular, how the implosion worked. This latter experiment was to be held at Los Alamos two days before Trinity. Dr. Edward C. Creutz would conduct it. The Trinity assembly was made under the close supervision of Kistiakowsky. Remembering his troubles with the lens molds, Kisty personally examined every explosive casting that day for chipped corners, cracks or other defects.

That night the assembly was "buttoned up" for its trip to Trinity. Each casting was given a final X-ray check. Every step was logged and photographed and a serial number affixed to each part. Leo Jercinovic and an ex-farmer from Pennsylvania named "Tiny" Hamilton took turns guarding the explosive charges whenever the scientists took a break from their work. Shortly before midnight the assembly was put in a special metal container covered with a waterproof casing. The whole contraption was then packaged in a wooden crate. An Army truck backed into the building. Under the glare of a pair of overhead lights the dozen men under Kistiakowsky loaded the crate aboard, lashed it to a special steel bed and covered it with a tarpaulin. Outside, three jeeps full of armed MP's, two sedans with security agents and a second truck loaded with spare parts waited for the signal to leave. Several of the enlisted men drew straws to see who would ride with the assembly. No one wanted to. Jercinovic drew the short straw.

At one minute past midnight the caravan gunned its motors and started down the mesa road for Trinity, 212 miles to the south.

FRIDAY, JULY 13 It had been Kisty's droll idea to defy the superstition attached to that date by waiting until just after midnight Thursday to leave. Now, as the caravan with its lethal cargo rolled along the first leg of the route through Espanola, Kisty fretted in the lead car every time the speedometer went above thirty miles per hour. Exhausted, he finally dozed off. Just outside Santa Fe he was jarred awake as the security car hit its siren and the caravan picked up speed. Any thoughts that this would be a quietly covert operation were dashed as the security car, siren blaring and red light flashing, led the convoy rocketing

169

through the silent streets of Santa Fe. The idea had been to warn off any drunken drivers who might veer into the convoy's path. It succeeded admirably while waking up half the town.

South of Albuquerque the convoy rumbled down a cracked two-lane highway bordered on the east by precipitous mesas and the rugged Manzano peaks emerging in the first gray of dawn. It glided through the sleepy farming town of Belen ("Little Bethlehem") and minutes before eight pulled up to a roadside diner at Socorro. The MP's scrambled off the jeeps, brandishing their automatic rifles, and surrounded the caravan. Inside, the explosives team breakfasted on wheat cakes and scrambled eggs. Three hours later the convoy bumped along a graded dirt road at Trinity, trailing clouds of dust as it approached the detonation area. Bainbridge and his staff, twenty miles away at the shot tower, watched the trucks coming. At noon the convoy reached the tower. The explosives truck backed into position at the tower's base and the core was lifted onto a special cradle, where Jercinovic and others began partially disassembling it. The charges were gingerly removed to allow the nuclear core to be inserted. For the next three hours the work progressed inside a hastily erected tent, Kisty barking orders and dispensing tools like a man possessed.

At the McDonald ranch house Robert Bacher's and Marshall Holloway's nuclear assembly team had gathered that morning to make the last delicate checks and final construction of the plutonium core. A small business matter was settled first. The scientists were about to sacrifice a nuclear treasure that had cost two years and nearly half a billion dollars to amass. They wanted to make sure that the Army, not they, got stuck with the bill. Bacher, representing the University of California, asked Groves's deputy, Brigadier General Thomas Farrell, to sign a receipt for the plutonium core in his presence. Farrell agreed and jokingly asked if he could feel the material to make sure it was all there. The general donned rubber gloves and for a full minute stood silent, fondling one of the heavy nuclear balls in his hands, feeling its glowing warmth and hidden power. Then he signed the receipt and handed it to Bacher.

At nine A.M. the final assembly began. The valises were opened and the parts carefully inspected. The eight-man team, dressed in white surgical coats, hovered over the table where the plutonium pieces lay on strips of sanitized brown wrapping paper. They worked out of field kits that had been packaged in an old icehouse at Los Alamos and which would shortly be used by the men at Tinian. The kits had everything from tools to K-rations. Geiger counters clicked nearby and MP's stood guard in the background. Outside, four jeeps stood parked, backs to the house and motors idling, ready for an immediate getaway in the event of an accidental chain reaction. The scientists searched painstakingly for holes in the core that might cause a deadly leakage of neutrons. They plugged the few they found with bits of Kleenex tissue. Metallurgist Cyril Smith rubbed the surface of the core with an emery cloth to smooth down whatever blisters remained. The gold foil had, thankfully, settled that crisis. Louis Slotin sat mesmerized before the plutonium hemispheres, tortuously prodding them across the table to the invisible point where they were almost critical. Harry Daghlian, a young Purdue physicist, stood at Slotin's side, watching the game in numbed fascination.

The atmosphere in the ranch house was electric. The assembly men tried to ease the tension with banter and jokes about the K-rations they would have for lunch. Oppenheimer dropped by every few minutes. It seemed to Oppie, at the time, that he should have been coming into the ranch house for a steaming mug of coffee after a long horseback ride instead of to observe the deadly work in progress. Oppenheimer was so fidgety that Bacher and Holloway

171

finally had to ask him to leave the premises until the assembly was done.

As each part fell in place and the core assumed the perfect symmetry the scientists had dreamed of, a murmur of satisfaction swept the room. There was a special esprit among this group unmatched elsewhere in the bomb project. It was not only that they were the first men ever to put together a device like this, or that they had lived more than the others in a world of fearful and arcane dangers. It was that they comprised the truly elite fraternity. Of the score of scientists who physically assembled the world's first atomic bomb in the final hours before its test, this band of men provided the heart of the weapon.

At 3:18 P.M., Kistiakowsky phoned from the tower. The explosives team was ready for the insertion of the nuclear core. In the ranch house only one small task remained. Louis Slotin picked up the minuscule cylinder that had been months in the making. He looked around the room at his colleagues. One by one they nodded, and Slotin deftly, like a master jackstraw player, wedged the plutonium hemispheres apart far enough to allow the initiator to slip between them. The core was complete. The hemispheres had virtually been joined in a single globe that would fit within the bowel of the bomb. The scientists called this globe the "plug." They laid its eighty pounds on a litter and carried it to a waiting sedan. Then, with Bacher at the wheel and Holloway and Morrison guarding it, the plug started for the tower.

At the tower, the plug, riding a manually operated hoist, began its slow descent into the explosives assembly. While Holloway cranked the hoist, Morrison steadied the plug with a pair of pincers. Sweat coursed down the faces of both men. Never before had so much nuclear material been handled at one spot. The stuff was so close to being critical that a minor jar the wrong way might set off a chain reaction. As the unit was lowered inch by inch into the bomb, the needles on the

Geiger counter fairly leaped. At one point Morrison leaned inside the bomb and inserted a three-foot-long hypodermic needle in the plug to monitor the rising neutron count. Several times the work stopped as "sand devils" swirled about the tent and threatened to sabotage the operation. The wind had risen and afternoon thundershowers began sweeping the area. The fear that lightning might strike the tower and somehow detonate the bomb heightened the tension. The dozen men inside the tent hurried to complete the job and leave.

Suddenly the plug stuck. Someone cursed softly. Oppenheimer froze in apprehension and General Farrell rushed over to see what had happened. Bacher stopped the excited officer and grappled with him a moment, trying to explain the accident. The plug had expanded from the heat of its casing and couldn't be forced into the cooler explosives assembly. A hurried conference ensued. It was decided to leave the core next to the assembly and hope that it, too, would cool and contract. Agonizing minutes later Holloway stuck his head in the opening of the assembly and signaled that the lowering could proceed. The plug dropped smoothly into place. The ordeal was over.

Kistiakowsky and his explosives team had stood by anxiously the past hour. When the nuclear crew departed, they moved in once more to replace the charges over the plutonium core. Kisty had relaxed a bit and the atmosphere was more joshing now. The reassembly went off without a hitch. Only once or twice did the scientists have to use Scotch tape on the charges to make for a snugger fit. At ten P.M. the last charge was placed, the assembled bomb laid to sleep in its cradle and the tent vacated until morning.

That day 500 U.S. Superfortresses rained incendiary bombs on strategic targets in four Japanese cities. Intelligence sources reported that the B-29's were destroying about half of every Japanese city they hit. Allied aircraft were also spreading destruction over Korea, Formosa and the Japanese Ryukyu Islands. While the bombers struck, U.S. Navy fighters broke up enemy attempts to run troop convoys from Shanghai to Tokyo to bolster their homeland defenses against the expected invasion. Italy declared war on her erstwhile ally.

The 3000 bombs that pounded Japan on July 13 represented less than one sixth of the potential destruction of the bomb that was about to be tested at Trinity.

Aboard the *Augusta,* Harry Truman kept in hourly touch with the commander of the Third Fleet off Japan. The President and his Secretary of State posed for newsreel photographers on the deck that afternoon and conferred the rest of the day on the Potsdam agenda.

General Groves put in a call from Hanford, Washington, to Mrs. O'Leary in Washington, D.C. She advised him, among other things, that Leo Szilard was circulating his petition at Oak Ridge, warning against surprise use of the bomb on the Japanese. She interrupted Groves's sigh to tell him that a number of Szilard's colleagues had reacted by circulating a petition of their own protesting his.

At Trinity the weathermen issued a disturbing forecast: the four days following the scheduled test date would be almost ideal; but for July 16 light thunderstorms were expected, with a deep layer of fresh easterly winds. Conditions for the test, the forecast concluded, would be generally unfavorable.

SATURDAY, JULY 14 The bomb began the trip to its final resting place atop the tower at eight A.M. The scientists surmised what might happen if a cable snapped and the five-ton gadget plunged to the ground. Before the hoist they inaugurated "Operation Mattress." The bomb was raised about fifteen feet. Trucks raced out from Base Camp and unloaded scores of GI mattresses at the tower. The scientists stacked the cotton mattresses crisscross fashion under the gadget until the pile was nearly twelve feet high. They prayed that, whatever happened, the mattresses would soften the impact.

A motor-driven hoist started hauling the bomb the last ninety feet to the top. The hoist moved slowly, about a foot a minute. The bomb could swing free inside the steel scaffolding, and the scientists feared the wind might rock it against the tower's side and jar loose the delicate mechanisms inside. The hoist proceeded with the aid of "skates" which ran on tracks along the tower's side. One of the skates slipped suddenly and racketed down the track. Everything stopped. The bomb swayed on its cable like a blunt sword of Damocles. The scientists held their breaths. Nothing happened. The skate was fixed and the hoist went on.

Leo Jercinovic and another Engineer, Arthur Machen, climbed the tower ahead of the bomb, removing the platforms at various levels to let the gadget pass through. At the very top they lifted the trapdoor that opened on the galvanized-iron shed which would house the bomb. Slowly they eased the sphere through the space, then placed the steel cradle beneath it. The bomb had been hoisted in a vertical position. For the test, however, it would assume the same position as a combat weapon in the bomb bay of a Superfort. Jercinovic and Machen gently maneuvered the bomb toward the oaken floor until it rested on its side. Then they anchored the baby in its cradle.

Major Robert Furman signed a receipt for a lead bucket that morning at Los Alamos. The bucket, slightly bigger than a large cookie can, had a handle. But Furman and his

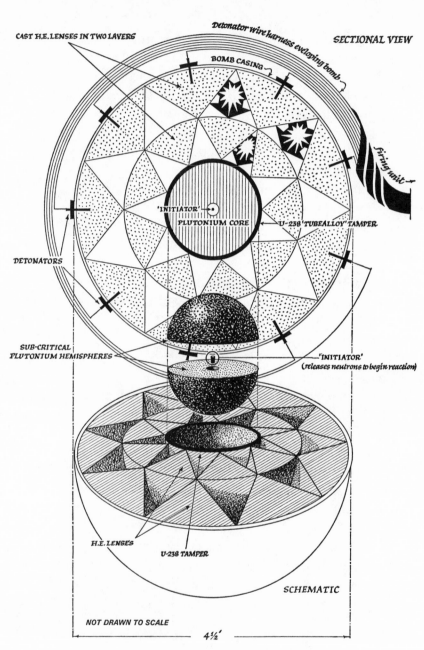

CAST H.E. LENSES IN TWO LAYERS

Detonator wire harness enveloping bomb

SECTIONAL VIEW

BOMB CASING

firing unit

'INITIATOR'

PLUTONIUM CORE

U-238 'TUBEALLOY' TAMPER

DETONATORS

SUB-CRITICAL
PLUTONIUM HEMISPHERES

'INITIATOR'
(releases neutrons to begin reaction)

H.E. LENSES

U-238 TAMPER

SCHEMATIC

NOT DRAWN TO SCALE

$4\frac{1}{2}'$

" The Gadget "

GUY FLEMING

Maj. Gen. Leslie R. Groves, chief of the Manhattan Project, and Dr. J. Robert Oppenheimer, director of the Los Alamos Scientific Laboratory, in mid-1945.

Klaus Fuchs, convicted atomic spy, at London airport en route to exile in East Germany after his release from prison in June 1959. Fuchs had served 9½ years of a 14-year sentence.

Tech. Sgt. Leo M. Jercinovic, one of the GI's who helped build the bomb, at a remote explosives-firing site at Los Alamos, summer 1944.

Trio of Manhattan Project leaders at the White House after a meeting with the President. Left to right: General Groves, Dr. James B. Conant of Harvard, and Dr. Vannevar Bush, director of the Office of Scientific Research and Development.

Dr. George B. Kistiakowsky, captain of the team that fashioned and assembled vital high-explosive lenses for the atomic bomb. He later became President Eisenhower's top scientific adviser. Below, the late Enrico Fermi, winner of a Nobel Prize for splitting the atom, initiated the first man-made nuclear chain reaction. Fermi played a leading role in the Trinity test.

Base Camp at Trinity a few days before the test. The camp was located 10 miles south of the detonation point where a 100-foot steel tower (*below*) awaited, with an iron shed at the top to house the bomb during the final hours.

The "gadget" was unloaded at the base of the tower on July 13, 1945. Shortly after this picture was taken, a tent was erected to shield the bomb during final assembly before it was lifted to the top of the tower. In Germany meanwhile the Big Three assembled for the Potsdam Conference (below): Soviet Premier Stalin (far left), British Prime Minister Churchill (far right, cigar in hand) and, midway between them, President Truman with Secretary of State Byrnes at his right.

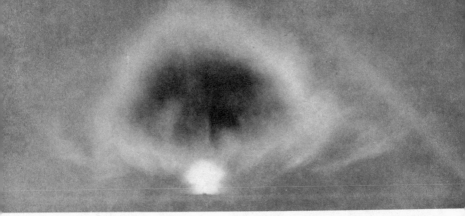

Dawn, July 16, 1945, 5:29:45 Mountain War Time. A brilliant pinprick of light heralds the explosion of the world's first atomic bomb.

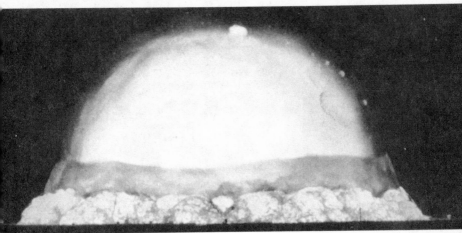

At .034 seconds after detonation a dazzling cloche of fire spills across the desert, acquiring a skirt of radioactive dust. The shot tower has already been vaporized.

Thousands of tons of boiling black debris are swept into the explosion's maw 2 seconds later . . .

. . . creating a vision of Armageddon as the detonation site is blotted out by a fire storm of exploding gases and churning sand and dirt.

At 9 seconds a white-hot fireball lifts from the desert, spewing a geyser of debris across the site, and (below) billows upward in a furnace of destruction. These photographs were taken from 6 miles away.

Three weeks after Trinity a similar plutonium bomb, of the "Fat Man" type pictured here, was dropped on Nagasaki. "Fat Man" resembled the Trinity device in all respects except the tail fins needed for an aerial drop. Below, Nagasaki, virtually wiped out by the bomb, which exploded with the force of 20,000 tons of TNT. Nearly 100,000 Japanese were killed or injured.

co-courier, Captain Nolan, couldn't budge it. It contained 200 pounds of lead insulation surrounding a core of enriched uranium that represented a cool $300,000,000 investment. Shortly after eleven A.M. Furman and Nolan started out from The Hill to deliver the bucket to Tinian.

Their journey was no easier than others that day. The sedan they were riding in blew a tire halfway down the mesa. For a moment Furman pictured himself and the bucket plunging off the mesa into eternity. The caravan made it without further incident to Albuquerque, where Furman and Nolan were supposed to pick up two Army DC-3's for the flight to San Francisco. Both planes were grounded with technical troubles. Furman rushed to the Kirtland base commander's office and whipped out a letter from General Marshall. The letter from the Chief of Staff explained the importance of the two officers' mission and requested assistance in case of emergency. Within an hour both were airborne.

At Hamilton Field, San Francisco, a knot of security agents escorted the couriers and their bucket off the plane and drove them to Hunters Point Navy Yard, where the *Indianapolis* was waiting. Naval forces on the West Coast had been alerted to the cruiser's departure, and tight security arrangements prevailed throughout the area. Furman took the U-235 to the commandant's office at Hunters and a twenty-four-hour guard was posted around it.

At noon that day the Creutz experiment was performed with alarming results in a canyon near Los Alamos. A mock replica of the Trinity bomb was set off to allow the scientists a final check on how the implosion process worked. Relay signals indicated a failure. Creutz sent a coded message to Oppenheimer at Trinity, telling him that the explosives assembly had performed badly. On the basis of Creutz's report, the scientists calculated that if the Trinity test worked similarly there would be no nuclear explosion.

The news hit Base Camp with a shock. Oppenheimer was almost visibly ill. An emergency meeting was held to decide whether to attempt the Trinity test in the circumstances. Bethe, at Los Alamos, was told to check with Creutz and see if there was any chance an error had been made in the relay signals. The tension gave way to recriminations. Kistiakowsky was accused of poor workmanship on his explosives assembly. Bacher and others were incensed by the prospect of Kistiakowsky's having caused a delay of the test.

Kistiakowsky stood his ground. He collared the disconsolate Oppenheimer and begged to reassure him that the explosives charge would work all right. "I'll bet you my month's salary against ten dollars that it will!" he blurted. Oppie looked at him sadly as the two men shook on the bet.

Hours later another misfire jolted the camp. Again it occurred in Kistiakowsky's division. But this time young Donald Hornig caught the blame.

Hornig's X-5 Unit was responsible for the firing circuits that would activate the detonators on the bomb. Hornig's special pride was the 500-pound firing unit which was finally hoisted atop the tower that afternoon. Before it went, though, the scientists ran off one more rehearsal with the dummy firing unit they had been using. The circuits blew out and the rehearsal collapsed. Hornig was as baffled as he was dismayed. He had checked every detail of the detonating system for weeks; the dummy unit had never missed before. Now, with only twenty-four hours left, one of the most critical parts of the bomb had failed. There seemed to be no explanation. Hornig wondered if his whole design was at fault and if it would wreck the test on the 16th. He would spend a sleepless night trying to find the answer.

* * *

178

At three P.M. Groves's private DC-3 approached the little airport at Pasadena, California. Aboard with the general were Conant and Bush. The smog almost hid the ground below, and Groves went up to the cockpit to help guide the pilot. As the plane thundered in on its approach, a high-tension power line loomed up ahead. The pilot spotted it at the last moment. The DC-3 reared up sharply to clear the wires, vaulting nearly 1500 feet in the air. Finally the plane sideslipped onto the field as fire engines and personnel rushed out to meet it. One of Groves's aides ran up to the general. Ashen-faced, the lieutenant sputtered, "Thank God, sir. If you'd crashed, we'd never have been able to explain what you and Conant and Bush were all doing together on one plane!"

By late afternoon the scientists had finished the final primping of the bomb. The work had been done amid an electrical storm so violent that they had debated bringing the gadget down from the top. The steel tower was a giant lightning rod on the desert, and no one wanted to be around if a bolt struck it. The bomb, however, stayed in the shack. Detonators had been clamped to its shell. Racks and brackets had been bolted around it to hold it firmly in place. A web of cables enveloped it. By five P.M., when the last mechanism had been attached, the bomb no longer resembled the marble-smooth vessel that had been borne aloft hours before. Crawling with switches and snakelike wires, it looked for all the world like an ugly Medusa bent on destruction.

The President stayed locked in the Admiral's Cabin, conferring with aides for most of the day. The *Augusta* had entered British waters and a British escort had sailed out to meet it. The sailors on the escort vessels shouted the traditional three cheers as they steamed past the *Augusta*. Truman strode jauntily on deck just in time to give them a broad smile. Early that evening the cruiser swung northward through the mists of the English Channel.

Bill Laurence arrived in Los Alamos after dinner that night. The reporter had just mailed a cheery letter to his editor at *The New York Times*. In it Laurence hinted at the coming events at Trinity and across the Pacific. "The story is much bigger than I could imagine," he wrote. "When it breaks it will be an eighth-day wonder, a sort of Second Coming of Christ yarn. It will need about 20 columns on the day it breaks."

But when Laurence reached the laboratory, he found to his utter amazement that the scientists were glooming over their coffee cups about the uncertainties of the coming test. They talked in flat tones of a "dud" or a "fizzle" at Trinity. The pool estimates on the bomb's yield particularly dismayed Laurence. Most of them seemed despairingly low. Not even the arrival of Isidor Rabi that day lifted spirits. The Columbia physicist had gotten off the train at Albuquerque wearing rubbers and carrying an umbrella in the hot sun. Now he took one look at the pool bets and again thumbed his nose at the odds. Rabi plunked down a dollar and wagered the bomb would yield a blast equivalent to that of 18,000 tons of TNT.

His colleagues thought it a comic gamble. The attitude on the mesa and at Trinity that day was best expressed in a satirical quatrain that had achieved notoriety as the "Los Alamos Blues":

> *From this crude lab that spawned the dud,*
> *Their necks to Truman's axe uncurled,*
> *Lo, the embattled savants stood*
> *And fired the flop heard round the world.*

VII

July 15, 1945

OPPENHEIMER awoke at Base Camp after a restless sleep of less than four hours. He had been up half the night with Hornig, trying to determine why the firing circuits had failed on Saturday. General Farrell heard him tossing on his bunk in the next room, coughing and coughing until it seemed he would fall apart.

A telephone call from Bethe reached Oppenheimer at the mess hall as he was finishing breakfast. The news brought a smile to his haggard features. The Creutz experiment had turned out to be meaningless. The scientists had received a distorted signal the day before. There was no reason why Kistiakowsky's explosives assembly shouldn't perform as expected. Hornig burst into the mess hall with more encouraging news. The answer to the blown circuits appeared exasperatingly simple: the scientists had overworked the dummy firing unit through countless experiments over the past weeks and the machine had finally rebelled. The real firing unit for the test was sitting on top of the tower in good shape and ready to perform.

Rejuvenated, Oppenheimer gulped his coffee and set out to tour the test site. He checked first with the weather people. The sky above Trinity was clear at the moment, but conditions for the morrow were still iffy. Oppie put in a long-distance call to General Groves in Riverside, California. Groves was about to catch a plane for Albuquerque. He listened impatiently to Oppenheimer's report on the Creutz experiment. "What about the weather?" he interrupted. "The weather is whimsical," Oppie replied.

It was the Sabbath and a day of special prayer for the men at Trinity. The bomb was assembled, in place, waiting only to be armed at the final moment. Those who had sweated through the nuclear assembly the previous day looked forward to a few hours' leisure. Norris Bradbury, in a memo to the explosives assembly team, designated it a day to "look for rabbits' feet and four-leaf clovers." Kistiakowsky borrowed a jeep and drove into the desert to seek the solitude and relief he needed from the past days' tensions. He was still unhappy over implications that his explosives assembly might come a cropper. Leo Jercinovic went off with a couple of pals to explore some abandoned silver mines on the edge of the site. Near Mockingbird Gap they spotted a herd of antelope prancing through the mesquite.

For most, however, there was no leisure that day. Last-minute procurement flaps had Harry Allen in a stew. Several pieces of cable and cadmium shielding were needed for a certain experiment. None was available. Out went a double-X priority request over the teletype. Wires hummed to the Chicago purchasing office and a special plane was dispatched to fly the materials direct to Albuquerque, where a truck waited to relay them to Trinity. Elsewhere on the site scientists by the scores checked their gauges and recording instruments, conducted "dry runs" of their timing equipment and tasked their memories to see if any contingency had been overlooked.

The desert within a five-mile radius of the shot tower was pocked with instruments of every description. Rugged crusher gauges to measure high blast pressures lay in burrows scant yards from the bomb; tiny gauges of quartz crystal, mounted on pipes, poked from the ground; strange wooden boxes with aluminum-covered holes peeked from behind yucca bushes. A half-mile from the tower, men worked over a pair of silver barrage balloons that would hoist some instruments just before the shot to measure the shock wave.

Julian Mack and his photography crew worked feverishly to adjust their cameras. The sun was so hot that whenever they touched the cameras the metal left flesh burns on their hands. There were thirty cameras in all: high-speed beauties that could record in color and black-and-white every angle of the explosion; delicate spectrographs that could capture each nuance of the fireball; and one thingumabob that could photograph the faces of six viewing scopes simultaneously through a maze of lenses and mirrors. The cameras were positioned at two key bunkers 10,000 yards north and west of the tower. They would "shoot" through bulletproof glass sheets set in concrete walls a foot and a half thick and reinforced with steel. Precise timing was needed to activate the cameras seconds before detonation and set them in motion at the right rate of speed. For maximum flexibility Mack had scrounged two surplus Army Air Force machine-gun turrets on which he had mounted cameras. He and an assistant would operate them like a pair of tail gunners from their bunkers.

Unfortunately, the circuit crisis the day before had ruined all the power batteries for Mack's cameras. His people scurried over the site on Sunday removing the dead batteries and soldering in new ones. Extra help was needed and there were idle members of the nuclear assembly team on hand. Cyril Smith, a distinguished M.I.T. metallurgist, worked all day soldering batteries with a buck private from Kearney, Nebraska. Marshall Holloway, who had run the core assembly, spent the Sabbath sandbagging shelters and digging up broken cables. The cables had been buried in trenches between connection points, but someone had neglected to give them enough slack to allow them to cling to the earth's

185

natural contours. Under the pressure of several feet of dirt they had stretched and snapped. Scores of connections were pulled out as a result, and some could not be replaced in time for the test. The accident cost some valuable experiments.

The bulk of the scientists still at Los Alamos planned to leave by bus for Trinity late that afternoon. A number of them departed earlier, however, to spend the day in Albuquerque. Bill Laurence took off with Sir James Chadwick and Dr. Edward McMillan, one of the discoverers of plutonium. Colonel Gerald Tyler, the post commander, joined them. He was on his way to Kirtland Field to meet General Groves and Bush and Conant.

Their big blue Buick was rolling down the mesa road when it suddenly occurred to Chadwick that he ought to inform the Prime Minister in London that the test was being fired on schedule the next morning. He turned to Tyler: "Colonel, stop the car. We must go back. I have to call Mr. Churchill." Tyler looked at the scientist as though he had gone awry. "Doctor," he said evenly, "I can't afford to miss the General while you're on the long-distance phone with the Prime Minister." The Buick rolled on.

At eleven o'clock that morning in Antwerp, Harry Truman and his party walked down the gangplank from the *Augusta*. Waiting to greet the President at the end of his 3800-mile voyage were General Eisenhower, various Belgian officials and members of the Secret Service. Truman looked tanned and fit. He had traded his rakish shipboard clothes for a somber double-breasted suit and gray felt hat. Accompanied by Byrnes, Leahy and special interpreter Charles Bohlen, Truman waved to the welcoming committee, then departed by car for the thirty-five-mile drive to

Brussels. From Brussels his private plane, the *Sacred Cow,* would fly him the last leg to Berlin. Churchill was already en route by air to the conference from Bordeaux, France, where he had spent a short holiday at his beloved easel.

Stafford Warren assembled the fallout team for a luncheon briefing at Trinity just before noon. The top weather specialists and officers in charge of evacuation attended. Their main concern was that the radioactive cloud might drift into a thunderhead. In that case the fallout would be swift and widespread. Warren reviewed for the last time all plans to cover such a contingency.

Teams of fallout monitors would take up posts along the highways bordering Trinity, with one roving monitor in charge. Their job would be to report the progress of the fallout cloud and to check the level of fallout in the towns and highways under their jurisdiction. At the site, medical officers would be stationed in each of the three main shelters and would take charge in the event of an emergency evacuation. Another medic would ride the B-29 observing the test; and one would man a duty desk in Albuquerque.

Warren had arranged to have his monitors report to him in code over radio transmitters in their cars. The monitors would use characters from the movie *Wizard of Oz* to identify themselves. Each of the towns in their vicinity was assigned a station number. Chief monitor Joseph Hoffman, in Carrizozo, was the Tin Woodsman of Station Six. Warren would run the fallout command post at Base Camp. He would keep an open line to another Army medical officer, Major Hymer Friedel, stationed in Santa Fe. If the Base Camp was wiped out by the explosion, Friedel was to assume command and direct any evacuations from nearby towns.

Shortly after the meeting broke up, the medical group began issuing protective clothing to all Trinity personnel:

187

coveralls, caps, gas masks, cotton gloves, even special booties to be worn over shoes.

When General Groves flew into Albuquerque at noon, air traffic was already shutting down throughout the Albuquerque–Santa Fe–El Paso area. Colonel Tyler and some other military brass were on hand to meet the general and his party. The scientists and various high-ranking officers stood around in knots at the airfield, chatting and waiting for their baggage. Groves, horrified by such lax security, ordered everyone into cars and on to Albuquerque. The bags could follow later, but Groves wanted no reporters or other snoopers spotting such VIP's as Bush and Conant.

At Albuquerque, however, he found things worse. A steady stream of scientists had filtered into town that morning to pass the day in window-shopping and other pursuits while awaiting the bus caravan from The Hill. They congregated at the Hilton Hotel. When Groves marched into the lobby, he was dumfounded. Scientists were everywhere— sprawled in the lounge, lunching in the dining room. The general ordered them out. Furthermore, he advised them to disperse in pairs and make themselves as inconspicuous as possible for the rest of the day. Dr. Ernest Lawrence, Bill Laurence of *The New York Times* and several others finally found a hamburger stand. They spent the remainder of the afternoon pacing the sidewalks of Albuquerque, feeling a little like Dead End kids on the lam from the police.

The weathermen held a conclave at Trinity. Their operation had spurred itself furiously during the last twenty-four hours. Teletype reports clacked continuously into Hubbard's office. Planes flew over the Oscura range in the morning to photograph smoke experiments, and weather balloons were launched in droves. By mid-afternoon the sky above Trinity was a carnival of balloons drifting in lazy clusters toward the northeast. The men below watched them rise, then drew a compass course of their paths at different altitudes. The forecast that day was a welcome surprise: The winds on July 16 would blow gently at dawn and there would be no rain in the immediate test area.

All afternoon the scientists fussed with their instruments or just marked time. Fermi and Weil tested their tanks in an artificial crater they had bulldozed a few days before. The tanks were painted silver-gray to cut down the sun's heat and make them easier to track against the dark hills. Weil suffered terribly that day from infected sinuses aggravated by the desert dust. In the middle of the frantic preparations he jotted a note to himself to be sure to buy some nosedrops. Herb Anderson, who was responsible for the recovery experiment, assembled his tank crews for a final briefing. He worried that the ancient machines might break down at the last moment. The GI drivers laughed. "Leave it to us," one of them assured him, "everything's in shape."

Someone had decided at the eleventh hour to make at least an effort to gauge the bomb's impact on building structures. Frank Oppenheimer walked around the site, positioning little boxes filled with excelsior. He also scattered pine shavings and pieces of lumber with corrugated iron strips nailed to them. The shavings and lumber represented portions of Japanese houses, and the excelsior was a sample of highly inflammable material. The scientists even procured some live "guinea pigs." Warren drove into the desert with a box of white mice and strung the beasties up by their tails from signal wires. That was one experiment that never had a chance. The mice all died of thirst before the shot.

Joe McKibben slouched in front of a control panel at the

South-10,000-yard shelter. McKibben was a spindly Lincolnesque character with a thick shock of hair and a soft Missouri twang. He talked with a slight stammer and his glasses were forever falling over his nose. For nearly two weeks he had been working without let-up on the timing circuits for the test. Everyone wanted to test his individual experiments against Joe's timer. They had finally worn him and his circuits out the day before, and there had been the hell to pay when the circuits blew. Now McKibben checked out for the last time the complex mechanism that would fire the bomb. Mentally he ticked off the segments. They would fall one after the other like dominoes: a signal would fire the detonators, the detonators would ignite the high explosive, the high explosive would implode the plutonium core—and whammo. If it would only, only work, he thought.

About four o'clock, as thunderheads began moving into the area, Ken Greisen climbed the tower. He carried a device called the informer. He would rig it to the detonators on the bomb and it would tell him what had gone wrong if the detonation failed. Inside the shed at the top of the tower he picked his way over coils of wire and carefully connected each of the sixty-four detonators to the informer. The north side of the shack, facing the biggest array of instruments and cameras, was uncovered, and Greisen could look out and see the storm clouds scudding in over the Chupadera Mesa and the Oscuras. Lightning, he thought—what if it should hit the tower and detonate the bomb? He laughed to himself. He could just as easily be blown to bits by the cubic inch of explosive in the tiny detonator he held in his hand.

Another scientist climbed the tower after Greisen had left. Robert Oppenheimer wanted to see for himself that nothing had been neglected in the bomb's final toilet. Perhaps, too, he wanted to feel the Gorgon's head one last time and stare it in the face with all its barbarous accouterments. Perhaps, more than anything else, he wanted to be alone where he could think, high above the busy desert with just the wind and the bomb for companions.

Below him an exodus was already taking place. All personnel not needed for the shot were vacating the site. The nuclear-assembly men cleared their kits and instruments from the McDonald ranch house. One or two took a last plunge in the lukewarm waters of the old cattle cistern. Leo Jercinovic and other enlisted men packed their gear and loaded it onto trucks. Some of them took along sandwiches for the long night's vigil on Compania Hill. By five o'clock all nonessential men and vehicles had departed Base Camp, and the barracks lay deserted.

Truman had arrived at the "Little White House" in Babelsberg. Tired from his trip, he had gone straight to his suite on the second floor. On the sunporch outside his room he had paused a few moments to look below at the garden stretching in a tapestry of shadowed green to the quiet waters of Lake Griebnitz. It was a tranquil setting for a man with the bomb on his mind. Churchill was due to arrive within the hour at his house two blocks away. And in a somber residence a mile distant, Soviet officials were awaiting Generalissimo Stalin.

Across the Pacific, Japanese coastal cities reeled from the second day of massed bombardment by ships of the U.S. Third Fleet. The battleships *Iowa, Missouri* and *Wisconsin* had joined in the attack, hurling salvo after flaming salvo of sixteen-inch shells into enemy iron and steel works along the mainland. The ships had approached unopposed to within three miles of the Japanese coast while more than a thousand carrier planes swarmed in to rake airfields and rail targets. The big guns of the battlewagons had howled their wrath under sunny skies while their shells streaked toward their quarry every fifteen seconds or better. The Navy reported that no Japanese shore batteries had even attempted to return the fire.

A hailstorm peppered the sidewalks at Los Alamos as members of the Theoretical Division entered the post auditorium to hear a final talk from their chief, Hans Bethe. He reminded them they were about to witness the first atomic bomb test. "Human calculation indicates that the experiment must succeed," Bethe reported with clinical solemnity. "But will nature act in conformity with our calculations?"

A half-hour later the scientists, their pockets stuffed with sunburn cream and snake-bite antidote, boarded three buses and set off for Trinity with a motorcycle escort. As the convoy slowed at the main gate, a sedan screeched to a stop in front of it and Richard Feynman scampered aboard one of the buses. Feynman had been in New York twenty-four hours earlier when he'd received a wire from Bethe: "Baby due to arrive July 16." He had caught the next plane out for Albuquerque. Now, at the back of the bus, he spotted his colleague Klaus Fuchs sitting alone. Feynman plunked down next to him.

At her lodge in the Frijoles Canyon, Mrs. Frey could see excitement written all over the face of her twenty-three-year-old son, Richard. He had been working as an enlisted man at Los Alamos for the last fifteen months. Mrs. Frey had seldom seen him in that time. For security reasons he was not allowed to visit the lodge. This evening, though, he had showed up mysteriously. "Mum," he said, "I'm leaving tonight for something big." Mrs. Frey knew better than to ask questions. "Good luck," she said as she kissed him.

The convoy of scientists stopped briefly in Santa Fe to pick up several passengers. The newcomers wore Army Engineer uniforms but they belonged to the Counter Intelligence Corps. They were a part of a twenty-five-man force of agents which had assembled at the La Fonda Hotel for a last briefing from Captain Frederick B. "Dusty" Rhodes. The agents had two principal duties as they fanned out to their various posts: to help perpetuate the "cover" story about an ammunition-dump explosion, and to summon the MP evacuation force if fallout inundated their areas.

In Carrizozo, forty miles east of Trinity, a husband-and-wife team were already helping set up part of the elaborate monitoring apparatus for the test. Alvin and Elizabeth Graves, a pair of Ph.D.'s from the University of Chicago, had checked into Harry Miller's Tourist Court the day before with a most untouristy set of baggage that included a seismograph, Geiger counter, short-wave radio and portable electric generator. In Cabin Number 4 the Graveses spread out their equipment on a creaky double bed and told the inquiring owner that they were on a cross-country trip and would stay only two nights. The owner seemed more interested in where the couple had gotten gasoline to make such a trip than in their weird instruments. In fact, Al Graves had frugally hoarded his ration stamps so he could drive from Los Alamos to Santa Fe every month for a cello lesson.

A leaden overcast marred the sunset at Trinity. Cyril Smith stood with Oppenheimer at the edge of the reservoir at Base Camp and watched the clouds coming. They chatted about casual things—family, home, life on the mesa—and at one point the conversation drifted into philosophy. Smith, a cultured Englishman, found surcease from the day's tension listening to Oppenheimer talk. The bomb might have been a continent away. Oppie gazed at the darkening Oscuras to the east. "Funny how the mountains always inspire our work," he remarked.

Nearby a young engineer named William Caldes listened

bug-eyed to a discussion among Enrico Fermi and several of his colleagues. The scientists were trying to relieve the tension in their own way by wagering how long it would take for the earth to be incinerated if the shot ignited a chain reaction in the atmosphere. Fermi was taking bets on whether such an event would merely destroy New Mexico or wipe out the world. Jokingly he suggested that even if the test flopped, it would have been a worthwhile experiment for proving that an atomic explosion was not possible.

Caldes was getting more upset by the minute. It seemed to him inexcusably cavalier talk to be coming from such noted scientists unless there was a grain of truth in it. Just as Fermi looked out at the landscape and sighed, "Ah, the earth on the eve of its disintegration," Caldes saw a tarantula slither into the circle of men. His fears evaporated as he watched the scientists scatter as though the bomb itself had dropped in their midst.

At dusk Bainbridge called a halt to further testing of the firing circuits. Donald Hornig had gone to the tower to arm the bomb. In the shed at the top Hornig unscrewed the harness of cables from the dummy firing unit and carefully clamped them to the real one, a stubby aluminum tank that lay a few feet from the bomb. Patiently he inspected each of the detonation points on the bomb. At the bottom of the tower he paused to make sure that the vital firing switch was still in "open" position and its covering box locked. Its counterpart was being checked that very moment at the control center at South-10,000-yards. The last step in readying the bomb was finished. All that stood now between the beast and its moment of truth was the closing of the switches and the signal to fire.

By seven P.M., when Groves arrived at Base Camp with Conant and Bush, the weather had deteriorated. The overcast had settled and begun to disgorge a blustery drizzle punctuated by lightning flashes. The rain had not yet reached the shot tower, but some of the scientists had succumbed to the tensions of the past week and were clamoring for a postponement. The rain threatened to ruin electrical connections, the plans for the B-29 observation plane and, most important, the extensive precautions taken to avoid fallout in populous areas. Not only would heavy rains bring down radioactivity in excessive amounts over a small area, but the mounting winds might shift and carry it much farther than had been anticipated. Groves was especially worried about the nearest large town, Amarillo, Texas, which lay 300 miles southeast. It would be impossible to evacuate Amarillo's 70,000 inhabitants.

At the same time, many of the group leaders at Trinity recognized the demoralizing consequences of a postponement. The men had been working day and night for weeks. Tension had built up to an unbelievable point and tempers were pitched for a shot on the morrow. Delay now would mean a wrenching psychological readjustment. It was also doubtful that any postponement could be limited to a day or two. The scientists badly needed several days of rest. It would take at least that long for them to recoup their strength and to dry out, reassemble and check their instruments. Oppenheimer and Bainbridge were besieged by conflicting advice.

Groves alone understood the political demands of an early test. He was also afraid that each day's delay would jeopardize the security measures he had taken and increase the chances of a sabotage attempt. He called Oppenheimer into an office and, after excusing the flustered weathermen, shut the door and quietly discussed the prospects with the director. They agreed that for the moment there was no need to postpone the test beyond possibly an hour or two. It was still hoped that the shot could go by four A.M.—or some time within the dark hours when conditions would be best for photographing the fireball and the sleeping countryside would be relatively undisturbed by the explosion. The two men agreed to confer again at midnight and review the situation then. "Get some sleep," Groves urged. The general promptly returned to his tent and turned in for the night. The canvas slapping in the high wind disturbed his slumber not a whit. But Oppenheimer stayed awake, chain-smoking and worrying through the endless hours.

The possibility that the rain might damage the circuits at the tower disturbed Oppie. He called Hornig, who knew every inch of the circuitry, and asked him to go back and baby-sit with the bomb. Once more Hornig went to the top of the tower. Huddled in the shed amid a coil of cables and discarded ropes and pulleys, he pulled out a cheap paperback, *Desert Island Decameron,* and began thumbing through it. The light flickered dimly from a single sixty-watt bulb hanging above the gadget. The *Decameron,* however, had lost some of its fascination. With each flash of lightning outside, Hornig dropped the book and began counting seconds to himself, trying to figure how close to the tower the bolt had struck.

Toward nine Bainbridge held a final briefing for the dozen group leaders. All personnel were to be out of the test area two hours before the shot. It was enough leeway for a man to walk safely from the blast zone if his jeep broke down. The MP's had a list of some seventy-five persons who would man the main shelters at North-, West- and South-10,000-yards. They would check the list against the bodies there to make sure no one had been stranded at the detonation point. Plans called for the largest group of scientists and officers to gather in the South-10,000 shelter: Oppenheimer, Bainbridge, Kistiakowsky, General Farrell, Lieutenant Bush, Joe McKibben and Don Hornig at the firing control panel, and Sam Allison in the countdown booth. At North-10,000-yards, physicist Robert Wilson would be in charge of a score of specialists making photographic and

196

nuclear measurements. A searchlight crew and more photo technicians would occupy the shelter at West-10,000-yards. The shelter chiefs were authorized to maintain discipline and enforce orderly evacuations if fallout threatened.

As the briefing broke up, Bainbridge was told that a handful of GI's had asked to be relieved from manning their stations. They had suffered a last-minute fright after hearing some of the wild predictions about the bomb. By ten o'clock, however, most of the scientists and GI's were manning their stations.

In Washington, Mrs. O'Leary set the alarm clock in her bedroom for 5:30 A.M. She would need an hour to breakfast and get down to her office at the War Department in time to receive an important message from the general. Groves had told his secretary to be on hand early Monday and to have her code sheets ready for deciphering.

In his apartment at the Woodley Park Towers, Theodore Koop, a Pentagon official handling voluntary press censorship, was listening to a news broadcast when his phone rang. It was one of Groves's security officers. "Something's happening in New Mexico at daybreak tomorrow," he said. "Censorship may have to take emergency action if things go wrong." In his highly sensitive position Koop had known indirectly for some time of the atomic-bomb project. He guessed immediately that the security officer was tipping him off to the impending test. He went to bed, but it was the only night of the war he was unable to sleep. Among his other worries Koop feared for the safety of his sister in Tucson, Arizona.

Winston Churchill was in Berlin that evening having a ripping time with the men of the famed "Desert Rat" armored division. About 400 of them had gathered for the ceremonial opening of a club in their name. They had fought

197

the Germans across North Africa from Alamein to Zuara, and they remembered warmly the Prime Minister's visits to the battle front. Churchill listened to them sing "For He's a Jolly Good Fellow" and thought, a bit roguishly, that he detected a certain sheepishness among some of them for having voted against him in the recent British elections.

In the "Little White House," Truman turned in. The Filipino mess men had served up a piping-hot dinner earlier, and the President had dined quietly with Byrnes and one or two other staffers. Ambassador Averell Harriman had dropped by afterward to pay his respects. The evening was hot and the house unscreened. Mosquitoes whined everywhere. Outside it was still light although the hour was past ten. The bomb, of course, was seldom far from Truman's thoughts. He tossed and turned that night in the bed of the former Nazi gauleiter.

The convoy of scientists from Los Alamos stopped at the Albuquerque Hilton to pick up those colleagues who had come down earlier in the day. Chadwick and Bill Laurence found room in a sedan and climbed in together. Chadwick, whose discovery of neutrons had played so telling a role in the drama now reaching its climax, was silent and moody. Sitting next to him, Laurence felt the shadow of the bomb between them. As the convoy resumed its journey, the reporter tried to feel out the scientist on the question of whether Britain and America should share the secrets of the bomb with their Russian ally. Chadwick reacted violently. "Why should we?" he blurted. "They don't give us anything." Behind them, in one of the darkened buses, Klaus Fuchs watched the MP's on their motorcycles racing by his window.

At Kirtland Field, Luis Alvarez and Deac Parsons stocked their B-29 for the flight to Trinity. Their equipment included every imaginable electronic device: radio receivers, cathode-ray tubes, special cameras and three aluminum canisters containing microphones and transmitters. The B-29 planned to fly over the shot tower just before detonation and drop the canisters by parachute. The plane would radio the control station at South-10,000, and the bomb would be fired a minute or two later. The microphones inside the canisters would register the speed and pressure of the fireball and radio the data to the B-29 for instantaneous taping. The cameras would measure the fireball's intensity, and the film would be parachuted to the ground for retrieval by security agents. In their airborne telemetry station Alvarez and Parsons hoped to learn everything possible about the bomb's behavior before they flew the first combat mission with it to Japan.

The war of jitters had begun in earnest at Trinity. The weather had put nerves on edge. But beyond that was the simple animal urge for self-preservation, the obsessive desire during these last hours to put as much distance as possible between the beast on the tower and oneself. A jeep broke down near the detonation point; the occupants left it there and scurried back to camp on foot. Several scientists got flats and drove their tires down to the rims rather than stop to change them. A few hardy souls still toiled on the desert, fighting the clock to get their instruments in perfect order.

Engineer Caldes had a moment of panic in the concrete bunker 1000 yards north of the tower, where his instruments were stored. Checking on them late that night, he found that the crude air-conditioner he had rigged had broken and the ninety-degree heat in the bunker was melting the insulation on his circuits. Some of them were already shorting and Caldes feared his particular experiment was doomed. Only frantic efforts to fix the conditioner saved the day. Staff Sergeant Benjamin C. Benjamin got momentarily careless and almost canceled his ticket to the big show. The scientists were using prima cord, an explosive shaped like a rope, in an experiment to record the shock wave. Some of the stuff was lying on the ground near Benjamin when an electrical surge ignited it. The prima cord exploded with a concussion that rocked Benjamin to his knees. He was still in a daze when his colleagues rushed up.

Louis Jacot, an SED on the evacuation detail, noticed his hand shook slightly when he lifted the beer can to his lips. He had washed down his C-rations dinner and was trying now to dull some of the trepidation he felt about the morrow. It was cold in the jeep, he thought, sitting there with the others watching the rain sweep in sheets across the highway. They were parked on Route 380 just north of Trinity. For half a mile east the road was lined with trucks and jeeps. The MP's, cloaked in ponchos, huddled in the trucks and cursed the weather. It was only 11 P.M. and the long night held no promise of sleep. Jacot, two officers and a sergeant named Vince O'Gorman swapped terse opinions on the operation they might have to embark on the next morning.

They knew that squads of other soldiers were sitting that very moment in a parking lot in Socorro, and they wondered how their mates would ever evacuate the town's 4300 citizens if they had to. The Special Engineers like Jacot, who had been ordered to supplement the meager MP force, carried no arms and would probably be no match for a shotgun-toting rancher who didn't want to leave his property. Jacot and his buddies carried only handmade maps of the region around Trinity which they might have to evacuate. And in recent weeks, during surveys, they had learned that the maps were antediluvian and that many of the landmarks on them didn't exist. An access road to a ranch or village would turn out to have a mine cut across it. Some roads existed only in the map-makers' imagination. The prospect of removing whole communities of people seemed nightmarish.

A strange tedium had settled over the test site.

In Oppenheimer's office and the weather shack worried frowns still prevailed. But elsewhere the mood was like that one experiences in the hours before the final girding for climax: that twilight time before the player departs for his Big Game, the groom for his wedding, the soldier for the invasion assault. Once in the stadium, the church or the landing craft, the tension mounts unbearably. But before that the hours pass slowly.

At Base Camp and in the shelters the GI's and scientists read, wrote letters or played cards. Oppenheimer found a moment between checks with the weathermen to dip into his anthology of Baudelaire. Fermi fiddled with his slide rule and mused on a homemade experiment he would try out for the shot. Bainbridge, already without sleep for twenty-four hours, checked the final dispositions of all personnel and slapped himself occasionally to stay awake. In more than one tent, bottles appeared from duffel bags and men fortified their spirits with bourbon and rotgut gin. Everything humanly possible had been done to assure success. The die was cast. Trinity waited on the weather.

Robert Wilson climbed the tower a few minutes before midnight. He had one last chore before leaving for his station at North-10,000 yards. He wanted to attach a small canister to the top of the tower. The canister contained tiny tubes for measuring the speed of the bomb's chain reaction. Wilson and Bruno Rossi had been rechecking it all evening. As he neared the top, Wilson recalled his dream of the last few nights. He would be almost at the summit, and then a misstep would send him hurtling off the tower. It was always a long, slow fall, and each time, before he struck the ground, he woke up sweating. Wilson strung the canister from a girder next to the shack. Before he descended, he opened the trapdoor and looked in. Donald Hornig was still huddled next to the bomb. He had given up worrying about the lightning and was lost at last among the nymphs and lagoons of *Desert Island Decameron.*

VIII

July 16, 1945: 0001 to 0400 Hours

I N THE darkness of his tent General Groves rubbed the sleep from his eyes and began fumbling with the buttons of his khaki shirt. Carefully he adjusted his overseas cap to a dignified angle. Then he marched into the chilling drizzle to keep his midnight appointment with Oppenheimer.

It occurred to the general, as he crossed the camp grounds, that the shot tower ten miles away had no adequate guard. There was always the danger that a saboteur might infiltrate the ring of MP's surrounding Trinity or that someone at camp might crack from the strain and take it on himself to disrupt the test. Only hours before, one young scientist had become hysterical and had had to be removed under sedation. Groves decided to dispatch an armed party to the tower.

Two jeeps and a sedan took off with an eight-man party that included Bainbridge, Kistiakowsky, Joe McKibben, weatherman Jack Hubbard and two sergeants, and Lieutenant Bush and an MP guard. Kistiakowsky kept muttering that Groves's idea was absurd and that the general was seeing spies and spooks under every cot. At the tower Kistiakowsky informed Don Hornig that he was being relieved. For Hornig it was almost the day's happiest moment. The loneliness, the lightning and the oppressive presence of the bomb had tautened his nerves to the breaking point. After one final brief check of the gadget, he slipped through the

205

trapdoor, the last man at Trinity to see the bomb in all its brutish trappings.

The party settled down for the long vigil. Hubbard and his men began sending weather balloons aloft every quarter-hour to gauge the winds' velocity. At the base of the tower Bainbridge, cradling a field telephone, talked anxiously about the weather with his chief aide, John Williams, at the South-10,000-yard control center. Thirty feet away Lieutenant Bush sat in his jeep, fingering a submachine gun and wondering for the thousandth time how he had ever wound up in such an assignment. Bush mused on what might happen if the B-29 observation plane lost its course in the murk and rammed the tower. The thought began to prey on him. He was a good soldier and he was very scared.

All over the desert men were busily devouring the night in a multitude of ways. They drank beer, played poker, read poetry, wrote their wives, fought their instruments and cursed the elements.

Bob Krohn and Jack Aeby, two young engineers, had a terrible time tethering Barbara Anne, an unwieldy barrage balloon that was being used in a critical experiment. While lightning crackled across the flats, they pumped inflammable helium into Barbara Anne. Once she was aloft, however, their troubles had only begun. A cable, coated with luminous paint, was harnessed from the balloon to a jeep on the ground, so that the scientists would be able to watch the shock wave snap the cable, and thus gauge its velocity.

But each time Krohn or Aeby grabbed the cable to steady it, lightning charged down the wire and stung their hands. Krohn felt his hair literally stand on end as the electricity surged through his heavy gloves. The winds were now beginning to blow with such force that the cable picked up the front end of the jeep and swung it about like a toy. The two engineers decided it was time to make tracks.

Carlton Hoogterp, a Dutchman, had last-minute business on the desert. He had set up small wooden boxes in every direction from the shot tower. The boxes were perforated with holes covered by aluminum foil. The shock wave breaking the foils would tell him how much blast pressure per square inch the bomb could deliver. Hoogterp was removing some rain coverings from the boxes at about one A.M. when his jeep developed steering trouble. He clambered out and rushed to the nearest shelter on foot.

In a blockhouse near the West-10,000-yard shelter John Fuqua, a twenty-eight-year-old Army private from Harrodsburg, Kentucky, checked his searchlight. He had been told very little of what the test was all about, except that there would likely be an explosion and he was to track the cloud from it with his light. Three other searchlight crews, stationed north of the shot tower, would help him. All at once, inside the blockhouse, Fuqua felt awfully alone and homesick. The blue-grass hills seemed eons away from the sand and mesquite of Trinity. He reached over and patted the German shepherd dog asleep at his feet. The dog was no coon hunter, but he'd been good protection against tarantulas. Fuqua picked up his pen and continued writing.

Fifty yards away, in West-10,000, John Manley asked the medical officer for some salve. Dust and lack of sleep had caused a painful infection in Manley's eyes. Here he was, the shelter's chief scientific officer, on the morning of the test and he could barely see. At North-10,000, Robert Wilson, the scientist in charge, stumbled into the shelter from his rounds of the site. Exhausted, he grabbed a telephone and rang the control center for a weather report. Seconds later, still holding the phone, he sank to the floor in a deep sleep. Louis Hempelmann, the medical officer at South-10,000, tried to keep out of everybody's way. The scientists and military observers were beginning to crowd the tiny bunker to its rafters. Hempelmann crawled under a table and shut

207

himself off from the turmoil with a good detective novel. In his tent at Base Camp, Emilio Segrè finished the last chapter of André Gide's *Faux-Monnayeurs*. He closed the book and lay on his cot listening to the rain beat a dirgeful tattoo on the canvas.

The tower was wrapped in a mantle of mist that all but obscured the pinpoint of light at its top. Every few minutes Lieutenant Bush and the guard left their jeep to shine flashlights on the tower. Their beams darted among the crisscross of girders and played on clumps of cable trailing from the bomb shack to the ground, undulating like pythons into the darkness. From time to time the short-wave radio in the sedan crackled with messages for Bainbridge or Kistiakowsky. McKibben, white-faced with fatigue, tried to doze in the back of one of the jeeps. A few minutes before two A.M. Bainbridge took a call at the tower from Base Camp. Oppenheimer and Groves had reviewed the weather situation and found nothing to encourage them. Bainbridge reported that conditions at the tower were no better. It was decided to call off the scheduled four-o'clock shot. There would be at least an hour's delay.

Harold Dean and his wife, the only inhabitants of Old Bingham, shared a late snack in the back of their combination post office and general store. Twenty-three miles due north of the shot tower, Old Bingham was the nearest community at hand. The Deans had tried vainly to sleep with what seemed like half the U.S. Army parked outside their door. Jeeps had been racing up and down the highway since midnight. The clatter and commotion annoyed the couple. What made them madder was that no one would tell them why the Army had picked the Deans' place to hold maneuvers.

San Antonio's only phone had been tied up all night long. It was located in Joe Miera's Owl Bar & Café, and Joe had handed out the key earlier that evening to the dozen Army Engineers who rented the cabins behind his bar. They had been camping on Joe's property for weeks with all their fancy equipment. He found them a clannish, close-mouthed bunch; but he was happy to see their money and to watch them teach his four-year-old grandson how to march. This had been a trying night, though. Joe's daughter, Carmelita Chavez, was having a baby, and the soldiers' bustling had kept her awake. "Calla la boca!" he yelled from his bedroom.

At Los Alamos only the wives slept soundly. Stanislaw Ulam, one of the few scientists who hadn't gone to Trinity, had one of his rare dreams. He saw quite vividly the plutonium ingots massed together within the clay-gray core, the explosives charges arranged like wedge-shaped slices of pie around them. He saw the core compress into a tiny ball, then vanish, not suddenly but as in a slow-motion movie. He awoke just as the flash seared his subconscious. Ulam would have similar dreams in years to come. With Edward Teller he would share the patent for the hydrogen bomb.

One look at the barren knoll twenty-five miles from the shot tower, and Bill Laurence bristled with indignation. How, he wanted to know, could he write an eyewitness account of the test so far from the scene? He got little encouragement from the mob of scientists and VIP's who stepped off the buses behind him. The drizzle was bone-chilling, almost everyone had forgotten overcoats in the rush to leave Los Alamos, and the company was tired and grumpy from the long trip. The scientists had reached Compania Hill at two A.M. only to learn that the test would be delayed an hour or more. Except for a lonely searchlight beacon to the southeast, there was nothing to mark the vicinity of the shot tower. The radio connection with the control center was out of order, and no one really knew when the bomb would go off or where to look for it. For a while the caravansary at Compania was a depressing scene. The only saviors were the ham sandwiches and hot coffee.

The coffee was a godsend at Base Camp too. Oppenheimer held court in the mess hall and consumed quantities of it. Flanked by such lieutenants as Rabi and Warren, he conducted an informal colloquy on the chances of holding the test that day. As he talked, Oppenheimer rolled himself one cigarette after another and puffed them down to the ash. The weathermen popped in periodically to reassure him, but the pelting rain outside did little to assuage his worries. Rabi tried his best to soothe Oppenheimer and had almost succeeded when Fermi rushed into the mess hall and pleaded for a postponement. Fermi feared for the safety of the camp if a sudden wind shift threatened a deluge of radioactive rain following the shot. Evacuation routes from Base Camp were inadequate and the rain would make them virtually unnavigable. "There could be a catastrophe," he warned Oppenheimer.

Groves, roving the mess hall like a caged bear, saw that Oppenheimer was becoming more and more agitated. The camp, with its palace guard of scientific advisers all converging on the laboratory director, was no place for cool decisions to be weighed. The general suggested that Oppenheimer accompany him immediately to the control center at South-10,000 yards, where the atmosphere was less hectic. Even that was grounds for dispute. Several of Oppenheimer's colleagues feared for his life and tried to dissuade him from watching the test from so near. Uncertain of the bomb's power, they worried that a runaway chain reaction might envelop the shelter and cremate Oppenheimer alive. General Farrell tried to cool the tension with an ingenuous remark. "We've all had a long joyful life," he suggested, "and maybe we'll all go out in a blaze of glory." In the end Oppenheimer followed Groves to the shelter.

Hubbard's forecasters held a 2:15 A.M. weather conference as thundershowers and thirty-mile-an-hour winds raked the test site. They reported there was still hope for a shot some time between dawn at five A.M. and sunrise at six. Predictions called for a lull in the storm at that time, followed by a northeasterly shift of winds above 20,000 feet. This would enhance the safety factor by ensuring that high-flying fallout would move toward the less populous areas around Trinity.

But fifteen minutes later, at 2:30 A.M., the storm hit the detonation area full-blast. Halfway up the shot tower a searchlight shorted and plunged the structure in darkness. From West-10,000, Julian Mack sent out a frantic call requesting that the light, on which his cameras had been focusing, be relit as quickly as possible. Kistiakowsky grabbed a powerful flashlight and climbed the slippery stairway to a platform fifty feet above the ground. He stood there for the next two hours, beaming the light at intervals toward Mack's cameras, while the downpour raged about him. Only later did his colleagues discover that Kisty suffered from vertigo.

Behind the bunker at South-10,000, the pair of shadows paced restlessly, dodging puddles of rain water, halting every few yards to hold silent communion with the bleak heavens. Communication between the shadows was felt rather than spoken. Groves and Oppenheimer had fought the battle of the bomb side by side for too long not to know instinctively what was in each other's minds at such pregnant moments. Now they studied the skies intently, searching for some small sign that would encourage hopes for a dawn shot. They hung on each fleeting glimpse of a star as lovers hang on a passing glance. Tiring at last of the futile game, the two men retreated to the shelter.

There they measured the consequences of scrubbing the test that day. Dawn was less than two hours away, the weather over the shot tower had worsened and, while there was hope, there was no promise that the storm front would dissipate before sunrise. Groves had grown impatient with the weather's vagaries and no longer put much stock in Hubbard's reports. He feared that further delay might subject the firing circuits to ruinous dampening. Oppenheimer kept repeating, "If we postpone, I'll never get my people up to pitch again."

Their decision was finally relayed to Bainbridge: Hold up the test another half-hour until 5:30 A.M. If there was no weather break by then, daylight would force a definite postponement.

In Potsdam it was almost noon. The President had slept until eight A.M., more than an hour beyond his usual rising time. Mary Churchill, the Prime Minister's daughter, had driven her father and Foreign Secretary Anthony Eden over to the "Little White House" to pay a social call on Truman and Byrnes. The four men spent a relaxed morning in the sunlit study of Truman's suite. No detailed business of the impending conference was discussed. But Truman, who had worked hard during his ocean voyage to prepare an agenda, asked the Prime Minister if he too had one ready. "No," growled Churchill, "I don't need one." The two leaders then turned the conversation to the war in the Pacific.

That day the marauding Third Fleet had resumed its bombardment of Japan from seventeen miles offshore. Carrier planes battered Japanese shipping along the coast of Honshu, and U.S. battleships fired 2700-pound missiles by the thousands at enemy steel and iron works. The factories burned and collapsed under the weight of more than a thousand tons of shells. There was no sign of response from either Japanese coastal batteries or the Japanese air force. A

U.S. general gave a succinct explanation: "Lack of fuel, pilots and spare parts."

The mess hall at Base Camp served a 3:45 A.M. breakfast of powdered eggs, French toast and coffee. Vannevar Bush walked in, his rumpled seersucker suit splotched with rain. Bush had been unceremoniously awakened by a violent gust of wind that had collapsed his tent and bared him to the storm. Other officials and scientists filed into the mess hall behind him. Some ate leisurely, as they anticipated watching the shot from Base Camp; others wolfed their food and moved out quickly to their shelter designations.

At four A.M. the rain quietly let up. Joe McKibben at the shot tower subconsciously felt the weather lift. He had been dreaming that Kistiakowsky was teasing him by sprinkling a garden hose in his face. McKibben woke up realizing the rain had stopped and that mist was gently falling on his face. Ken Bainbridge was leaning over him, saying, "Come on, Joe. It's time now."

IX

July 16, 1945:
Zero Minus One Hour

VISIBILITY was poor at Kirtland Field in Albuquerque, but the B-29 was ready for take-off and the control tower had finally given its consent. Alvarez and Parsons were boarding the plane at 4:30 A.M. when a telephone call reached them from Oppenheimer at Trinity. Alvarez took the call in a booth near the landing apron. His face dropped as he heard Oppenheimer say, "I'm sorry, but it's too dangerous. We're calling off your operation."

Alvarez argued heatedly. He reminded Oppenheimer that the plane was radar-equipped and that both he and Parsons were radar experts. They could find the tower despite the weather. "Everything's set up," Alvarez pleaded. "If we don't go in and drop these things, we'll have no way of knowing the bomb's effect on a plane overhead." Oppie was adamant. "I'm responsible for your life," he repeated, "and I forbid you to go near the tower." He warned Alvarez to have the observation plane steer a course at least fifteen miles west of the detonation point.

Bitterly disappointed but determined to make the best of a bad bargain, Alvarez joined the twelve-man party aboard the plane and directed the pilot to take off immediately. Just as the wheels went up, the ventilation system collapsed and smoke filled the craft. People coughed and yelled for oxygen masks, and for a moment the whole expedition seemed doomed. Finally the bomber gained altitude, the cabin cleared of smoke and the big Superfort veered sharply toward the south and into the enveloping murk.

The crew of the *Indianapolis* was watching a mysterious crate swing aboard the heavy cruiser at that hour. They nudged each other and solemnly nodded. Floodlights illuminated the crate and its stenciled markings: "Secret—U.S. Government." Surely this was the forbidden cargo the *Indianapolis* had been assigned to trundle across the Pacific. The ruse worked. A few yards away in the darkness, officers Nolan and Furman, unnoticed, boarded the ship by a rear gangplank. Behind them two sailors followed with the bucket. They carried the U-235 coolie-style, swaying from a crowbar on their shoulders. In the flag lieutenant's vacant quarters, the officers attached the bucket to eyebolts welded to the deck and crisscrossed it with restraining straps. Furman snapped a padlock on the whole package and pocketed the key.

At 4:45 A.M. at Trinity, as the deadline neared for a final decision on the shot, Bainbridge received the weather report he had been waiting for at the tower. It told him that the high-altitude winds had considerably lightened and that their speed above 10,000 feet was no more than an average eleven miles per hour. The overcast was breaking and within an hour would be effectively scattered. The current wind conditions would hold for the next two hours. Bainbridge held a hurried phone conference with Oppenheimer, Groves and Hubbard. Should they proceed? One dissenting vote was enough to call off the test. Unanimously they agreed to go ahead. The scientists would need a good half-hour for final preparations in all three shelters. The zero hour was set, and Bainbridge phoned John Williams at South-10,000 with this curt order: "Prepare to fire at five-thirty."

The last arming ritual began. Bainbridge, McKibben and

Kistiakowsky would now close all the switches connecting the bomb with the complex firing and timing equipment at the shelters. The trio moved out first to a small pit 900 yards west of the tower, where a control station was located for all timing relays. McKibben lifted the lid over the hole and began pulling switches that would send automatic timing signals to all the experiments. Kistiakowsky, holding his flashlight on a set of printed instructions, repeated each step in a low, heavily accented voice. At 4:55 A.M. they returned to the tower, where Bainbridge turned on a dozen "aiming" lights to guide the B-29. Then, while Lieutenant Bush and the guard loaded the jeeps for departure, McKibben and Kistiakowsky carefully checked Bainbridge as he unlocked a coffin-like box directly under the tower and threw the switch to close the tower end of the firing circuit. Only one last step remained.

Just before they departed, Lieutenant Bush phoned the blockhouse at West-10,000. A searchlight would be needed on the tower as an extra precaution against saboteurs in the last half-hour while the bomb lay unguarded. Private Fuqua roused himself from his letter writing and trained his light on the tower six miles away. He flicked on the powerful beam and watched it slice the darkness until it came to rest on the bomb shack at the tower's pinnacle. In the control center at South-10,000, Bainbridge completed the arming ritual. The switches that would close all arming and timing circuits at that end were kept within a padlocked box for which he had the only key. While McKibben took his seat in front of the control panel, Bainbridge opened the box and threw the all-important firing switch into the ready position. The gadget was now fully armed.

Bainbridge's final chore was to broadcast the decisive weather report to the heads of the three shelters. The winds, he noted, were blowing generally to the east. At North-10,000, Robert Wilson snorted derisively when he heard

219

that. Everyone at his station knew the winds at that moment were blowing directly from the tower toward them. They were not amused by the prospects of having the fallout cloud pass overhead.

At five A.M. on Compania Hill the stentorian snores of reporter Bill Laurence routed his two companions, physicist Joseph Kennedy and Monsanto chemical executive Charles Thomas, from their slumbers in the back of an Army sedan. An officer poked his head in the car and informed them the test would come some time within the next half-hour or not on that day. Frantically the three tried to make radio contact with South-10,000. With some of the world's most prodigious scientific brains assembled on that knoll, no one seemed able to cure the short-wave set of its troubles. Richard Feynman had been tinkering valiantly but to no avail. The scientists stood around in the dark and munched candy bars as they waited for some divine revelation to tell them when the shot would go.

The final countdown began at 5:10 A.M. with a crashing rendition of the "Star-Spangled Banner." Just as Bainbridge gave the signal to Sam Allison in the control center, radio station KCBA in Delano, California, crossed wave lengths with the Trinity frequency. The station, operated by the Office of War Information, was opening its morning Voice of America broadcast to Latin America. The National Anthem provided stirring accompaniment for Allison as he intoned the announcement: "It is now zero minus twenty minutes."

Across the desert, men heard the words and their pulses quickened. The countdown had started, and now the boredom of the long night evaporated with miraculous swiftness. Books were closed, poker hands dropped and beers abandoned as their owners marshaled every wit to concentrate on the disembodied voice that flowed from loudspeakers throughout the site. At Base Camp, Phil Morrison stood beside a sound truck and relayed Allison's countdown to the scientists assembling at the old reservoir, where trenches had been dug for them.

At South-10,000, Allison sat in a cubicle on the right-hand side of the shelter. He held a telephone mouthpiece in one hand and gripped a microphone on the table with the other. The microphone would transmit information by short wave to the B-29 when it reached Trinity. At the age of forty-five, Allison was capping a successful science career by inaugurating what would be one of the tersest, most exclusive broadcasts in history. If that thought escaped him then, it was only because activity in the control center had intensified to a distracting degree.

Across the room from Allison, a man half his age was balancing on a stool, his eyes fixed on the panel in front of him. Don Hornig cautiously moved one hand toward the switch that could halt the test immediately if some last-second crisis occurred. Joe McKibben had just thrown a "minus twenty minutes" switch to synchronize all timing and firing signals with Allison's countdown. The twenty-foot-square room was jammed with a dizzying assortment of dials, monitoring screens and electrical fuses all mounted on crude panels that sat on tables or tottered on the shelves of GI clothes lockers. Men hovered before the panels and twisted the dials, nodding to one another as lights flashed on and weird lines wiggled across the oval screens. Outside, dozens of jeeps, sedans and carryalls stood by, facing away from the shelter, their motors idling. The drivers, tensed at their wheels, were seasoned veterans of Trinity, men who knew every road on the site and had driven each one at night countless times. One of them looked up to see a pair of silver stars winking at him from a foot away and heard a calm voice saying, "It's General Groves, soldier. Take me back to Base Camp."

The phone rang on a bed table in Santa Fe's picturesque La Fonda Hotel, 175 miles north of Trinity. Major Hymer Friedel picked it up and heard Stafford Warren at the other end. "Let's synchronize watches," said Warren. "It's five-fifteen here, fifteen minutes to zero." Friedel adjusted his watch and asked his superior how things were going. Warren said he was staying close to his radio transmitter and getting position reports from his field monitors. "Everything's okay so far," he added, "but keep this line open, no matter what." If disaster enfolded Trinity, both men knew the line would carry Warren's last orders, turning over the whole far-flung evacuation exercise to Friedel.

Sixty miles south a security officer in Albuquerque's Hilton Hotel walked across the room to shake Captain Thomas Jones awake. "Leave him alone," said Jones's deputy, Lieutenant Philip Belcher, "he's exhausted. There's still time." The two officers resumed their watch at the window while Jones dozed fitfully on the single bed. At 209 North High Street, David Greenglass pushed his chair from the breakfast table and got ready to leave. For Greenglass and hundreds of other GI's at Los Alamos it was just another working day at the laboratory. He disliked the way these weekend passes ended, disliked having to crawl in the dark from the snugness of the double bed and breakfast alone before taking the long bus trip back to The Hill. He lingered at the bedroom door, watching Ruth turn in her sleep, then tiptoed out of the apartment.

"I've got it!" yelled Feynman to the cluster of men around the radio truck at Compania Hill. Allison's voice crackled faintly over the short-wave set, faded amid static, then charged ahead loudly with the countdown. The GI's and scientists hearing it began scrambling up the slope of the hill. Within five minutes Allison's voice had faded again for good. The countdown to Compania Hill had been discontinued so that the frequency could be used solely to guide the B-29 now approaching Trinity.

A CIC officer at Base Camp monitoring the communications network threw a momentary fit. He had been listening to a conversation between Julian Mack at West-10,000 and Berlyn Brixner, Mack's alternate at North-10,000. No proper names were supposed to be used over the airwaves at Trinity. The two men, who were discussing a technical problem, referred to each other as "Aches" and "Pains." Suddenly the shelf holding Mack's radio gave way. "Aches to Pains, Aches to Pains," Mack screeched. "Oh, hell, Brixner," he bellowed, "the radio's collapsed!" At this point the security officer interrupted with a choice expletive of his own and the two scientists hastily resumed their code.

Joe McKibben shifted his eyes from the firing console and turned a knob to heat up the filaments on the automatic timing circuitry. The tiny panel meters told him that the signals were going out properly. He unhooked the Lucite cover over the automatic timer, the device that would activate all timing and firing circuits in the last minute. Beside him Hornig tightened his grip on the "stop" switch. His eyes never left the panel for a split second. He would need to react at least that fast if the switch had to be thrown suddenly. To McKibben's and Hornig's right, at the very front of the bunker, sat an Englishman named Ernest Titterton, a detonator expert whose sole responsibility was a tube called the thytratron. At the instant McKibben's firing signal flashed across his viewing scope, Titterton would fire the tube which would activate the bomb's detonators.

It was 5:20 A.M. in the bunker and getting warmer.

On Compania Hill the scientists half listened to their final instructions as they jockeyed for positions on the slope. They were told to lie or sit down on the ground and cover their eyes with pieces of dark welder's glass, a precaution that seemed absurd to those who had been having trouble seeing more than a few feet ahead of themselves in the murk. They were warned to stay prone until the shock wave had passed over, two minutes after the shot. Many of the scientists who had bet that the bomb would fizzle pooh-poohed the orders. Some took them to heart. Bill Laurence, still bridling at the remoteness of his observation post, heard a voice behind him say: "Don't worry, you'll see all you need to. We want our chronicler to survive."

In San Francisco Bay the *Indianapolis* was under way, gathering steam as she slipped beneath the graceful span of the Golden Gate, past Point Bonita and out into the ghostly fog of the Pacific. Below decks Nolan and Furman sat on their double-decker bunk and flipped a coin to see who would pull the first four-hour watch over the bucket. For the next ten days one of them would always stay with it.

The first siren sounded at zero minus five minutes. It was a short alerting wail. At Base Camp people started moving toward the trenches. Marshall Holloway approached his with a sinking feeling in his chest that perhaps some flaw would mar the shot and it would be traced to the nuclear assembly. Fermi, in a jocular mood now that the storm had died and the fallout scare diminished, stood atop the mound surrounding the abandoned reservoir and made some final notations on his slide rule. He began tearing up sheets of paper with a flourish and stuffing them into his pockets. Herb Anderson watched him wonderingly. Fermi, his leprechaun grin flashing, said, "Just watch, I'll know the yield before anyone."

Observers on Compania Hill saw a green Very rocket arch in the sky to the south, slowly descend, flash briefly, then dim and vanish in the blackness. That was their signal that the shot would go in five minutes. Reporter Laurence

224

shivered in the cold and moved forward on the knoll now dotted with murmuring shadows. He was an atheist by nature, believing firmly in the inevitability of events. But even Laurence, like others on that hill, sensed he was about to share in a profound religious experience, an event bordering on the supernatural.

Far to the south, in a trench near Mockingbird Gap, a quartet of Military Policemen smoked and waited for the dawn to end their troubles. Someone figured this was the 210th night they had pulled guard duty at Trinity. Relief was not far away, though. They would be packing up soon after the test was over. As the night wore on, the MP's wondered if perhaps the camp had suddenly been deserted and the whole site vacated by some last-minute fright. From their lonely outpost the desert seemed so motionless, so quiet. One of their number emerged from behind a boulder and shambled back to the trench. "Too damn scared to piss," he muttered.

Oppenheimer was a wax statue in the yellowish light of the control room. He stood immobile in the doorway, clutching his battered sombrero. Only the weedy neck moved as he peered first at the activity in the shelter, then at the weather outside. The sky had cleared to the east; a screen of mist still blanketed the west. The gusty ground winds had slowed to gentle zephyrs. Inside South-10,000, Oppenheimer could see General Farrell looking over Hornig's shoulder at the dial-studded panels. He saw Kistiakowsky twitching with excitement next to Allison, and felt the studied gaze of Lieutenant Bush. The young officer had been ordered to keep a weather eye on Oppenheimer. There was concern that the high-strung director might have a breakdown at the last minute.

All the uncertainties of the reckoning at hand had flooded Oppenheimer's consciousness. His emotions oscillated between fear that the bomb would fail—that all the faith and funds lavished for this surpassingly important moment would be dissolved in a whimper—and fear that the weapon which he had suckled from birth would perform with all too terrifying exactitude. And what of the world if it works? he thought. In his misery Oppenheimer turned to an officer beside him and murmured, "Lord, these affairs are hard on the heart."

Zero minus two minutes.

Inside the shelter there was a quiet movement toward the door, where a translucent screen hung. A periscope atop the bunker would project the image of the shot on the screen, and scientists had begun clustering expectantly around it. Only the men at the firing consoles remained rooted. Oppenheimer walked over for a last check with McKibben and Hornig. Hornig's eyes never wavered from the panel, but, sensing the director's tension, he cracked, "What's likely to happen, Oppie, is that at minus five seconds I'll panic and say, 'Gentlemen, this can't go on,' and then pull the switch." Oppenheimer, unamused, shook his head and moved slowly toward the door.

At Base Camp the siren had sounded a long wail for everyone to take his place in the trenches.

Jack Aeby braced his camera on the back of a chair facing the shot tower. Then he donned a pair of welder's goggles, noticing too late that one of the lenses was cracked. Phil Morrison interrupted his countdown relay to pull up his socks and pull down his pants legs so that the least amount of skin would be exposed. Major Alexander Stephens, a special Engineer observer, returned with a tarpaulin to his trench only to find it occupied by a row of VIP's including Conant, Vannevar Bush and Groves. Stephens gallantly spread out the tarpaulin and squeezed in beside them without a word. They lay there peering over the mound toward the tower. In the orderly room, where he had been leashed to Lieutenant Bush's desk, "Toff MacButin" began howling with fright.

The two-minute warning rocket for the Compania Hill group sputtered out prematurely, and several scientists remarked that it was an ominous sign. Leo Jercinovic absently tapped the steel helmet on his head and felt the heavy metal ping in his ear. The GI's had been ordered to wear the combat hats for the test. Some of the scientists were taking extreme precautions too. Edward Teller wore heavy gloves and an extra pair of dark glasses under his welder's goggles. He and Hans Bethe had smeared their faces with sunburn oil for protection against ultraviolet rays. Twenty miles from the bomb, in the predawn gloom, it seemed a ridiculous safeguard.

Fifty miles north of Trinity, eighteen-year-old Georgia Green was riding in a car along Highway 85 near the town of Lemitar. Her brother-in-law, Joe Wills, was driving her to an eight-o'clock music class at the University of New Mexico in Albuquerque. She would stay there for a week before returning home to Socorro. "Is it daylight yet?" she asked. "No," answered Wills gently and turned to look at the girl staring straight ahead through the windshield. Georgia Green was blind.

In Carrizozo, Al Graves anxiously watched his wife puttering with the Geiger counter that rested on the window sill facing Trinity forty miles westward. Diz Graves was seven months pregnant, and Al worried that the strain of the last hours might injure her health. He put a steadying arm around her and drew her to him. Over the short-wave set they could hear Sam Allison conversing excitedly with the pilot of the B-29. The Graveses made a last check of their instruments. Then together they waited for the jagged crests of the Oscuras to emerge from the night, bringing with them,

227

hopefully, a dawn that would light the mountains as never before.

In San Antonio the GI's rapped on Joe Miera's door and told him to come out and stand in front of the café. The soldiers promised Joe he would see something the world had never seen before. Hugh McSmith, a store owner in Bingham down the road from the Deans, stumbled over his pet cat on his way back to bed. He'd gone to the window to catch a glimpse of the plane he had heard groaning in the clouds overhead. It was an odd hour, he thought, for a plane to be aloft.

The B-29 groped through the darkness along the western edge of Trinity. From the cockpit Alvarez and Parsons searched the overcast below for the "aiming" lights at the shot tower. Frustrated, they slipped on their Polaroid glasses as they had been instructed. It seemed a futile gesture as both men wondered if they would see anything in the next minutes to justify their trip. Subconsciously their thoughts turned to the future. In three weeks they would ride into history—Parsons to arm the ugly uranium bomb aboard the Superfortress "Enola Gay" en route to Hiroshima; Alvarez, aboard another plane, to record its impact on the city.

It was lunchtime in Potsdam. The Prime Minister had concluded his social visit and the President had spent the next hour at the "Little White House" attending to mail, signing legislative bills and squeezing in a sandwich. Stalin still had not arrived, so the conference scheduled for that afternoon had been postponed. Truman decided to take advantage of the delay by making a spur-of-the-moment visit to Berlin. He asked Leahy and Byrnes to join him. Before they set off, Truman was heard to remark about Trinity and its effect on his talks with the Russians: "If it explodes as I think it will, I'll certainly have a hammer on those boys."

IX: *July 16, 1945: Zero Minus One Hour*

Leo Jercinovic watched the one-minute warning flare burst briefly in the heavens. By reflex he checked his watch: 5:29 A.M. "This is it," he whispered to a buddy. For a fleeting moment he thought of his wife and kids and wondered whether the fireball might roll over Compania Hill and as far north as their house in Santa Fe. Then he flattened himself on the sharp pebbles of the slope and made his eyes into slits. Richard Feynman leaned into the cab of a truck and peered through the windshield. He wore no goggles, worrying only of the danger of getting burned by ultraviolet rays. Bill Laurence wetted the tip of a pencil and brought out his note pad. What he would jot then and in the days to come would bring him a second Pulitzer Prize.

Alone, on the saddle between two hillocks, Klaus Fuchs remained standing. If the bomb's yield was what he had predicted, there would be no need to grovel on the ground. And his predictions, he might have reminded himself, were as finely wrought as a jeweler's timepiece and as seldom wrong. Indeed, most of what he had accomplished in the last years, from science to spying, had seemed to him undeniably right. Methodically Fuchs slipped the welder's glass over his spectacles.

Base Camp from above resembled an outpost of the dead: bodies scattered about in shallow graves, no movement or whisper of activity, only a voice blaring out of the shadows, "Minus 55 seconds, minus 50 seconds . . . " The Voice of America program now punctuated Allison's countdown with rapturous background music. Ken Greisen, lying next to I.I. Rabi, listened dreamily to the waltz from Tchaikovsky's Serenade for Strings. The violins seemed to rise in crescendo with Allison's excited blurts. Rabi, annoyed by his colleague's calm, turned on him scornfully. "Tell me when you get excited, Greisen," he snapped.

*   *   *

229

At 45 seconds before zero McKibben flipped the switch for the automatic timer. The robot device began triggering circuits in rapid precision. The score of persons in the control shelter tensed in frozen cameos. Oppenheimer grasped a beam for support and thought: I must remain conscious. General Farrell thought of the Scripture, "Lord, I believe; help Thou mine unbelief." Hornig, hand poised on the "stop" switch, stared at the voltmeter in front of him, where four small lights would turn red when the firing unit at the tower was completely energized. At minus 30 seconds all four blinked on and the needle on the voltmeter swung sharply to the right. The firing unit was fully charged.

At 10 seconds a gong sounded over the public-address system. John Williams and Kistiakowsky dashed from the control shelter. Williams squatted behind a ridge of dirt, and Kisty clambered on top of the bunker. Bainbridge, lying on a foam sheet twenty-five yards away, turned his gaze from the shot tower to the top of Little Burro Peak behind him. In Carrizozo the Graveses' short-wave radio failed momentarily and Diz Graves stammered out the last seconds on her own. At Base Camp, Conant turned to Groves and remarked laconically that he had never imagined seconds could be so long. Greisen nudged Rabi and said with a straight face, "I'm excited now."

At 5 seconds the cameras began churning at North- and West-10,000 yards. Julian Mack perched in his machine-gun turret at the West station and counted off the seconds to himself. Suddenly he smelled smoke. The power generator in his turret had overheated and caught fire. The turret was ablaze. An assistant shouted that he was turning off the power. "No, no!" Mack screamed. "The cameras are still running, let it burn!"

* * *

In the control center Sam Allison was seized by a sudden fear that the explosion would create a lightning effect and pump electrocuting volts into the microphone he gripped. At minus one second he dropped the microphone and screamed as loud as he could: "Zero!" In that instant a final surge of high voltage engulfed the firing unit, and the signals from McKibben and Titterton charged across the desert to galvanize the detonators on the bomb.

Fermi and the others heard Allison's last scream. Then silence for what seemed an eternity. And in that millisecond only the toads spoke at Trinity.

X

Trinity

A PINPRICK of brilliant light punctured the darkness, spurted upward in a flaming jet, then spilled into a dazzling cloche of fire that bleached the desert to a ghastly white. It was precisely 5:29:45 A.M.

Georgia Green felt the flash and a sudden loss of breath. "What's that?" she gasped and clutched the arm of her brother-in-law. The car shook and swerved off onto the shoulder of the road. In the floodlit control center Joe McKibben was aware of an even brighter light paling the instrument panels. Across the test site everything suddenly became infinitely tiny. Men burrowed into the sand like ants. Oppenheimer in that blinding instant thought of fragments from the sacred Hindu epic, Bhagavad-Gita:

> *If the radiance of a thousand suns*
> *Were to burst at once into the sky,*
> *That would be like the splendor*
> *of the Mighty One . . .*
> *I am become Death,*
> *The shatterer of worlds.*

For a fraction of a second the light in that bell-shaped fire mass was greater than any ever produced before on earth. Its intensity was such that it could have been seen from another planet. The temperature at its center was four times that at the center of the sun and more than 10,000 times that at the

235

sun's surface. The pressure, caving in the ground beneath, was over 100 billion atmospheres, the most ever to occur at the earth's surface. The radioactivity emitted was equal to one million times that of the world's total radium supply.

No living thing touched by that raging furnace survived. Within a millisecond the fireball had struck the ground, flattening out at its base and acquiring a skirt of molten black dust that boiled and billowed in all directions. Within twenty-five milliseconds the fireball had expanded to a point where the Washington Monument would have been enveloped. At eight tenths of a second the ball's white-hot dome had topped the Empire State Building. The shock wave caromed across the roiling desert.

Human response may have been the same as on that first dawn in the basement of time when Man discovered fire: fright at first, giving way to impetuous curiosity, then an awed realization of the phenomenon and, finally, primitive glee.

Men turned to look at the fireball, inflated now a half-mile wide, and wondered if it would ever stop growing. In their excitement many threw off their dark glasses and instantly lost sight of what they had waited years to see. At Base Camp there were silent handclasps and murmurs of amazement; at South-10,000, a squabble of excited voices that rose to a deafening din; and on Compania Hill, a piercing whoop followed by a mad jig that suggested to one observer the fire rites of prehistoric savages.

Robert Wilson, at North-10,000, watched the red dots on his viewing scope dance off the screen at the zero moment. The test is a failure, he thought, and ran outside into the noonday glare of the explosion. Ernest Titterton watched the same thing happen on his scope at South-10,000 and wondered aloud what had happened. "Off scale!" someone yelled. Then the light smote the shelter. General Farrell turned despairingly to a fellow officer. "The long-hairs have let it get away from them!" he exclaimed.

Kistiakowsky swayed on top of the control bunker, dazed by the light. The shock wave hit him seconds later and bowled him into the mud. Scrambling to his feet just as Oppenheimer dashed up, he threw a grimy arm around the director. "Oppie, Oppie," he cried deliriously, "I won the bet, you owe me $10!" Oppenheimer, trembling, reached for his wallet. "It's empty, you'll have to wait," he said with utter seriousness. The two men embraced.

The intercom at South-10,000 came alive with a babble of voices as scientists at Base Camp and other shelters filled the air waves with congratulatory cries. Someone started a snake dance and the happy line curled around the control room. Asleep in an empty barrack a Tennessee soldier who had gone on a beer binge the night before felt nothing until the blast jolted him from his stupor. He opened his eyes to the north and screamed in pain. In a trench by the reservoir Bill Caldes winced at the fireball and ground the palms of his hands into his eyes. My God, he thought, is it never going to stop?

Enrico Fermi didn't notice the crack of the shock wave. The blast sounded across the desert like a thunderclap of doom, mounting in resonance as it raced to the very rim of the Jornada's bowl and reverberated off the lighted peaks. Fermi was too engrossed in dribbling scraps of paper from his pockets. He watched them slowly fall then sweep suddenly across the reservoir as the shock wave struck them. Within seconds Fermi had paced the distance the scraps had blown and estimated the force of the explosion as the equivalent of 20,000 tons of TNT.

A few feet away Jack Aeby watched Fermi, thinking, "That man has flung clear off his rocker." A needle of light marred Aeby's vision where the flash had pierced the crack in his welder's goggles. In their crowded trench Conant,

237

Bush and Groves solemnly shook hands as they lay there awe-stricken by the explosion. Groves pictured himself at that moment as a successful Blondin who had just crossed his personal Niagara by tightrope. When Bush remarked that the shot seemed brighter than any star, the general lapsed into one of his rare flings at wit. "Brighter than two stars," he cracked, pointing to his shoulder insignia.

On Compania Hill, Richard Feynman stumbled from the truck he had been sitting in, a bright purple splotch dancing in front of his eyes. Edward Teller lifted his glasses and flinched as the unearthly light assaulted his retinas. The GI's and scientists saw the fireball splash upon the desert, then spiral upward in a vivid kaleidoscope of colors that seemed to unfold from its interior, merging within seconds from an eerie yellow-green into orange, peach, pink and finally a deep purple. The effect staggered even such blasé foreigners as Britain's Sir Geoffrey Taylor and the imperturbable James Chadwick.

As the statues on the hill broke into a momentary jig of ecstasy, Ernest Lawrence slapped Chadwick on the back. The Englishman grunted and leaped in the air. Everywhere on the slope silent silhouettes of a minute ago mimicked him, cheering and stomping the earth in a festival of joy. "It worked, my God, the damn thing worked!"

The sight beggared description.

For a split second after the moment of detonation the fireball, looking like a monstrous convoluting brain, bristled with spikes where the shot tower and balloon cables had been vaporized. Then the dust skirt whipped up by the explosion mantled it in a motley brown. Thousands of tons of boiling sand and dirt swept into its maw only to be regurgitated seconds later in a swirling geyser of debris as the fireball detached itself from the ground and shot upward. As it lifted from the desert, the sphere darkened in places,

238

then opened as fresh bursts of luminous gasses broke through its surface.

At 2000 feet, still hurtling through the atmosphere, the seething ball turned reddish yellow, then a dull blood-red. It churned and belched forth smoking flame in an elemental fury. Below, the countryside was bathed in golden and lavender hues that lit every mountain peak and crevasse, every arroyo and bush with a clarity no artist could capture. At 15,000 feet the fireball cleaved the overcast in a bubble of orange that shifted to a darkening pink. Now, with its flattened top, it resembled a giant mushroom trailed by a stalk of radioactive dust. Within another few seconds the fireball had reached 40,000 feet and pancaked out in a mile-wide ring of graying ash. The air had ionized around it and crowned it with a lustrous purple halo. As the cloud finally settled, its chimney-shaped column of dust drifted northward and a violet afterglow tinged the heavens above Trinity.

Leo Jercinovic blinked his eyes and for one terrified instant thought the entire atmosphere was afire. Then, numbed by the brilliance, he crawled to his knees and realized slowly that the world was still there and that people were yelling inarticulately all about him. He heard Charles Thomas of Monsanto shout to Ernest Lawrence that they had just seen the greatest single event in the history of mankind. And he heard a GI behind him say, "Buddy, you just saw the end of the war." He did not see Klaus Fuchs standing in the semidarkness twenty yards away, his face an inscrutable mask as he watched the fireball ascend.

The shock wave on Compania Hill was only a slight caress. But its roar, which reached the outpost nearly two minutes after the blast, caught some observers unawares. "What was that?" asked the startled *Times* reporter, convulsing the knot of scientists around him. In his excitement

Laurence had forgotten that the shock wave would create an ear-splitting thunder. The Graveses' motel in Carrizozo lay behind the protective wall of the Oscuras, but so powerful was the explosion that the building shuddered to its foundations and Diz Graves ducked behind the bedroom wall. Tom Jones bolted upright in his bed at Albuquerque's Hilton Hotel. It was as though someone had shot off a flashbulb in his face. A red glow filled the southern sky outside his window and he wondered if anyone was alive at Trinity. In Santa Fe, where a fainter light had suddenly suffused his bedroom, Major Friedel had the same thought. He picked up the open line to Stafford Warren at Base Camp and heard a voice on the other end say, "All is well."

When the shock-wave boom reached his trench, Groves's first reflex was to announce: "We must keep this whole thing quiet." Major Stephens leaned over and said, "Sir, I think they heard the noise in five states." Still Groves was determined to preserve the secret for as long as possible.

The enormousness of that task was already being realized by CIC agents hundreds of miles from Trinity. In Alamogordo, Albuquerque and Amarillo, Texas, agents watched and shook their heads at the awesome pyrotechnic display. For every agent, a hundred other citizens saw or felt the blast.

The Deans in Old Bingham thought the Japs had invaded. Hugh McSmith had the bed-sheet ripped off him and heard the water cisterns in his back yard shatter. He thought the B-29 had crashed behind his house. In San Antonio, Joe Miera heard the shock wave—"a noise like an airplane, freight train and thunder rolled into one"—and the sound of breaking windows in his home. The GI's in front of his bar were yelling, "Now we've got the world by the tail!" Passengers aboard a train near Mountainair, seventy miles northeast of Trinity, thought they saw a bomber explode in mid-air. On the Arizona-New Mexico state line, 150 miles away, Mrs. H. E. Wieselman saw "the sun come up and go down again." David Greenglass, approaching a bus stop in Albuquerque, looked over his shoulder as the whole southern horizon flared in brightness. That must be the test, he thought with a curious pang of pride.

The entire southern part of New Mexico, portions of Arizona and the El Paso panhandle of west Texas felt the explosion's tremors. Many citizens reported they had heard at least two or three successive blasts. Houses shook and windows blew out in Gallup, New Mexico, 235 miles northwest. Forest rangers near Silver City, in the state's southwest corner, placed frantic calls to the local Smithsonian Observatory, asking if an earthquake had struck. The Associated Press bureaus in Arizona and New Mexico were swamped with queries.

Engineer Ed Lane of the Santa Fe Railroad was highballing through Belen, en route to El Paso, when he saw what he imagined to be either a severe electrical storm in the Sandia Mountains or a fiery meteor. By the time he reached El Paso he had decided to tell his story to the local papers. The El Paso *Herald-Post's* city editor thought Lane had had an optical illusion. But calls from the paper's far-flung correspondents, plus corroborating reports from the Associated Press, finally convinced the editor that something unusual had happened. He ordered a replate for the front page of the afternoon editions.

Luis Alvarez calmly sketched the mushroom cloud on a piece of yellow tablet paper as the B-29 circled the southern extremity of Trinity and began cruising up the eastern rim of the site. It had been five minutes since he and Deac Parsons had watched the overcast split open and seen the fireball hurtling up. Now the ball had transformed into an ugly grayish cloud. A vast pall of smoke covered the earth beneath. In another five minutes the variable winds had torn the cloud into three distinct sections, which drifted off in different directions. The largest and topmost section, a dense white mushroom trailed by a dusty-brown streamer, began riding the winds of the troposphere toward the northeast. Within another half-hour the pall had begun dissipating. Alvarez thought: What can you do for an encore after this? The very next day he would leave for Tinian—and Hiroshima.

The euphoria at Trinity was intense and short-lived. Paper cups and bourbon were passed around at Base Camp. One tipsy young physicist offered General Groves a jug of whisky. Another approached him in tears, complaining that the unexpectedly powerful blast had wrecked all his measuring instruments. "Well, if the instruments couldn't stand it," said the general, grinning, "it must have been a pretty big bang. And that's what we wanted to know most." To a colleague Groves announced matter-of-factly: "The war is over as soon as we drop two of these on Japan."

At North-10,000, Julian Mack sat in his camera turret and watched the cloud disappearing. The fire in his turret had been only momentary and had left him unsinged. But the shock of what he had witnessed had seared his memory for years to come. Like others, Mack was already contemplating the future. He heard an assistant by his side exclaim, "My God, it's beautiful." "No," Mac said, "it's terrible."

Just before he left the control center for Base Camp, Oppenheimer shook hands with Ken Bainbridge. Bainbridge looked him in the eyes and said softly, "Now we're all sons-of-bitches."

At 5:55 A.M. Groves called Mrs. O'Leary in Washington. He told her he would be returning to the capital that afternoon and asked her to give George Harrison, Stimson's deputy, the first word that the test had been an astounding success. The conversation between Groves and his secretary was in code, but two of Groves's aides standing by Mrs. O'Leary's desk could tell from her smile what had happened. Minutes after she hung up the phone Mrs. O'Leary had decoded the full message and carried it to Harrison's office in the Pentagon. There she helped the deputy draft the first preliminary cable to Stimson in Potsdam.

Oppenheimer tried to relax at Base Camp over a brandy with General Farrell and Oppie's brother, Frank. But as soon as Groves had finished with the phone, the director excused himself and put in a personal call to Los Alamos. He asked his secretary to locate his wife, Kitty, immediately. "Tell her she can change the sheets," said Oppie.

The mood at Base Camp had turned reflective. The exhaustion of the past week had overtaken many, and as the first euphoria faded, the impact of the shot began to settle on consciences. A strange oppressiveness hung in the air like the humidity. Men noticed small things: horses in their stables, still whinnying in fright; the windmill above the reservoir slowly spinning in the wake of the shock wave; a little dog huddled near the orderly room, shivering in the morning heat; and the sudden silence from the rain holes, where the toads had stopped singing.

In the mess hall, normally garrulous KP's and mechanics sat speechless over untouched eggs and sausage. Others listened to the moans of pain coming from a nearby barrack. The medics had given the Tennessee soldier morphine and tried to convince him that he'd lost his eyesight only temporarily. But the shock of the flash had induced hysteria, and the fellow lay on his cot raving about the "wrath of the Lord" and the sin of getting drunk on the Sabbath. It would take several weeks of psychiatric treatment before he would return to duty, sight restored, with a pledge never to drink again.

I. I. Rabi, who had just won the betting pool's $102 pot for his estimate of the bomb's yield, moped about the camp, oblivious to congratulations, groping in his thoughts for the ultimate meaning of the event he had witnessed. Sam Allison felt a chill run down his spine as he listened to one of the Washington VIP's explain why it would be better to cremate Japanese civilians with the new weapon than lose a million American boys in an invasion. General Farrell, a religious man, was stunned by what seemed to him the blasphemy of ordinary mortals toying with forces hitherto reserved to the Almighty. Kistiakowsky felt the joy of that dawn dissolve in forebodings of doomsday. To another observer he remarked lugubriously, "I am sure that at the end of the world, in the last millisecond of the earth's existence, Man will see what we have just seen."

Oppenheimer, still shaken, allowed Rabi to drive him into the hills for an hour or so to let him unwind. As their jeep passed through the camp's main gate, Dr. Conant and Vannevar Bush stood at attention, their hats off in salute. Behind them the fallout cloud drifted in the distance, its dusty streamer assuming the shape of a huge black question mark.

Philip Moon, a normally reserved Britisher, first spotted the trouble at North-10,000 shortly after six A.M. The needle on his Geiger counter began fluctuating wildly. He looked outside and saw that a section of the fallout cloud had sheered off and was heading toward the shelter. He shouted to Captain Henry Barnett, the station's medical officer, who rushed over and confirmed Moon's fears: the Geiger's count had already passed the 35-roentgen mark, way above the safety limit.

Barnett, Moon and chief scientific officer Robert Wilson took one look at the nasty reddish-brown cloud bearing down on them. They could see at least a mile into it. "Let's get out of here," Wilson ordered. The scientists scooped up whatever records were on hand and frantically packed their equipment. Jeep drivers gunned their engines and men cursed their slower colleagues. Several GI's who had been ordered to track the cloud with their searchlight refused to leave. Wilson unleashed such a torrent of invective that the astonished sergeant grabbed his men and raced without another word to the waiting motorcade. A minute later the caravan had evacuated North-10,000 and was barreling back toward Base Camp. Several of the cars were riding their hubs when they finally reached camp.

In Albuquerque, Captain Tom Jones took a phone call from General Groves at 6:30 A.M. "It worked," Groves reported. Jones beamed and said, "How about an easy job now, sir, like hiding the Mississippi River?" Groves harrumphed and told the security officer to inform Kirtland Field that all air traffic was to remain barred from the Trinity area until further notice. The captain, unshaven and in civilian clothes, sped by car to the air base and routed the commandant from bed to give him the order. For a moment, before he saw his credentials, the commandant considered tossing Jones in the stockade.

Minutes after the skies above Trinity cleared, the scientists had their first chance to view the destruction they had wrought. The honors fell to the men in the tank-recovery group. George Weil, Herbert Anderson and Enrico Fermi donned white surgical costumes and boarded their tanks. Then, with Anderson in the lead and Weil and Fermi following, the two tanks raced across the flats toward the detonation area. The occupants conversed in code lest the Carrizozo taxi service on the same frequency overhear them. A mile outside camp Weil's tank stalled. Fermi climbed out disgustedly and hiked back to camp. But Anderson clanked

245

on. As he approached the zero point his Geiger counter went berserk.

Anderson was unprepared for the sight that greeted him. A half-mile away he saw what looked like a great jade blossom amid the coppery sands of the desert. Where the shot tower had once stood, a crater of green ceramic-like glass glistened in the sun. The fireball had sucked up the dirt, fused it virescent with its incredible heat, then dumped the congealing particles back on the explosion point. They lay there inside a 1200-foot-wide saucer some twenty-five feet deep at the center. The bomb, even from 100 feet up, had so pulverized the earth that the tower's concrete stumps, which once stood above ground, had been crushed to a depth of seven feet beneath the sand. The tower itself had completely evaporated. Within a mile of the crater there was no sign of life or vegetation.

Anderson stopped his tank at the crater's edge and fired the rocket with its clawlike retriever. The dirt samples he recovered sent his Geiger counter soaring off scale. Even had he not witnessed the explosion, Anderson would have known immediately from the radioactivity in the samples that the bomb had been a fantastically powerful one. He lingered for a moment, gazing through his periscope at the thousands of emerald beads that would one day be known as the "pearls of Trinity," or trinitite. Then, wary of the danger of overexposure, he ordered the driver to head back to Base Camp.

Had Anderson been able to leave his tank, he would have discovered countless other tokens of the bomb's ravage that morning. A half-mile beyond the crater, Jumbo's 215-ton bulk had been knocked askew by the blast. A seventy-foot-high steel tower that had encased Jumbo lay crumpled on the ground, its mangled girders severed from one another as cleanly as a small wire snipped by pliers. The tower had been the equivalent of a six-story steel building, and when Groves later saw its wreckage he decided that the newly erected Pentagon was no longer a safe shelter from the bomb.

The stench of death clung to the desert in the vicinity of the detonation. No rattlesnake or lizard—nothing that could crawl or fly—was left. Here and there carbonized shadows of tiny animals had been etched in the hard-packed caliche, where the rampaging blaze had emulsified them. A herd of antelope that had been spotted the day before had vanished, bound, some said later, on a frightened dash that ended in Mexico. The yuccas and Joshua trees had disappeared in the heat storm; no solitary blade of grass was visible. The only green on that burned, discolored desert was the trinitite.

Scientists checking on their instruments learned all too quickly how devastating the blast had been. Only a few instruments had survived to record with any effect the mightiest man-made explosion in history. The electromagnetic storm paralyzed and bent scores of expensive gauges and measurement recorders. Radioactive gases blew into equipment and ruined it with condensation. The bomb's overwhelming light raised havoc with cameras; those not protected by thick shields of lead were totally demolished; even those surrounded by sand or concrete barriers had their films blackened and destroyed by the tremendous gamma-ray emission. Few films were salvaged that had not been uniformly fogged by the intense radiation.

The building specimens laid down by Frank Oppenheimer were never recovered. The boxes of excelsior, the lumber and corrugated iron strips had been blown into eternity on the cruel wind. There was little doubt now of the bomb's capacity to smash all but the strongest building structures into nothingness.

Detailed interpretations of Trinity would take weeks to conclude. But by mid-morning of July 16 it was obvious that the gadget had surpassed all expectations and produced an explosive yield greater than the scientists' most optimistic predictions. It confirmed that implosion was probably the most efficient way to detonate an atomic weapon. It also illustrated for the Hiroshima planners one vital aspect of their mission. The Trinity bomb had emitted a terrific amount of radiation, which had encircled the explosion in a radioactive dust skirt as it rolled across the desert. The radioactivity had created a reverse smothering effect and had actually weakened the blast power of the bomb at great distances. Had the gadget been detonated at a level much higher than 100 feet, the radioactivity would have been far less and the blast power much greater. As the Army desired to kill Japanese by blast rather than radiation, Trinity confirmed their judgment that the Hiroshima bomb should be detonated from an extremely high altitude.

Up to four days before Trinity, the combined air power of the United States and Britain had assaulted Germany with two million tons of bombs containing about one million tons of high explosive. It was now apparent that fifty planes, each carrying an atomic bomb, could deliver in one night all the destruction that the Allies had meted out to Germany in forty-three months of air raids.

Three hours after the Trinity explosion Harry Truman saw at first hand the devastation of Berlin.

It was 4:30 P.M. German time, and a hot sun beat down on the open car in which the President rode with Byrnes and Leahy. They had passed triumphantly under the Brandenburg Gate after taking the salute from the U.S. Second Armored ("Hell on Wheels") Division drawn up in formation along their route. Now their caravan moved slowly past the burned-out hulks of buildings along Bismarckstrasse and Berlinstrasse and through the charred debris of the Tiergarten to Unter den Linden. There, before the smoked walls of the Reichschancellery, where Hitler had met his death, the car stopped and Truman got out. The President walked over to a group of reporters, shaking his head. "I never saw such destruction," he told the newsmen. "It's a terrible thing, though they brought it on themselves. I don't know whether they learned anything from it or not. But it demonstrates what can happen when man overreaches himself."

In Albuquerque a quartet of Trinity observers arrived at the Hilton Hotel shortly after ten A.M. and rushed to a room to put in a long-distance call to the British Embassy in Washington. Reporter Bill Laurence was among the group, which included Ernest Lawrence, James Chadwick and British explosives expert William Penney. While the Americans showered, the two Englishmen argued over the correct way to address the British Ambassador. When the call was finally connected, Chadwick reported to Lord Halifax the success of the test and asked that the information be relayed to Winston Churchill in Potsdam. Halifax, however, had decided to observe protocol and not send a report to his government until it had been advised first by U.S. authorities.

News of the explosion, meanwhile, was threatening to break wide open. Every newspaper, wire service and sheriff's office within a 300-mile radius of Trinity was besieged with anxious queries and eyewitness reports. Counter Intelligence Corps agents in Alamogordo called superiors in Washington for advice: unconfirmed reports from bystanders in that town had been picked up by the International News Service. In the city room of the Albuquerque *Journal*, news editor Millard Hunsley's suspicions were aroused when a pair of Army officers strolled in and asked casually if he had seen a flash to the south that morning. Hunsley, whose phone was ringing like a fire alarm, was sure both men were security "creeps" checking up on him.

249

CIC chief Tom Jones received a call from one of his agents in El Paso that the *Herald-Post* was going to front-page its afternoon editions with the mysterious story of engineer Ed Lane. While Jones phoned General Groves about this development, the agent in El Paso tried desperately to get *Herald-Post* city editor "Mike" Michael to kill the story. Michael, a crusty green-eyeshade type, refused. Just before eleven A.M. the AP bureau in Albuquerque alerted Jones that it could no longer sit on the story and that unless the Army put out something on its own, the bureau would have to move the story on its wire.

The commanding officer of the Alamogordo air base had been provided weeks before with a news release in which each word had been numbered for security. Groves now ordered the release to be distributed at once. A copy of it was rushed to the AP office in Albuquerque. The wire-service story that appeared in a modest half-column on the front page of the Albuquerque *Tribune* that afternoon carried the lead:

> An ammunition magazine, containing high-explosives and pyrotechnics, exploded early today in a remote area of the Alamogordo air base reservation, producing a brilliant flash and blast which were reported to have been observed as far away as Gallup, 235 miles northwest.

The AP carried the Alamogordo commandant's cryptic statement that "weather conditions affecting the content of gas shells exploded by the blast may make it desirable for the Army to evacuate temporarily a few civilians from their homes." At the last moment Groves, fearful of excessive fallout, had inserted that reference in the release.

By one P.M. local security agents had informed Washington that the story had reached four states and was beginning to get out of control. Radio stations even on the Pacific

Coast were carrying reports. The El Paso *Herald-Post* had splashed the story on page one and included colorful eye-witness yarns. The Army security people stuck to their guns, however. Assisted by the Office of Censorship in Washington, they managed to keep the news out of any Eastern paper and thus out of circulation in the communication centers of Washington and New York. The only explosion *The New York Times* reported the next day was that of an ammunition magazine in Strasbourg, France. The "cover" story out of Alamogordo was accepted, and few editors bothered to question the crass stupidity of the Army for storing high explosives next to flares and gas shells in one magazine.

The pall had cleared above Trinity, but now began the tense hours of waiting for fallout reports. It was an uncomfortable period for Groves and Stafford Warren. The medical dangers were most immediate first of all. But in addition both men knew that the Army was not eager to pursue too diligently the possibilities of widespread fallout. The specter of endless lawsuits haunted the military, and most of the authorities simply wanted to put the whole test and its aftereffects out of sight and mind as quickly as possible. Within the bounds and time allowed them, however, Groves and Warren sought to do a conscientious monitoring job.

The cloud drifted northeastward at about ten miles per hour, dropping its trail of fission products across a region measuring 100 miles long and 30 miles wide. In the deep ravines, where cattle grazed, the radioactivity settled in a white mist; but in the populous uplands there was far less activity. The monitors feared, however, a phenomenon known as inversion. The canyons north of Trinity are like the teeth of a comb, and the sun and the cool air in them squeeze together to produce thermal updrafts that cause sudden wind shifts. These wind shifts, or inversions, might lift the fallout as it began to settle and carry it far beyond the expected limits, dumping it in some remote area unknown to the monitors.

By noon Warren's teams had identified heavy fallout in an oval extending ten miles north of the Trinity crater. Their counters in some places showed readings of 35 roentgens an hour. At three P.M. the Graveses began getting disturbing readings on their Geiger counter at Carrizozo. At 4:20 P.M. the counter shot off scale and Al Graves phoned Warren at Base Camp. The fate of little Carrizozo hung in the balance while the scientists and military decided whether to evacuate it. They held off, and within an hour the radioactive cloud had passed over and the fallout readings had dropped.

As the radioactive cloud drifted beyond Carrizozo, however, with the monitors in full chase, the scientists suddenly realized they had overreached the limits of radio contact with Base Camp. Fallout was dropping on northern communities like Coyote, Ancho and Tecolote, and the monitors were unable to relay the news to Warren. Sections of the cloud had reached Vaughn, 112 miles to the north, and some radioactivity was dropping on towns as far as 120 miles from the test site. Even as officials at Base Camp were advising Washington that the fallout danger was diminishing, the monitors were racing back toward Trinity with reports that fallout had hit a number of areas beyond their jurisdiction. Vaughn was thought to be especially "hot." The situation was still much in doubt.

By dusk most of the monitors had returned to Base Camp with their reports. Monitor Joe Hirschfelder drove his sedan into Base Camp with his Geiger counter showing the car's interior alive with radioactivity. His tires were radioactively hot, and he himself was carrying a surface dose of fallout. Even after a shower and medical check Hirschfelder was so suspect that he was unable to hitch a ride back to Albuquerque with several colleagues. The situation, however, had improved, and the tension over excess radioactivity had diminished. The fallout level within a forty-mile radius of Base Camp had dropped considerably. Farther north the cloud appeared to have dissipated finally over the vicinity of Vaughn. There had been no alarms of excessive fallout after Carrizozo, and most officials at Trinity were convinced that the bulk of the fallout had been confined to the detonation area and about ten miles north of it. General Farrell notified the Pentagon a few minutes before five o'clock that, while they had come awfully close to evacuating in several spots, the danger had passed.

Unknown to the scientists, an inversion *had* occurred and part of the fallout cloud had skipped out of its predicted path to spew a load of radioactive ash on cattle ranches along the Chupadera Mesa west of Carrizozo. That incident would precipitate a round of legal headaches for the government in weeks to come. The main cloud had finally wrapped itself around Gallinas Peak, sixty-five miles to the north, there to break up and disappear for good.

On their way back to Trinity some monitors met the exodus of scientists returning to Los Alamos. The test had worked and already the scientists were anticipating the fabrication of a second plutonium weapon that would follow the Hiroshima bomb across the Pacific to Tinian.

Outside Belen a monitor spotted Enrico Fermi and Sam Allison. Their jalopy had finally collapsed and Allison was trudging into town to find some spare tires. Fermi, ingenious to the last, borrowed a tank of methane gas from the monitor and inflated his tires with it. The Italian Navigator was still so wrought up from the test that he had asked Allison to chauffeur him all the way back to Los Alamos. Fermi didn't trust himself at the wheel that day.

Aboard the homeward-bound buses scientists sprawled exhausted in their seats. Though weary, they were bursting to tell the world of their secret; but strict security was still enforced along the route. In towns where they stopped to catch a bite of supper, the scientists talked of inconsequential things and the occupants of one car studiously ignored those of another. Not until they reached the gates of Los Alamos could they shout to the heavens of their triumph. Even then the message was far more graphic in the grim, silent faces of many of them. Those who watched as the scientists stepped from the buses and cars that evening, knew instinctively from their expressions that the shape of war had changed forever.

At Base Camp a small crew remained to clean up. The captains and the kings had departed. Groves and his entourage had flown back to Washington to prepare their report for the wise men at Potsdam. Ken Bainbridge and John Williams had commandeered a car and driven off to the south to unwind with a week of fishing and solitude along the creeks of the Rio Grande. The MP's held a little party for Lieutenant Bush and toasted him with beer and orange pop.

Oppenheimer had telegraphed his Chicago colleague Arthur Compton: "You'll be interested to know we caught a very big fish." Then the director had taken one last walk along the cooling desert. The first flush of satisfaction had left him and the full import of Trinity had begun to register. He had reason, he felt, to enjoy some sense of tranquillity because the bomb might help to end all future wars. In his heart, though, Oppenheimer knew that the world would never be the same again; that, whatever surcease from war the bomb might soon bring, it had opened an age in which peace would become an even more tenuous quantity and peace of mind a will-o'-the-wisp forever.

He stopped a few feet from a turtle lying on its back. The creature had been flipped over by the shock wave and was

waving its feet helplessly in the air. Oppenheimer kr
down and righted the turtle. He watched it paddle aw₋ᵧ,
thinking, "That's the least I can do."

The cablegram reached Stimson at 7:30 P.M., Berlin
time. It was from the War Department in Washington and it
read:

> TOP SECRET
> URGENT
> WAR 32887.
> *For Colonel Kyle's Eyes Only. From Harrison for
> Mr. Stimson. Operated on this morning. Diagnosis not
> yet complete but results seem satisfactory and already
> exceed expectations. Local press release necessary as
> interest extends great distance. Dr. Groves pleased
> He returns tomorrow. I will keep you posted. End.*

Although the message was general and inconclusive, it
was enough to indicate to Stimson and Truman that the
United States now had in its possession a weapon of unparal-
leled power. To Byrnes, who was somewhat less impressed,
the message made it clear that further diplomatic efforts to
bring the Russians into the Japanese war were pointless. All
three men felt a great surge of relief at the news, however.
The bomb as a probability had been a weak reed on which to
rely in bargaining with the Russians. As a reality it seemed a
galvanic force in the hands of the American negotiators.

Elated, Stimson wired back to Washington this message:

> TOP SECRET
> *From: Terminal*
> *To: War Department*
> *To Secretary General Staff for Mr. George L. Har-
> rison's Eyes Only. From Stimson. I send my warmest
> congratulations to the Doctor and his consultant.*

At Los Alamos the party in Oppenheimer's home lasted far into the night. Relief and joy at being home again had rejuvenated the scientists. The house rocked with their cheers, and the liquor flowed. One physicist pretended he was General Groves guarding the shot tower; another leaned over the stair railing and announced he was going to dive off and detonate a foot above the floor. In the middle of the festivities Oppie walked up to Teller and pulled him aside. "Edward," he said gravely, "we have done an excellent job. It will be very many years before anyone will be able to match this weapon."

Klaus Fuchs may have celebrated the successful explosion in the solitude of his bachelor dormitory. Perhaps, sitting on the edge of his bed, he fought off fatigue and a splitting headache while he finished checking some notes on a crumpled pocket pad that had accompanied him to Trinity. He could probably hear the sounds of mirth echoing faintly through the village on the mesa as he placed the pad in a corner of his bureau drawer and turned out the light. He had one last appointment to keep with Harry Gold.

XI

Aftermath

ON JULY 17, 1945, few persons knew that a new era had dawned at Trinity.

Winston Churchill first learned of it shortly after noon that day. He had just held a luncheon for Stimson and was walking the Secretary to the gate of his Potsdam villa when Stimson turned and said, "Mr. Prime Minister, I think I should tell you that the test in New Mexico has exceeded our expectations." Churchill had not heard from his own people on the matter and the news braced him like a whiff of brandy. He fairly bubbled with excitement and calmed down only long enough to warn against any disclosure to the Russians.

In an ornate, paneled room in the 300-year-old Cecilienhof Palace, the Big Three convened the first session of the Potsdam Conference later that afternoon. Stalin, surrounded by scowling NKVD agents, finally arrived to take his seat at the circular table. He and Truman and Churchill settled down in red-upholstered chairs that sported carved cupids on their backs. Two immense wrought-iron chandeliers lighted the scene as the leaders posed for pictures and exchanged formal greetings. It was a stiff and unproductive opening session.

George Harrison's second cable reached Stimson early on the morning of July 18. Its coded message bore sensational news:

TOP SECRET

PRIORITY

WAR 33556.

To Secretary of War from Harrison. Doctor has just returned most enthusiastic and confident that the Little Boy is as husky as his big brother. The light in his eyes discernible from here to Highhold and I could have heard his screams from here to my farm.

Decoding clerks at Potsdam thought the seventy-seven-year-old Stimson had just become a father. The Secretary, however, correctly translated the message for a delighted Truman: The Hiroshima bomb already crossing the Pacific would probably be every bit as powerful as the Trinity device. Trinity's flash had been visible for 250 miles, or the distance between Washington and Stimson's "Highhold" estate on Long Island. Trinity's blast had been heard for fifty miles, the distance from Washington to Harrison's farm in Upperville, Virginia.

Truman called in Byrnes and his military advisers immediately. This second cable confirmed the prospects of a merciful abridgment of the war in the Pacific. The bomb, properly used, could give the Japanese forces an excuse to surrender with honor and release them from any obligation of resisting to the last man. U.S. military leaders, however, did not yet know what effect the new weapon might have, physically or psychologically, on an enemy. For that reason they urged that existing plans for the invasion of Japan proceed. Truman, approaching his final decision on the bomb's use, waited impatiently for more detailed information from Trinity.

It arrived by courier at 11:35 A.M. on July 21, a thirteen-page document containing General Groves's semiofficial account of the test and a dramatic description of the scene by his deputy, General Farrell. The report was buttressed by photographs of the bomb's damage. The officers had labored two sleepless days and nights on the document, realizing its historic importance as the first complete account of the test. Farrell at one point had sent aides scurrying around Washington to verify a Biblical quotation he wanted to use.

At three P.M., in the sunroom of the "Little White House," Stimson began reading the report aloud to Truman and Byrnes. The President and his Secretary of State sat spellbound as Stimson tripped over the words in his excitement. "For the first time in history there was a nuclear explosion," began the report, "and what an explosion!" The document detailed highlights of the tension before the test and vividly depicted the fireball and the damage that attested to the bomb's power. At the end of the reading Truman seemed a new man as he departed for the next session of the Conference.

There was now no question in the President's mind that the bomb should be used if the Japanese rejected the Allied ultimatum. Truman had weighed all the possibilities and implications, and the decision seemed inescapable. A man accustomed to making up his mind abruptly with minimum fuss and feathers, Truman had not found this decision easy to make. But that afternoon at Cecilienhof Palace, he behaved as though he were king of the lair. Churchill watched him face down the Russians, advise them in no uncertain terms just where the United States stood and generally boss the whole meeting.

He understood it better the next morning when Stimson called with a copy of the Trinity report. Churchill, who was relaxing in his zippered siren suit, read the report, then waved his cigar with a flourish. "Stimson," he rumbled, "what was gunpowder? Trivial. What was electricity? Meaningless. This atomic bomb is the Second Coming in Wrath."

261

Now the final steps before the wrath was unleashed on Japan swiftly followed one upon the other.

On July 23 at Los Alamos the scientists completed the plutonium core for the first implosion combat bomb. The weapon would be earmarked for one of several possible Japanese targets, among them a major shipbuilding and troop-embarkation point whose twelve square miles were jammed with flimsy eave-to-eave dwellings that gave the city its name, "Sea of Roofs"—Nagasaki.

Early the evening of July 24 in Potsdam, following adjournment of a particularly discordant session, Truman sauntered around the conference table and confronted Stalin. The President purposely left behind his special interpreter, Charles Bohlen. He wanted this moment alone with the Soviet leader. Churchill and Byrnes stood about five yards away, intently gauging the effect of what Truman was about to tell Stalin. The United States had just exploded a weapon of unusually destructive force, Truman informed the Premier through the Soviet interpreter. He waited for the news to sink in. Stalin looked up through hooded eyes and replied with no trace of emotion, "I am glad to hear it and I hope you make good use of it against the Japanese." That was all. Stalin asked no questions and Truman offered no elaboration. The President had taken the minimum step of advising the Russians on the bomb. He did not follow it up with any reference to the bomb's postwar role. Indeed, Truman was probably too nonplused by the Premier's response to do so. It seemed obvious to him that Stalin did not appreciate the significance of the revelation.

The *Indianapolis* reached Tinian on July 26, and Major Furman and Captain Nolan delivered their "Bowery" shipment of U-235 to the waiting airmen of the 509th Composite Group. Already being flown across the Pacific was a shipment of material code-named "Bronx"—the first plutonium charge for Trinity's combat twin, a bomb known as the "Fat

Man." Another Bronx shipment had been promised from Los Alamos within a few weeks.

On the evening of July 26 the United States, Britain and China issued the ultimatum to Japan that was to become known as the Potsdam Declaration. The document, calling on Japan to surrender or suffer annihilation, was signed by Truman, Churchill and Chiang Kai-shek. Russia, not yet at war with Japan, did not participate. There was no mention of the bomb in the ultimatum, although the force and sternness of its language bespoke the Allies' new confidence. The signers stated their terms boldly and added: "We will not deviate from them. There are no alternatives. We shall brook no delay."

Two days later the Japanese Premier rejected the ultimatum out of hand as "unworthy of Public notice." What followed will be forever argued as a moral issue by historians. But there can be no quibbling about the clarity of the warning in the Potsdam Declaration, a warning that would have been far less unequivocal had it not been for Trinity. As Herbert Feis wrote later, the light of Trinity's explosion "filtered into the conference rooms at Potsdam only as a distant gleam. It was the fire, however, concealed in the final call for Japanese surrender that was issued from Potsdam."

The last days of July presented a marked contrast between the scientists, soldiers and statesmen most intimately involved with the bomb and their counterparts who watched from the sidelines as final preparations were made for use of the weapon.

Trinity had been a tonic to Groves, Stimson and other military and political planners. Back in Washington, where he met with aides to revise the public announcements that would be issued after the atomic-bomb raids, Stimson found that the test had altered his disposition to the point where he could infuse fresh gusto into the statement being prepared for the President. In Los Alamos, Oppenheimer was so spurred by success that he was urging a redesign of the plutonium bomb to give it even more lethal punch.

Removed from such exhilaration, other atomic scientists and military leaders either maintained their skepticism about the bomb's effectiveness or pondered in fear the verdict to drop it. Admiral Leahy still professed little confidence in the weapon and told Britain's King George VI shortly after Trinity: "It sounds like a professor's dream to me." Generals Marshall and Eisenhower brooded on the President's decision. Marshall, who had earlier suggested that Soviet observers be invited to the Trinity test, was deeply disturbed at the idea of a surprise atomic attack on Japan. Eisenhower, after Stimson advised him of the decision in Berlin, told the Secretary flatly that he abhorred the thought of the United States being the first nation to use such a weapon, and against a nation that seemed ready to surrender. Stimson was furious at the general's response.

In Chicago the dissent led by Szilard and Franck continued. Compton finally conducted a poll of the Metallurgical Laboratory, which showed that 46 per cent of the scientists there favored a military demonstration of the bomb in Japan before invoking its full use as a weapon. Others advocated varying forms of warning demonstrations. Only 15 per cent of those polled supported the idea of using the bomb in whatever way possible to achieve prompt Japanese surrender.

Groves's Target Committee, meanwhile, had drawn up an execution list of four Japanese cities considered militarily strategic. The choice had not been easy because General Curtis LeMay's B-29's had already ripped the guts out of Japan's major cities, and only a completely untouched target would demonstrate the effect of the new weapon. Japan's five biggest industrial centers—Tokyo, Nagoya,

Osaka, Kobe and Yokohama—had long since been devastated. The victims nominated for the atomic bomb were Hiroshima, Kokura, Niigata and Kyoto. All were approved by Stimson except Kyoto, the ancient capital and cultural mecca of Japan. In Kyoto's place Nagasaki was picked. A key consultant in the Target Committee's deliberations was Robert Oppenheimer.

On August 6, Oppenheimer strode down the aisle of the Los Alamos auditorium to deliver an announcement to his colleagues. As he mounted the podium, he clasped his hands above his head like a prizefighter. Then he told them what had happened that morning over Hiroshima.

The first atomic bomb had blown three fifths of the city off the face of the earth.

Edward Teller remembers walking by a colleague who shouted to him exuberantly, "One down!" It was the cry of the boy whose slingshot had just felled the neighborhood bully, of the factory worker whose bolts may have fashioned the Superfort "Enola Gay," of every daring young man—from dragon tickler to explosives expert—who had contributed in some measure to the bomb's inexorable progression. None that day could picture the staggering statistics of Hiroshima:

Twenty per cent of her population wiped out; 60 per cent of the city destroyed; 37,000 persons injured; 13,000 missing; rail stations, bridges, factories and scores of other buildings reduced to flaming rubble. Three months before, Oppenheimer had estimated for the Interim Committee that no more than 20,000 Japanese would be killed in such an attack. It had not occurred to him or to anyone else that the sight of two lone B-29's would fail to frighten the citizens of Hiroshima into their air-raid shelters. In their innocence, 92,000 men, women and children died.

That morning, on the way back to Tinian, Luis Alvarez

wrote a letter to his young son. "Dear Walter," it said. "This is the first grown-up letter I have written to you, and it is really for you to read when you are older. . . . What regrets I have about being a party to killing and maiming thousands of Japanese civilians this morning are tempered with the hope that this terrible weapon we have created may bring the countries of the world together and prevent further wars."

Captain William Parsons, who had armed the bomb en route to Hiroshima, forwarded a report on the mission to Tinian: "Clear-cut, successful in all respects. Visible effects greater than Trinity." When Parson reached Tinian five hours later, he scrawled a four-line note on the official receipt for the bomb. The note read: "I certify that the above material was expended to the city of Hiroshima, Japan, at 0915, 6 Aug. 45. W. S. Parsons."

Seventy-five hours after Hiroshima the death blow fell on Japan.

At 12:01 P.M. on August 9 a duplicate of the Trinity bomb rolled out of the belly of a silver Superfort called "Bock's Car." It plummeted 29,000 feet down on Nagasaki and disemboweled the city within a fraction of a second. Nearly 100,000 Japanese were killed or maimed in the fire storm. The bomb carved a crater across one square mile of the city, destroying factories, shrines, tea houses and rickety homes in a blast wave of unprecedented might. Twelve hours later Nagasaki was still a mass of flame, palled by acrid smoke that shot up like a whirling waterspout. Its funeral pyre was visible to pilots 200 miles away.

Nagasaki in all its horror told the Japanese that Hiroshima had been no fluke or lone experiment. It said in effect: Here is a second example of what the bomb can do, and there are more. Indeed there were, though not in any quantity. The Nagasaki bomb had already rendered Hiroshima's

uranium bomb obsolete, and on August 12 a second plutonium Fat Man was ready for shipment to Tinian. At the last
minute, however, Groves got approval to delay the shipment. The general, like others, could already sense Japan's
death rattle across the Pacific. There was no need, he reasoned, to jeopardize further the nation's image for posterity.
Two days later the Japanese had surrendered and the war
was over.

On August 14 bells clanged, sirens whined and automobile horns blared in Los Alamos. Kistiakowsky set off a
small arsenal of leftover explosives in the canyons around S
Site. That day the exultation of victory swept the mesa, and
on the surface it seemed authentic. The plaudits of a grateful
nation rang in the scientists' ears. Recalling the race against
Germany, President Truman lauded the physicists for having won the Battle of the Laboratories.

"What has been done," he declared, "is the greatest
achievement of organized science in history. It was done
under high pressure and without failure. We have spent two
billion dollars on the greatest scientific gamble in
history—and won."

For the scientists there were medals and letters of merit.
Local citizens and the townspeople of Santa Fe and Albuquerque viewed them in a new light. For three years they
had been suspected boondogglers. Now they were heroes,
demigods. Reporters queued up to interview the scientists,
and some of the bomb makers became celebrities overnight.
Oppenheimer confessed to one newsman that he was a "little
scared of what I have made." But, he added, "A scientist
cannot hold back progress because of fears of what the
world will do with his discoveries."

After Hiroshima and Nagasaki, however, those fears
would settle like specters on the mesa. Deepening moral
doubts would begin to pull the physicists one by one from

267

their bomb work back to the serenity of the classroom. That summer on The Hill would leave graphic psychological scars: children in the laboratory's kindergarden bragging "My daddy made the atom bomb," or dashing into their carefully built sand castles with cries of "4–3–2–1–zero!" Finally, there would be the reproaches from their fellow men. A sense of opprobrium would be visited on each and every scientist who had labored on the bomb, and feelings of guilt, however undeserved, would become embedded in some of them.

In Italy the Vatican expressed its displeasure at the unleashing of the new force, and the Italian scientists at Los Alamos suffered special pangs of remorse. Fermi received a bewildered letter from his sister in Rome, ending, "For my part, I recommend you to God, who alone can judge you morally." A saddened Peggy Church, whose husband had three years before turned over their home and ranch school to the scientists, wrote of Robert Oppenheimer: "I could hardly bear to think that such destruction had been rooted in the heart of our once sacred world on the mesa; that the man who had put the bomb together just before it was dropped over Hiroshima had lived for a while in my own house."

Such was the new world that would gradually descend on the scientists in the wake of Hiroshima and Nagasaki. For one glorious moment they had seen the efforts of their years on the mesa crowned in the flashing triumph of Trinity. Then their invention had passed into other hands for a baptism that men would argue over for decades, perhaps forever. V-J Day at Los Alamos was a celebration of profound relief for those scientists who sought liberation from life with the bomb. But it was a bittersweet cup. For there would be no liberation from Hiroshima or Nagasaki, ever. And more than one scientist walked cold sober into the dark of that August night and retched.

* * *

For a month after the explosion a stench pervaded the atmosphere at Trinity. It was an indefinable odor, a mixture of vanished smoke, chemicals and animal life. Trinitite still sparkled in the hollow of the crater. A few yards away Jumbo leaned into the winds of the desert like a forgotten sentinel. The McDonald ranch house stood deserted, its floor littered with shards of glass, a broken door swaying gently on bent hinges.

In the orderly room at Base Camp, Lieutenant Howard Bush emptied his desk and watched the last truckload of furniture and equipment depart through the gates. He made a final check of the survey report that he would deliver to his superiors. He was not sure how they would react: the lieutenant had written off approximately $5,000,000 worth of equipment. But it was a bit difficult to explain to one who had not seen Trinity the complete disappearance of a 100-foot steel tower, a $20,000 hoist, a couple of abandoned jeeps and several tons of expensive instruments. Nor was Bush sure how to report the demise of a 215-ton steel container, two Army tanks and a small village of barracks and other buildings. They were of no further use to anyone. Bush shook his head apprehensively as he signed the report. His supply officer, wise in the ways of government spending, tried to cheer him. "Don't sweat," he said. "If it was five thousand, you'd be in trouble, but five million—pffft."

Among the last to leave Trinity were the fallout monitors. For weeks after the test they had poked about the desert searching for clues to the amount of radioactivity that had infected the area: discolored birds and rats, sore paws on dogs and cats. The job had been made no easier by the reluctance of the ranchers to co-operate with the scientists. More than one inquiring monitor was greeted with a hail of buckshot for his efforts. By mid-August the first indication that the scientists had deceived themselves on the extent of the fallout came from a cattle rancher on the Chupadera

Mesa. He reported that a number of his Herefords had lost hair along their backs and sides and had suffered severe blistering on their skins. Other ranchers began reporting similar symptoms in their herds. When new hair grew back on the wine-red steers it was of a roan color, giving the cattle an off-breed appearance. Lawsuits were filed with the commanding officer of the Alamogordo air base.

Inspection teams came down from Los Alamos and discovered radiation burns on the cattle. About seventy-five contaminated steers were bought up at premium prices by the government and shipped to Los Alamos and Oak Ridge for detailed analysis. The news spread around southern New Mexico, and a few really smart ranchers learned how to make bigger money. In Alamogordo, crowds flocked to see Arnie Gilworth's celebrated "atomic calf," a frost-colored beast that had been born shortly after the Trinity blast. "The mother was scared by the bomb," said Gilworth solemnly. Other citizens got the P. T. Barnum complex. A housewife exhibited her shriveled physique in public and claimed she'd lost twenty-two pounds right after the test. One rancher made the local tabloids with pictures showing how the whiskers and hair on his head had turned a premature gray from the explosion. And Hugh McSmith renamed his black tabby cat "Atomic" after it developed a rash of white spots. A West Coast entrepreneur offered McSmith $50 to let him put the cat in a freak show.

Amid all the medals and awards that flooded the Trinity participants in the weeks following the test, none was more surprising than the Good Conduct Medal which the Army bestowed on Lieutenant Bush's Military Police detachment. The Army had noted with pride that the detachment had suffered no venereal disease cases in the six-month period beginning in January 1945. The inspector general thought it amazing and gently suggested to Bush that perhaps he wasn't giving his troops enough freedom. On the contrary,

the lieutenant explained, he had given his men passes ev
Saturday night to the nearest town—Pope, New Mexico.
Bush thought it unnecessary to add that Pope was a railroad
siding populated solely by jack rabbits and mesquite.

On August 21 the atomic bomb's first peacetime fatality
occurred in Los Alamos. At Omega Site the dragon had
lashed back at young Harry Daghlian and sprayed him with
a mortal dose of radioactivity. The doctors took pictures of
him for clinical use. His hands were swollen unbelievably,
and the skin fell from his body in patches. Louis Slotin,
whom Daghlian had watched tickle the dragon's tail in the
McDonald ranch house, was at Daghlian's bedside constantly during the month it took him to die. Afterward a colleague told Slotin, "You won't last a year if you keep on
doing that experiment."

Guilt, boredom and the lure of teaching began emptying
the ranks of scientists at Los Alamos. Many who left felt a
special responsibility to speak out in their communities,
warning their countrymen of the perils ahead and the need
to chain the hideous new weapon to some responsible international authority. Others, tired of the constraining atmosphere of secrecy, departed out of longing for the openness
and freedom of academic life. Much of the exodus was due
to uncertainty over the laboratory's future. Those scientists
who had developed a kinship with the bomb, and who preferred to remain amid the beauty of the hills and mesas,
wondered what their mission would be.

On September 18 General Groves alleviated some of the
anxiety in a briefing on The Hill. Los Alamos would become
a weapons-research center devoted to improving the bomb's
design. At the same time, it would play an important role in
the nation's program to amass a stockpile of atomic weaponry that no enemy would ever dare test. The laboratory's

mission, in short, would be a vital one in the interest of America's defense. A new federal agency would soon take charge of all atomic affairs, Groves announced, and the harsh security regulations would be relaxed a bit. The general added, however, that security would still be energetically enforced over the most sensitive aspects of the bomb work.

At 6 P.M. on the day after Groves's briefing Klaus Fuchs met Harry Gold for the last time by a large adobe church on the outskirts of Santa Fe. The meeting was a long one, as Fuchs turned over to the Soviet courier a résumé of his entire work up to that date on the bomb. Gold, who found Fuchs's technical explanations tedious and quite beyond him, glanced at the package of sixty note pages crammed with sketches and equations in Fuchs's small crabbed hand—data that told the size of the plutonium bomb, what it contained, how it was constructed and how it was detonated, even minute calculations on the actual dimensions of the parts. He asked Fuchs if there was other news.

The test, Fuchs reported with unusual animation, had been successful, so much so that the scientists had been thunderstruck by its light and power. Gold listened closely as Fuchs described the roar and rainbow of colors that attended the explosion. Unfortunately, Fuchs added, the test marked the culmination of the British mission at Los Alamos. Co-operation between the Americans and British had dwindled in recent weeks to the point where the Britishers' further presence seemed fruitless. Fuchs would be shortly returning to England, where he would willingly continue his espionage activities.

Gold was prepared for that eventuality. He instructed Fuchs on how to contact his new courier in London. He was to show up at a certain subway station carrying five books bound with string and look for someone carrying a book by Bennett Cerf, *Try and Stop Me*. Fuchs jotted down the information and shook hands good-by. Then he drove his Buick to the nearest liquor store and purchased a case of whisky for a party that night in honor of several of his British colleagues. Within the year he would be back in England, safely removed from any retribution by the country he had most injured.

The old order was being replaced by the new as the Manhattan Project prepared to fold its tent at summer's end in 1945.

Kenneth Bainbridge and George Kistiakowsky returned to Harvard; Donald Hornig had accepted a teaching post at Brown University; Hans Bethe was going back to Cornell; Enrico Fermi and Samuel Allison to Chicago. Robert Oppenheimer would resume his career at the University of California and from there help lead the struggle to control the new force and employ its powers constructively. He would be succeeded as director by Norris Bradbury, the slim young explosives expert who had once been morally repelled by the thought of working on the atomic bomb.

For Bradbury and Oppenheimer, as for so many of their colleagues, the experience of the bomb had brought the realization that scientists could no longer indulge themselves as privileged hermits living and working aloof from the mainstream of political thought and decision making. After Trinity the scientists sensed they would be involved forever, politically as well as spiritually, in the new age they had created. From now on, at least for the foreseeable future, they would be a growing factor in the debate over how best to preserve and enhance their nation's security.

At Los Alamos the scientists had worked grudgingly under military supervision. Henceforward they would have to work willingly in tandem with the politicians and the generals. For the scientists had discovered belatedly that they could not simply build the atomic bomb, then run back to their universities and forget it. Even without Hiroshima

273

and Nagasaki, such a course would have been presumptuous. The price they would pay for fostering the bomb would be a share in the awful responsibility of its management. As spiritual custodians of the bomb, they would have no choice but to accept. In time the scientists would come to realize that such responsibility—like that which compelled the decision to drop the bomb—entails frequent moral revulsions that can only be equated with the overwhelming national interest as perceived by the Government.

What the scientists could not know was that their newly established eminence in the postwar nuclear era would be short-lived. The shift in power and responsibility for the new weapon and its progeny, from its scientific creators to the military-political leadership, had begun inexorably under the Pentagon's firm guidance of the Manhattan Project. It had accelerated after Trinity during the deliberations on how best to employ the new device. Control of the bomb after the war's end continued to ebb from the scientists' grasp even as their pride soared amidst all the celebrity accorded them.

The irony was implicit in one warrior's parting words to the man who more than anyone had mid-wifed the bomb's birth.

Late in September, Henry Stimson said his final good-by to Washington. The War Department had arranged for every general officer in the city to be at the airport that day to salute the Secretary on his departure. Just before he left, Stimson had his hair trimmed, and he asked Oppenheimer to sit with him while he was in the barber's chair. They talked a bit of the bomb and the experience that both had shared in so deeply. When it was time to go, the old man rose and turned to Oppenheimer. "Now it is in your hands," he said.

But it was not to be.

274

XII

The Arms Game, 1946–84

DECAY settled on Los Alamos the year following Trinity. In the aftermath of Oppenheimer's departure the exodus of topflight scientists was headlong. The bomb makers loaded their cars and moving vans with furniture and local souvenirs of every variety from Indian bracelets to Mexican saddle horses. Contractors watching the convoys snake down the mesa, shrugged and waited expectantly for the city to become a ghost town. Roads went unrepaired, hedges uncut. The houses became more dilapidated than ever. Only the water situation improved.

While the scientists returned to university campuses, many of the GI's, including Jercinovic, found permanent jobs with the newly opened Sandia weapons laboratory in Albuquerque. One departing soldier who wanted no more of bomb work was David Greenglass. In February he was honorably discharged from the Army. He had risen to head foreman of his explosives shop and had been promoted from corporal to sergeant. The Army had given him a Good Conduct Medal as a parting gesture.

In May, Louis Slotin became the second atomic scientist to die of radiation poisoning. When his screwdriver slipped and the plutonium hemispheres started to lock in a chain reaction, Slotin had torn them apart with his bare hands and saved the lives of seven other scientists in the room. He himself had absorbed 880 roentgens of radiation. Even as he carefully sketched on the blackboard the positions of each of his colleagues so that the doctors could determine how much radiation each had been exposed to, Slotin knew that he was doomed. He lost his mind within a week. Nine days after the accident he died in agony. It was one of the last jobs of Klaus Fuchs to report, as a matter of physics, what had happened in that fatal moment to the young scientist who had determined the nuclear size of the first atomic bomb.

The evening before Slotin died, scientists who had visited his bedside were compelled to attend a cocktail party for some visiting dignitaries. Their smiling presence was required to dispel any suspicion that something had gone wrong. It was still too early in the atomic game to allow news of an accident like Slotin's to slip out and scare the public. At the same time, the details of the accident, which Fuchs compiled, could have tipped off an enemy on the process the United States was using to determine the nuclear size of its bombs. By then, however, there was no need for Fuchs to pass along such information. The Russians already had it and Fuchs was angling for bigger fish.

While the report on Slotin's death was being locked up in a file, Fuchs was gathering information on a new and mightier weapon than the Trinity gadget—the hydrogen bomb. During a conference of some thirty physicists at Los Alamos, Fuchs had listened with interest while Edward Teller argued for starting immediately on production of "the Super." Before he left America in June, Fuchs had prepared a report on the H-bomb's prospects for his contact in London.

The irony of the whole secrecy business would be bared shortly. It was enough for Oppenheimer, Niels Bohr and others at that time to launch a crusade to break down the most offensive of the security barriers and try to free the nation's scientific and political leaders from what Oppenheimer later described as "our rather blasphemous sense of omnipotency and our delusions about the effectiveness of secrecy." Those of Oppenheimer's and Bohr's colleagues who felt strongly on this point banded together in the Federation of American Scientists. With little funds or public support, they lobbied to convince parochial politicians in Washington that the bomb must be placed under some form of international control if peace was to endure. It was Bohr's special prerogative to reiterate with all the passion at his command the futility of maintaining state secrets on atomic matters if true international co-operation was to ensue.

By mid-June 1946 the efforts of the scientists and certain farsighted policy makers resulted in the Acheson-Lilienthal Report, which outlined a plan for placing atomic energy under international control. The report was the work of several minds appointed to a special advisory board by Under Secretary of State Dean Acheson. Key members of the board were David Lilienthal, head of the Tennessee Valley Authority, and Robert Oppenheimer. The report they submitted to Truman and Byrnes warned that there was no prospect of security against atomic war in any international agreement controlled only by inspection and other policing methods. "Only if the dangerous aspects of atomic energy are taken out of national hands," it concluded, "is there any reasonable prospect of devising safeguards against the use of atomic energy for bombs."

On Bernard Baruch's shoulders fell the task of presenting the report to the United Nations. "We are here to make a choice between the quick and the dead," he told the twelve member nations of the U.N. Atomic Energy Commission one summer morning. The United States proposed the immediate establishment of an international authority that would oversee all aspects of atomic development from cradle to grave. The Atomic Development Authority would control the world's supplies of raw materials, all nuclear reactors and separation plants—in short, every nuclear operation potentially dangerous to world security. Once the plan was in effect, further manufacture of atomic bombs would halt and existing stockpiles would be dismantled.

It was a sincere effort made by a nation that believed its nuclear superiority was unquestioned and its nuclear secrets inviolate. The United States was making a magnanimous gesture to divest itself of its atomic sword and to share its atomic secrets. It assumed that Russia would welcome the idea of not having to live under America's nuclear shadow. The cruel joke perpetrated on America by the atomic spies was evidenced a month later when the Soviet representative at the United Nations denounced Baruch's proposal. The Soviets had no need of it. In Klaus Fuchs's and David Greenglass's reports they had enough information to start an atomic arsenal of their own.

On an August day in 1949 detection instruments in a U.S. B-29 over Asian waters picked up unmistakable traces of radioactive matter in the atmosphere. The fallout could not have come from the massive bomb tests conducted by the United States at Bikini three years earlier. Shocked officials in Washington realized all too swiftly that Russia, years before most Americans had anticipated, had exploded an atomic weapon of its own. A month later, after feverish discussion on whether to withhold the news for fear of panicking the American public, Truman announced the event.

The furor that followed provided a new lease on life for the bomb makers of Los Alamos. Their sense of purpose was restored. The hydrogen-bomb project, viewed reluctantly at first in Washington, assumed fresh immediacy. Over Oppenheimer's misgivings, work on the Super began in earnest and the scientists at Los Alamos plunged into another challenging realm of atomic physics. The Hill surged with a new vigor. Teller, who led the H-bomb program, entreated his old colleague Oppenheimer to lend his support to the project. Oppenheimer, morally repelled at the thought of building a new and more destructive weapon of war, refused. His obstinacy did not go unnoticed in certain government circles.

Faced with the fact of a second and menacing nuclear power, the United States found itself trapped in a race to preserve its stockpile superiority over the late-starting Russians. The responsibility for this new arms outlay rested no longer with the military but rather with the new civilian Atomic Energy Commission. The Manhattan Project had disbanded and General Groves had retired to an executive's life in Connecticut. The Commission, led first by David Lilienthal and numbering among its members Robert Bacher, father of Trinity's nuclear core, was charged with directing the anticipated vast civilian and industrial uses of atomic energy. For the immediate future, that turned out to be a pipe dream. The AEC over the next decade would devote the lion's share of its energy to helping arm the nation with defensive atomic missilery.

The arrest of Klaus Fuchs in February 1950 sent violent shock waves through Washington and the scientific community. The Russians' premature explosion of an atomic bomb had alerted U.S. authorities to the probability of a major "leak" of atomic secrets. In late 1949 the F.B.I. advised British counterintelligence that the "leak" had originated with the British atomic mission in this country. Klaus Fuchs, with his almost forgotten Stalinist record, became a prime suspect. Three months before his arrest Fuchs was placed under investigation, and British authorities even arranged to have him promoted to a senior position at Harwell Laboratory so as to forestall any suspicion on his part. When the noose was ready for tightening, Fuchs was taken in hand by police inspector William Skardon, to whom he gave the full, incredible report of his double life for the previous eight years.

"At Los Alamos," he told Skardon, "I did what I consider to be the worst I have done, namely to give information about the principle of the design of the plutonium bomb." Fuchs's pitiful recital of his childhood in Germany and the traumas that led him to cloak himself in a divinity in which his private judgment could supersede the public's led officials to conclude that they were dealing not only with a spy but with a confused egomaniac who had never really emerged from adolescence.

Now the small dramas at Potsdam and the United Nations took on fresh meanings. Stalin's lack of interest in the news of Trinity and Gromyko's out-of-hand rejection of Baruch's proposal seemed tied to the perfidy of Fuchs. The realization that Fuchs's spying had contributed substantially to the premature emergence of Russia as a nuclear power attested to the magnitude of his crime.

Few presumed that Fuchs alone was responsible for the Russians' remarkable breakthrough on the bomb. Soviet scientists had been scouting the fringes of atomic physics long before World War II, and such U.S. leaders as Vannevar Bush and James Conant had predicted before Trinity that the Soviets had the resources to overhaul the U.S. lead within several years. What the Russians lacked, however, was the financial and industrial base to engage in the sort of unstinting experimental effort which the United States had made before determining the best way to build its bomb. Fuchs saved Russia that ordeal and by so doing advanced their program by as much as eighteen months to three years.

For that, the Lord Chief Justice condemned Fuchs with these words: "You have done irreparable and incalculable harm both to this land and to the United States, and you did it, as your statement shows, merely for the purpose of furthering your political creed." His trial was over in eighty-seven minutes. Because Fuchs had given information to a wartime ally and not an enemy, he was not charged with high treason, for which the penalty is death. Instead he was given the maximum sentence for violating the Official Secrets Act: fourteen years' imprisonment.

In Los Alamos, where it took longer to absorb the full shock, Klaus Fuchs the baby-sitter was still remembered with affection. "He was such a quiet, sweet, reticent little guy," said one scientist's wife. "He was always mild and pleasant," said another, as though describing her favorite cigarette. Hans Bethe, Fuchs's chief in the Theoretical Division, expressed the bewilderment of many of Fuchs's colleagues. "He was one of the most valuable men in my division," Bethe told a reporter. "Everybody liked him. If he was a spy, he played his role absolutely perfectly." That he did. One physicist who had been close to Fuchs wasn't quite so incredulous at the news. "I realized that, no matter how well I knew him, I really *didn't* know him," Richard Feynman explained. Most, however, reacted like Norris Bradbury, who spoke poignantly of the most personally callous aspect of Fuchs's crime—his forsaking of his colleagues who had been misled into befriending and confiding in him. Said Bradbury: "For the first time Fuchs raised the question among the scientists, 'Who can you trust?' We felt as if we'd all been betrayed."

The inconsistencies of Fuchs's twisted psyche followed him even to jail. To the very last he refused to divulge to Inspector Skardon the detailed information on the bomb which he had passed to the Russians, on the grounds that Skardon wasn't cleared for such data. And from his cell at Wormwood Scrubs he petitioned the courts with righteous indignation not to deprive him of his British citizenship. He had, he said, already received the maximum punishment for his crimes. The petition was denied.

283

Four months after Fuchs's arrest the net closed around David Greenglass and the Rosenbergs. At the last, Greenglass spurned his brother-in-law's pleas to flee the country and elected to stick by his wife and eight-day-old baby. In a moment of remorse he even tried to flush $4000 down the toilet—"dirty money" which Rosenberg had pressed on him to pay for traveling expenses. The final step for Greenglass was to plead guilty and turn state's evidence against Julius and Ethel Rosenberg. Mrs. Tessie Greenglass said sadly as the FBI took her son, "I hardly heard from Davy during the war. I thought he was pushing a wheelbarrow or something."

The trial began on March 6, 1951, and lasted about three weeks. Copies of Greenglass's meticulous sketches of the Trinity bomb's lens molds—sketches that Harry Gold had passed on to the Rosenbergs—helped the government build up a towering case against the couple. Greenglass's data was hardly as erudite or encompassing as Klaus Fuchs's, and some doubt was expressed as to its accuracy. But knowledgeable witnesses testified that it described the inner workings of the bomb and, in one case, a substantially perfected version of the Fat Man weapon dropped on Nagasaki. At the very least, Greenglass's material had been a highly useful supplement to the documents which Fuchs supplied the Russians.

Greenglass could only smirk uncomfortably as he heard the Rosenbergs' enraged attorney describe him as "arrogant," "repulsive and revolting," "a tricky, crafty man—not a man, but an animal" who had "disgraced the uniform of every soldier in the United States" and who was now "trying to murder" the Rosenbergs for money. Judge Irving Kaufman accepted the U.S. Attorney's description of Greenglass as a man who had "told the truth and tried to make amends." While the Rosenbergs received the death penalty, David

Greenglass was sentenced on April 6, 1951, to fifteen years in Federal prison.

The unmasking of the atomic spies brought under suspicion the entire security apparatus of the atomic-energy project. And the first and most prominent figure to feel its repercussions was Robert Oppenheimer.

All his life a curious paradox had marked Oppenheimer. It was in his character, his actions and his words. He was the gentle philosopher and tough-minded organizer of the bomb makers. With balanced equanimity he could minister to a turtle and help select the target cities for the first atomic massacres. He could wish, as he did, for the success of Trinity while hoping at the same time that the secret of the atom would remain undiscoverable.

Oppenheimer had urged his hesitant colleagues not to abandon Los Alamos at the war's end but to remain and perfect the technology they had developed. Yet three months after Trinity he had gone, and his departure had dismayed and in some cases embittered his colleagues who had stayed on. Many of them saw in Oppenheimer, when he left, no longer the unalloyed physicist and devoted practitioner of science. His new celebrity had changed him. Oppenheimer had become the great "Gray Eminence" of the Pentagon and the State Department, a scientific statesman who moved about Washington's salons with the ease and confidence of an inbred politician. He was on a first-name basis with many of those hallowed figures whom the scientists regarded as quite outside their limited purview. President Truman had awarded Oppenheimer the nation's Medal of Merit and credited him "more than any other man" with the achievement of the atomic bomb. The National Baby Institution had made him its Father of the Year. "He was exhilarated," says Stanislaw Ulam, cofather of the hydrogen bomb, "and

285

he began to think of other things beyond physics." Another colleague put it less charitably: "I think the sudden fame and the new position Oppenheimer now occupied had gone to his head so much that he began to consider himself God Almighty, able to put the whole world to rights."

Much of this was sour grapes, though some of it doubtless was true. In fact, Oppenheimer in Washington was practicing with all the eloquence and persuasion at his disposal the credo that men of science should somehow bridge the gulf between themselves and their contemporaries. It must have come as a signal shock, therefore, when the government he had served throughout the war chose to isolate him for one of the most harrowing probes of a man's conscience and personal associations ever conducted in peacetime. All the ambivalences of Oppenheimer's complex personality were laid bare during three weeks in the spring of 1954, when a government board met to decide whether he could be trusted henceforth with the nation's top nuclear secrets.

A combination of factors led to the Oppenheimer inquiry. The revelations of the atomic spies had given Washington a disruptive case of the jitters and fueled the Communist-hunting antics of Senator Joseph McCarthy's followers. The mood of the times demanded scapegoats, and the background of Robert Oppenheimer was a fertile place to start. He had been a part-time consultant to the Atomic Energy Commission since the war and had top "Q" clearance to the AEC's most sensitive secrets. Now his contract was up for renewal and once again Oppenheimer's indiscreet past was under scrutiny. This time the violent emotions of the McCarthy era, plus the fact that Oppenheimer was no longer an indispensable wartime figure, militated against him. The highest agencies of government were already quietly erecting a wall between Oppenheimer and the nation's nuclear secrets. When Lewis Strauss, the new AEC chairman, advised Oppenheimer in late 1953 that his security clearance was about to be suspended, Oppenheimer demanded an inquiry so that he might answer the charges against him.

The inquiry took place in a second-floor room of one of Washington's dreary "tempos"—temporary office buildings—erected during the war. Oppenheimer lounged on a leather sofa facing the panel of three judges headed by former Army Under Secretary, Gordon Gray. The board had summoned forty witnesses and was considering the allegations against Oppenheimer contained in a 4½-foot-high pile of documents. He was accused of keeping company with known Communists and ex-Communists, deceiving U.S. security officials and leading the opposition to the hydrogen bomb's development. Before the inquiry was very old it became patently clear that he was guilty of all three charges. In addition, Oppenheimer had brought to the Los Alamos project a number of young scientists with Communist case histories. If that had been all there was to the inquiry, however, it would never have become the cause célèbre it did.

For if it was clear that Oppenheimer had kept bad company, it was also clear that he had abandoned most of it years before. The great bulk of the charges referred to his Communist flirtations in the 1930's and the fact that Oppenheimer's wife and brother had at one time been Communists—facts known to General Groves and the Counter Intelligence Corps at the time of Oppenheimer's appointment as director of Los Alamos. If it was true that Oppenheimer had opposed the hydrogen-bomb project and hindered its development by refusal to lend his moral support, it was equally true that he was entitled to do so as an independent scientist no longer in the full employ of the government. His refusal to compromise with his conscience was now apparently construed as a security threat.

It was on the grounds of his admitted deception of Intelligence officials that Oppenheimer's right to continued security clearance was most forcefully challenged. The incident, which involved an old friend of Oppenheimer's, constituted the most damaging evidence lodged against him and was the dramatic highlight of the hearing.

In August 1943 during a series of interrogations by CIC officers Oppenheimer had mentioned that earlier that year at Berkeley, before he left for Los Alamos, a friend had broached the possibility of transmitting technical information to Soviet scientists. The friend, he said, had suggested that atomic data might be funneled to Russia through an intermediary he knew. Oppenheimer had cut the suggestion off curtly at the time, but, convinced that his friend's remarks had been quite "innocent," he had neglected to report the incident to intelligence authorities. During the subsequent interrogation by the CIC, however, Oppenheimer had offered the story as a tip-off to the kind of attempt that might be made in the future to persuade atomic scientists to divulge information. Oppenheimer had apparently believed he was salving his conscience for not reporting the incident earlier and that the CIC would accept the tip in the spirit in which it was offered.

The security agents, however, had pounced on Oppenheimer's tip and asked for details. Oppenheimer, unwilling to divulge his friend's name, had thereupon concocted a yarn of intrigue that would have outdone an Ian Fleming plot. He had introduced new characters and new episodes in a clumsy attempt to fuzz up his friend's identity by embroidering what he believed to be the "innocent" truth of the Berkeley episode. Instead, as the CIC pressed him to identify his friend, Oppenheimer had found himself trapped and had finally been forced by General Groves into revealing that the man in question was one Haakon Chevalier. The idea that he had caused Chevalier's name to be blackened was to haunt Oppenheimer. It was the reflection on Oppenheimer's veracity, however, that especially interested the Gray Panel. By his own admission Oppenheimer had told the CIC a "cock and bull" story and a "tissue of lies." Why? "Because I was an idiot," he said.

General Groves, one of the witnesses, suggested that Oppenheimer's behavior in the Chevalier incident reflected "the typical American schoolboy attitude that there is something wicked about telling on a friend." That piece of character reference might have given the board some insight, if they had not had it already, into the puerile and essentially ingenuous ego that motivated Oppenheimer's actions in this instance. Groves, however, couldn't resist noting, in addition, that the breakdown of compartmentalization at Los Alamos, which he had opposed and which Oppenheimer had effected, had helped Fuchs to obtain information for the Russians. As a final nail for Oppenheimer's coffin, the general offered his own interpretation of the security requirements under the Atomic Energy Act and concluded, "I would not clear Dr. Oppenheimer today if I were a member of the Commission on the basis of this interpretation."

From then on, despite testimony from his colleagues and peers in government attesting to his loyalty and basic truthfulness, the inquiry slid downhill for Oppenheimer. At times the atmosphere in Room 2022 seemed more inquisitorial than inquiring. The attempts to entrap Oppenheimer into damaging statements often made the board's chief counsel seem more like an avenging prosecutor. But Oppenheimer submitted himself to the counsel's arrogant lashes like a penitent bowing to flagellation. He could muster none of his fire or eloquence to combat the mounting charges. Perhaps his troubled conscience prevented him from doing so. His old colleague I. I. Rabi, watching Oppenheimer's Kafka-like ordeal, turned to the board and said, "This is what novels are about. There is a dramatic moment and the history of the man, what made him act, what he did and what sort of person he was. That is what you are really doing here. You are writing a man's life."

The list of suspected Communists whom Oppenheimer had allowed to work at the laboratory was presented as evidence of his laxity in security control. The suspects were few in number, and whatever mischief they attempted at Los Alamos, of which none is recorded, they were bushleaguers compared to Fuchs and Greenglass, neither of whom was hired by Oppenheimer. Oppenheimer's opposition to the hydrogen bomb was made to seem sinister. It mattered not that he was in good company on that issue: Conant, former AEC chairman Lilienthal and Enrico Fermi. It was pointed out that he had led the development of the bomb which had destroyed Hiroshima and Nagasaki and therefore had little right to be squeamish about the hydrogen bomb. There seems to have been no consideration that a man may reach the point where he becomes unwilling to condone further the production of instruments of mass death.

So Oppenheimer, whom President Truman had once commended for his "unswerving devotion to duty" in developing the greatest military weapon of all time, was stripped of his security status. He was, as the massive volume of testimony shows, stripped of much more than that in the end. The board did not condemn Oppenheimer's loyalty. Instead it censured him for his "susceptibility" to influences that could endanger the nation's security; for his "serious disregard" for the requirements of the security system; for his conduct in the hydrogen-bomb program and for being "less than candid in several instances" during the inquiry. This last was especially mystifying, considering the almost helpless candor and naïveté with which Oppenheimer had sealed his fate.

In seeking to explain and expiate the sins of his past, Oppenheimer had, as Rabi said, laid the book of his life

290

before the three judges. After their verdict Oppenheimer's loyalty, but not his image, remained intact. He no longer stood in the public eye as an atomic-age immortal blessed with supernatural powers. Oppenheimer could appear now only as a very extraordinary human, one, in author Robert Jungk's words, "tormented by conflicting impulses, weak and wanting in that underlying steadiness of mind which probably only some faith above and beyond reason could have given him."

On June 28 the Atomic Energy Commission voted to uphold the Gray Panel's decision. Two days later Oppenheimer's consulting contract with the AEC terminated. It was a supreme irony of the affair that Oppenheimer could have let the contract run out quietly without requesting the inquiry to uphold his honor—an inquiry which became instead a soul-searing mea culpa ending in rejection.

The Oppenheimer case stirred the scientific community as no single event, including Fuchs's arrest, had since Hiroshima and Nagasaki. It was not only the humiliation of their wartime leader that grieved the scientists. It was the hearing's reflection, in its pages and pages of searching testimony, of the scientists' own collective dilemma: their bedazzlement at the overwhelming nature of their discoveries and the realization that they were woefully unprepared for the fame and responsibility which followed. For years afterward there would be little peace of mind for those scientists who had looked at Oppenheimer in the dock and thought: *There but for the grace of God go I.*

In the decades following Oppenheimer's mortification death took many of the giants of Trinity. Men like Compton, Fermi, Kistiakowsky, and Ernest Lawrence passed into the history of the age they had fathered. In the dusk of their lives many of them had grown weary and disillusioned by

291

the lost promises of that age. The limitations of the bomb as an instrument of political power had already become apparent, to the dismay of those who had believed it could be used to bend the Soviets to accept a postwar American blueprint for world peace. Even as America hoped that its nuclear monopoly in the late 1940s would induce Moscow to forego its territorial objectives in exchange for curbing further nuclear arms production, the Soviets were mocking the very concept of a just international peace.

The Cold War era saw Soviet aggression and expansionism move from the communist coup in Czechoslovakia and the Berlin blockade to the crushing of the Hungarian revolt. As the Soviets consolidated their takeover of Eastern Europe, Americans confronted the challenge posed by Communist belligerence in other parts of the world: the invasion of South Korea; the rise of a hostile Marxist dictatorship in Cuba. (In the Korean conflict the issue of whether to employ nuclear weapons against an enemy, in this case the North Koreans and their Chinese allies, was raised for the first time by President Eisenhower.) Even Sputnick, the first successful launch of an orbiting satellite, was viewed with alarm by Americans who believed the Soviets had demonstrated a dangerous advantage in missile-delivery technology. As Soviet–U.S. relations plummeted, the nuclear arms competition ratcheted upwards.

Between 1945 and 1955 the U.S. stockpile of nuclear weapons grew from two—"Fat Man" and "Little Boy"—to more than two thousand. In 1952 America had detonated "Mike," the code name for its first thermonuclear device, with a blast that was more than 500 times the size of Trinity's. "Mike" 's explosive yield, a shattering 10.4 megatons (millions of tons), wiped out the tiny South Pacific island of Elugelab and dug a crater a mile long and 175 feet deep in the ocean's floor. Within a year the Soviets had followed with their own first hydrogen bomb test. The birth of the

H-bomb, the so-called Superweapon, marked the last great conceptual achievement in the science of nuclear weaponry: the release of vast amounts of energy through the fusion of nuclei.

For many scientists, mindful of Oppenheimer's and others' warnings about the new weapon's potential for unlimited destruction, it also signaled a fateful determination by the United States and the Soviet Union *not* to reverse the arms race momentum, but to accelerate it.

In 1961 the Soviets broke a three-year moratorium on nuclear testing. At three different sites they conducted the most intensive series of tests in the world's history up to that point. The climax was a monster 58-megaton burst in the atmosphere above Novaya Zemlya. The device used was actually a 100-megaton bomb, tamped down by lead casing, that could be hung on the Soviet's largest missile and hurled across 3,500 miles to the continental United States. The U.S., which had adhered to the moratorium, responded by holding its own test series the following year over Christmas Island in the Pacific. The rationale, President Kennedy explained, was to maintain the U.S. lead in total military strength: "We do not propose to lose it." The new round of nuclear testing was necessary to preserve America's "superior capability."

The seventeen-year span from Trinity to Christmas Island had encompassed nearly 200 atomic explosions, about 100 megatons of nuclear energy rupturing the atmosphere, and more than 350 fruitless test-ban talks at the diplomatic level.

Small wonder that men like Fermi died saddened that the world had turned away from its chance for international control of the bomb and arrestment of the arms race. Niels Bohr died in 1962, still hoping against hope for an "open world" in which all secrets of the atom would be shared among nations. That year Leo Szilard and James Franck, those two outspoken consciences of the scientific community, lived to see the world teeter on the brink of nuclear holocaust—the Cuban missile crisis—before they, too, passed on. Just before he died, Szilard warned once more of the insanity of the arms race: the world would very soon have to live with itself, he said, before it was too late.

And in 1963 a glimmer of sanity *did* appear. A limited treaty banning nuclear tests in the oceans, atmosphere, and outer space was signed by the United States and Russia as well as Great Britain; and the wheel came full circle with the vindication of Robert Oppenheimer.

He walked through the doors of the White House Cabinet Room on a darkening winter afternoon, a stooped and wizened figure who seemed shriveled into his shirt collar. Under the short-cropped hair he wore the same frail, inquiring look that had peered from newspapers ten years before at the height of his celebrity. As President Johnson read the citation for the $50,000 Enrico Fermi award, the Atomic Energy Commission's highest honor, Oppenheimer, overcome with emotion, groped for his wife's hand. The forty or more scientific and government leaders gathered in the room heard the President extol Oppenheimer for his wartime leadership at Los Alamos and for his role in the climactic first test of the bomb.

When Johnson had finished, Oppenheimer stood for several seconds quietly studying the citation. He looked up then and said, barely audibly, "I think it just possible, Mr. President, that it has taken some charity and some courage for you to make this award today. That would seem to me a good augury for all our futures."

The augury, like Oppenheimer's eloquently wistful words, drifted out of that room and into the charged atmosphere of geopolitical reality, there to dissipate like so many particles of rejected atoms. The scientists' belief that official atonement for the past sins of McCarthyism had finally won them and their leader renewed respect, perhaps even a proprietary seat at the nuclear policy making table, was a delusion. In a quite different sense, General Farrell had been right at Trinity about "the long-hairs letting it get away from them." From then on, the scientists' advisory role in nuclear matters would be increasingly a technical one.

I. I. Rabi was to observe years later that the scientists had "abdicated" their magistery over the bomb, relinquishing it to people "who didn't understand it" or the scientists: the political and military leaders who, in Rabi's thinking, were less equipped than the scientists in terms of superior knowledge and humanitarianism to deal responsibly with the new weapon. In truth, it was a forced abdication to the Constitutional prerogatives of a political-military establishment which, in turn, distrusted the scientists' unworldliness and preachy utopianism. The Oppenheimer case served to estrange the two camps further, diminishing even more the scientists' weight in nuclear policy making. Fewer scientists sought to serve a security-obsessed government that had the power to destroy men's reputations; fewer political leaders found it necessary to bring scientists of dubious philosophy or loyalty into the nation's highest councils. Oppenheimer's vindication did not dramatically alter the trend.

In a world where nuclear arsenals were fast reaching overkill proportions—31,500 warheads barely twenty years after Trinity—those scientists who were not a part of the weapons-building process or privy to the war-gaming strategies evolving in Washington understandably lamented the turn of events. The bomb in its postwar incarnation, declared Rabi, had been used to subvert the original ideal of those who built it to end World War II. In seeking to protect its atomic nest egg, the U.S. had spawned an arsenal of them. The ideal was no longer to *save* civilization, but rather how to *extinguish* another civilization if necessary.

* * *

In fact, there were no longer ideals in the nuclear world, only stark challenges. And the most formidable of these was not how to win a nuclear war or how to survive one, but how to *prevent* one. Toward that end the U.S. embarked on a series of strategies, the sum purpose of which was to discourage any nuclear adversary from ever risking a first strike against America's homeland. A cardinal article of faith was that, while it was impossible to will nuclear weapons out of existence, it *was* possible to contain their use. By not being used the weapons would achieve their purpose. Another postulate was that neither superpower would take military steps that could threaten the survival of the other's strategic nuclear forces.

America's strategic forces gradually merged into a mighty triad composed of intercontinental ballistic missiles (ICBMs), manned bombers, and submarines. Each force complemented the others. The land-based ICBMs were the dray-horses of the arsenal, massive, powerful carriers of destruction, targeted to attack the enemy's homeland while protecting their own; locked in stationary positions, they were also highly vulnerable to an enemy first-strike. The missile-carrying subs, sleek insurers of ruinous second-strike potential, were more flexible, less accurate, most difficult to detect. Manned bombers, quickly airborne, could retaliate with a rain of megatonnage against an enemy that had unleashed a first strike, even as American ICBMs lay devastated in their silos. Bombers could also be recalled in the event of miscalculation.

The annihilating capacity of such a force made massive retaliation an appealingly simple, strategic concept. Indeed, the U.S. appropriated the idea through most of the 1950s even though it had not yet fully developed two of the triad's vital components, an operational ICBM system and a ballistic missile submarine fleet. Washington was confident, however, that it could respond overwhelmingly to any Soviet attack via its superior B-52 bomber force: 2,000 Strato-fortresses armed with as many nuclear weapons, enough to reduce the Soviet Union's cities and much of its citizenry to ashes many times over. That confidence subsided before the end of the decade when the Soviets unveiled a new intercontinental bomber of their own, Bison, and in 1957 sprang Sputnik on an unsuspecting West. The emergence of Bison and Sputnik denigrated the idea of a strategic defense based on massive retaliation by bombers, forcing the Pentagon to speed up its own intercontinental missile capacity. By April 1958, the first Atlas ICBM was in place; in 1960 the first Polaris missile subs were deployed.

By the early 1960s, with the U.S. in possession of a more credible nuclear defense force, massive retaliation had given way to flexible response: the U.S. would respond in kind to an enemy strike according to the nature and dimensions of the attack. The Cuban missile crisis, and Washington's carefully focused way of defusing it, had underscored the rationale for such a strategy. American leaders had become convinced that the risk of a massive nuclear exchange, touched off by a local confrontation, was not worth the candle. Although the U.S. had prevailed, thanks to superior conventional forces in its own Caribbean sphere of influence, the public had been shaken by the episode; there was a run on fallout shelter construction, and the first sizable antinuclear protest movement formed. A further stabilizing shift was the Kennedy administration's decision to redirect U.S. nuclear targeting away from Soviet cities and onto Soviet military installations.

Within five years, as short a time as it took for the Soviets to install their own ICBM system and for Kennedy's successor to be engulfed in the Vietnam war, the strategic concept had changed again. The ominous sounding new doctrine: Mutual Assured Destruction (MAD). MAD would ensure that under any conditions of nuclear attack by Russia the result could be nothing other than Russia's certain obliteration by all or part of the U.S. strategic forces. Soviet cities and industries became targets again. Even if it were ravaged first, the U.S. would be able to destroy in response up to 30 percent of the Soviets' population and up to 70 percent of their industry. In a Soviet retaliation, a mere 1 percent of their strategic forces reaching the U.S. could destroy more than fifty of America's largest cities, each to a greater extent than the havoc wreaked on Hiroshima.

For nearly a decade, through the Johnson and Nixon administrations, MAD was a doctrinal fixture in U.S. defense circles until changes in weapons technology dictated a new strategy and the era of counterforce: the ability to spike an attacker at any level of violence by concentrating selective firepower on elements of his nuclear force. The advent of smaller, more accurate weapons with the ability to surgically eliminate an enemy's missile sites meant that military installations, not civilian populations, were again the main emphasis of strategic targeting. The numbers of warheads in both U.S. and Soviet arsenals far exceeded the number of *non*military targets, thus compelling most weapons to be aimed at military sites if they were to be aimed at all. Like the earlier flexible response, the new doctrine, which was disclosed in 1974 by the Ford administration, also allowed the U.S. to counterattack with limited nuclear options instead of being forced to a reflexive spasm of massive retaliation using all available weapons.

Counterforce remains the basic strategic doctrine at this writing. But two new theories suggest possible changes in nuclear defense policy that would upset established wisdom about the unthinkability of nuclear war, the use of outer space to conduct it, and the risks of deploying an antimissile defense system.

For the first time in an American administration the idea of *fighting* a nuclear war, not simply preventing one, was breached at high levels of the Reagan administration in the early 1980s. The proposition that the U.S. should be prepared to *use* nuclear weapons under extreme provocation, to control or dominate any resulting escalation, indeed to *win* at whatever level a nuclear exchange might be waged— all this challenged the very underpinning of mutually assured destruction, the presumption that nuclear war was suicidal and therefore unthinkable. Limited nuclear wars *were* thinkable, it was argued, if their planners were prepared to manage the consequences. Small kiloton skirmishes, employing tactical battlefield weapons to wipe out enemy tank concentrations, were especially thinkable to those strategists concerned with Soviet supremacy in conventional forces and the threat of a Soviet invasion of Western Europe.

The danger of this theory, quite aside from its presumptions of control, lay in the irreconcilability of Soviet and U.S. doctrines: the U.S. would not launch a first *strike* against Russia with strategic weapons, but might use tactical nuclear weapons first; the Soviets rule out first *use* of nuclear weapons, but would strike preemptively against the U.S. with their full strategic arsenal if Soviet forces anywhere came under a first-use nuclear attack by the U.S. The theory has therefore elicited disbelief from those who see no way to keep battlefield nuclear shoot-outs from turning into full-scale armed conflict. "You suffer a defeat, you escalate," says Hans Bethe today. "The other side suffers a defeat, they escalate. As long as you have the means to escalate, you use them." In a 1982 magazine article, a quartet of distinguished national security experts urged that the U.S. adopt a no-first-use strategy. Any use of nuclear weapons, they warned, "carries with it a high and inescapable risk of escalation into the general nuclear war which would bring ruin to all and victory to none."

A second proposition, President Reagan's 1983 Strategic

Defense Initiative, revived the antiballistic missile (ABM) issue: whether an ABM system to protect America's military network and cities would enhance national security or endanger the nuclear balance. The proposal raised questions as well about the role of space satellites, their vulnerability, and the inclusion of outerspace as a potential "star wars" battleground. What Reagan sought, to replace the suicide pact that MAD and counterforce implied, was development of a shield of future-generation missile interceptors that would provide a nearly impenetrable defense against Soviet attack—a deterrence that threatened to destroy weapons, not people. The studs in this shield would be weapons hitherto associated in the public mind with science fiction or video arcade games: orbiting sensors that detect an attack at launch, then trigger giant remote-control ray guns to thwart it; ground-launched x-ray lasers, powered by nuclear blasts, flashing across the void at the speed of light to destroy enemy missiles; particle beam accelerators firing high-velocity nuclear "grapeshot" to knock down intruders at long range.

This space-age exotica was largely the work of a younger generation of nuclear scientists, championed by none other than the aging father of the H-bomb, Edward Teller. The weapons were no longer fantasy but achievable within the law of physics. They could, Teller claimed, "replace MAD with a *true* defense, one not only more moral but more practical." Others were less persuaded. A system of this magnitude, requiring for its development the estimated equivalent of eight Manhattan Projects, might bankrupt the defense establishment. There were technological doubts. The perfection of aiming required seemed unattainable to many: a laser beam so precisely focused on a single tiny area of a distant missile traveling at five miles per second that it could pierce the missile's metal skin and disable it. The space-supported wonder weapons would also be vulnerable to attack from antisatellite (ASAT) devices which the superpowers were already testing. The U.S. would have to entrust its fate to a handful of orbiting battle stations and supercomputers that could be shot out of the sky on command. The very idea that satellites, with their mutually reassuring watchdog role, might become prey to a race for dominance in ASAT weaponry worried people.

Finally, ABM seemed a dubious substitute for the doctrine of deterrence. If the strategic balance of the invulnerable offensive forces of the U.S. and Soviet Union owed its stability to neither side's trying to emplace an offsetting defense system, then any U.S. move toward an ABM plan might well upset the equilibrium. A nation impervious to attack would be in a position to attack another with impunity. To avoid that and neutralize an American ABM effort, the Soviets would likely expand their already bulging offensive-weapons arsenal.

For it is ordained. Each new strategy and counterstrategy has meant structuring a new military mission to deal with it, requiring in turn the right mix of new weapons systems each of which breeds its own new arsenal of warheads. The governing nuclear theology of mutual assured destruction may seem a futile one on which to base a lasting peace, but it has had a certain brute prohibiting effect thanks to a brace of weaponry unimagined by the builders of the first Trinity bomb. The weaponry to insure mankind against the MAD theory ever working is itself, in its reproductive process, a form of reasoned madness.

Four decades after Trinity, with its comparative popgun blast of 20 kilotons, more than 200,000 people, and an annual budget of $35 billion tend to the development, production and care of a U.S. arsenal totalling about 26,000 warheads with an explosive potential of more than 4,400 megatons. The largest warhead in stock has a yield of nine megatons, or 450 times that of "Fat Man." Comparative Soviet figures are unknown, but their share of the arsenal probably brings the total number of warheads in the world to 50,000, possessing a yield close to 20,000 megatons—twenty *billion* tons of TNT—or 1,250,000 times the yield of the 16-kiloton bomb that flattened Hiroshima. To raise the scale again by illustration, the megatonnage in world arsenals contains the potential firepower of at least 6,000 World War Two's. The total firepower expended in that conflict was a mere three megatons. A single U.S. Poseidon submarine is armed with weapons of triple that power; a single new Trident sub carries warheads the equal of six times that power, enough to destroy every major city in the Northern Hemisphere.

The road from Trinity to Trident has been as technologically fertile as it has been fearsome, but one more of extraordinary refinements than of seminal breakthroughs. The Trinity and Mike tests resulted from scientific discoveries that changed the nature of physics; no such high theoretical achievement has attended the subsequent history of weapons design, although the "star wars" weaponry, if realized, may break new ground. Nor has the weapons work spun off any great beneficial side technologies, as the space race spawned the phenomenon of miniaturization. It has been since the early 1950s primarily a scientific-engineering exercise in refinement, particularly the refinement of weapons' throw-weight: that is, insuring the most destructive explosive yield from the lightest warhead possible. Thus, a Trident sub today can pack below its deck the equivalent firepower of six world wars. Where the four-ton Trinity device yielded a puny 5,000 tons of explosion per ton of weapon, a one-ton device today can generate a million tons of blast.

What the weaponeers have been doing these past forty years, then, is improving on the magnitude of mass destruction that the advent of nuclear weapons signaled. It has also been an exercise in refining the *economics* of mass destruction. Pre-Hiroshima, it took one thousand bombers to level a city; post-Hiroshima it takes just one bomb. At the outset, therefore, nuclear weapons proved to be 1,000 times cheaper per target destroyed. The weaponeers have been seeking to better that ratio ever since.

For the decade of the fifties, producing the biggest bang seemed to be the trademark of technological superiority. But the enormous expenditure of money and material to explode the supermonsters, the dangers to the environment, and the outcry of public opinion changed the emphasis in bomb building after the Soviets' 58-megaton blast in 1961. Smaller weapons of high precision became the goal: "smart bombs" of lightning velocity and pinpoint accuracy with inboard guidance systems that could deliver them from the mouth of a battlefield cannon or the belly of a supersonic jet to targets hundreds of miles away. What transformed the work of the bomb makers in the sixties was the computer revolution. Computers not only enabled the accurate delivery of small weapons, they altered the pace and nature of the whole weapons building process, modernizing it overnight as surely as mechanized plows did the farming business. Scientists no longer had to undertake laborious, time-consuming tests of a weapon's effectiveness at different levels. The computers could construct a testing model and gauge or simulate how a new weapon would react in battle conditions, how the various features of a warhead—weight, shape, design, composition—would interact according to the always changing requirements of the military. A cluster of computer microchips could comprise the inboard guidance system of a weapon programmed to take out a Soviet SS-20 missile site tucked away in the Urals.

The coming of these new weapons with smaller warheads in the 100-kiloton range (still six times the yield of the

303

Hiroshima bomb) dictated the development of more efficient delivery systems, the next technological milestone. The debut of the MIRV (Multiple Independently-targeted Reentry Vehicle) in the late 1960s, followed by the Cruise missile, afforded the means of delivering low-yield strategic weapons in large numbers accurately and cheaply. As many as a dozen to fourteen MIRVs could be piggybacked on a single booster and released above the atmosphere over enemy territory to plunge down on a host of targets. MIRV, the congenial new ballistic missile, bolstered the force of American offensive weaponry while greatly complicating the enemy's detection capability. The Cruise by comparison was a small, pilotless subsonic jet that could be launched from planes, submarines, surface ships or land vehicles; with speeds of 450 miles per hour, plus the ability to maneuver within 200 feet of the ground, it too was among the toughest of weapons to detect.

These and other developments, like the move from liquid-fuel to solid-fuel rockets, have energized the arms industry, setting the foundations for new families of versatile weapons that can perform in a variety of roles from naval and strategic to theater and tactical. The Cruise for example has bred offspring whose nicknames sound like a men's toiletry display: "Glickum," "Slickum," and "Alcum" for GLCM (Ground-Launched Cruise Missile), SLCM (Sea-Launched), and ALCM (Air-Launched). As the bomb making or ordnance technology reached a plateau of sorts, the drive to perfect missile *accuracy* became the weaponeers' signature of the seventies and eighties. Each new weapons class has sired a more accurate and speedier descendant, from Pershing I to Pershing II, from Minuteman I to III, and now the planned MX (Missile Experimental), from Trident I to its second generation which may be operational by the end of the decade. The accuracy potential alone of these systems has increased 200 percent since the early 1970s;

their range, targeting flexibility, and payload strength have also markedly improved. Not without cost. Merely to develop fifteen major weapons systems now in production or blueprinted for the rest of the 1980s and early 1990s, including the top-secret Stealth bomber and something called the Midgetman missile, could cost American taxpayers as much as $400 billion.

Changing nuclear strategies; the variety of military missions; the diversity of weapons systems to fit the missions; and the technological sea change from mass-destruction behemoths to smaller, easily transportable weapons—all these have generated the most awesome stockpile of killing machines the world has known: warheads.

From the warheads of the early 1950s, which were largely bombs of a single type carried by the B-52s, the stockpile has reached its present level of sophistication with some two-dozen separately configured types of warheads, incorporating more than fifty different modifications and yields. The typical warhead is a package of fission or fusion materials that also contains chemical high explosives, an arming system, a firing system, a fuzing mechanism to regulate the detonation, and various safety devices. Eighty-five warhead types have been designed and tested since 1945, the newest a thermonuclear warhead with a 200-kiloton wallop, built for the Air-Launched Cruise Missile. There are categories of warheads to match each of the delivery systems: strategic missiles, defensive missiles, tactical or theater intermediate-range missiles, artillery projectiles, and manned bombers.

The history of warhead development has had little to do with any Strangelovian notion that the greatest number of warheads per se is best for everyone's health and security. Had that been the case, the superpowers could as easily have capped their nuclear armories at a credibly deterrent 500 megatons each and saved themselves a hatful of change. Quantity means little in military terms. The destruction of the enemy's cities and civilization is not the endgame, although it could come to that; destruction of his military order is. What is required then is the technological excellence to produce a superior mix of warheads, enough to fortify each of the triad's defense systems, enough to destroy the enemy's multiple military targets. It has been this striving for weapons *quality*—the precise match of warhead to missile, of weapons system to mission, of mission to strategic doctrine—that has accounted for the bloated size of the warhead arsenal.

For the past couple of decades, there has been unspoken relief that the scientists have devised no doomsday weapons, no post-thermonuclear device that could rearrange the science of atomic warfare and spell the earth's sudden finish. Yet a cycle has been occurring over that same period in which, in its most recent phase, the production of smaller, lower-yield, but undeniably lethal weapons has inflated the warhead stockpile to world-threatening levels. The cycle is an object lesson in how the obsolescing of weapons has perversely helped accelerate rather than slow warhead production.

It started when the simple free-fall Hiroshima and Nagasaki bombs were replaced after a few years with new guided offensive missiles. Counterweapons shortly made these new offensive missiles obsolete; in turn the counterweapons were rendered obsolete by the deployment of many even more sophisticated offensive ones. By the mid-1950s a quantum jump in warhead production was taking place as the military unveiled a bevy of new weapons systems to meet the demands of massive retaliation. Thirty thousand new warheads were pumped into the U.S. arsenal. The peak was reached in 1967 with 32,000 warheads. Thereafter, the numbers declined modestly while the explosive yield dropped dramatically. The phasing out of giant warheads for bombers, along with many heavy battlefield weapons, and their replacement with lighter missile warheads and artillery shells led to the gradual decrease, by two-thirds, of the arsenal's megatonnage.

But now the cycle's more familiar phase is underway again in the era of the MIRVs and mininukes. As demand increases for multiple-warhead missiles to fix on more widely dispersed Soviet targets, the number of warheads climbs. Today, even with old warheads being retired at the rate of three a day, new warheads are being born faster—at the rate of five each day. The U.S. is thus producing a net of two warheads daily, the Soviet Union about four. And, through at least the early 1990s, it is estimated that nineteen new types of warheads and approximately 30,000 individual warheads will enter the United States nuclear arsenal.

When people ponder the cold, hard, and quite plausible rationale for the immense numbers of weapons in the world's nuclear stockpiles, the many carefully calibrated controls for insuring against their accidental release, it is that much harder to condemn this condition as the certified madness it is. It makes it that much harder to reduce the arms race to a cartoon of two men standing waist-deep in a pool of kerosene, each angrily waving a fistful of matches at the other, never mind whether one has ten more matches than the other. And when the public reads of these numbers, then contemplates what might happen if one of these weapons was fired, triggering a nuclear exchange, the Dantesque vision of the ensuing horror informs the literature of the times. Right or wrong, and there is no way or desire to know for sure, the scenarios of this literature bear a certain truth based on history, empirical and theoretical science, and the sayings of wise men.

Robert Oppenheimer years ago acknowledged that forty

million Americans in twenty of their largest cities could perish in one night of nuclear terror. Hiroshima is history and the vignettes of its agony are familiar: families scorched, blasted, crushed to death, vomiting, shrieking, losing their minds from radiation sickness, watching their skin blacken and shred from burns, the survivors recalling children with their heads like boiled octupi, the naked man standing in the nuclear rain holding his eyeball in his palm. And the bomb that did this would be classed a mere tactical weapon in today's arsenals.

History, too, records man's carelessness with all this lethal ordnance. In July 1984 at Severomorsk on the Kola Peninsula in northwestern Russia, an accidental explosion devastated the Soviets' huge naval munitions depot there, destroying by some counts as many as a third of the surface-to-air and Cruise missiles stored for use by the Soviet northern fleet, killing between 200 and 300 workers, and causing Western analysts to believe at first that a nuclear bomb had detonated. Five months later an unarmed, misguided Soviet Cruise Missile landed on Finnish soil.

History and science have merged to produce informed speculation about the consequences of a nuclear exchange. The pattern of destruction caused by the air burst of a one-megaton bomb would start with initial nuclear radiation killing unprotected humans in an area of some six square miles. As Jonathan Schell has written, electromagnetic pulses would damage or knock out electrical circuits over a vast area, crippling much of the country's economy. The thermal pulse, a wave of blinding light and searing heat, would char the skin of exposed humans with second-degree burns at a distance of nine-and-a-half miles. The blast wave would crush all but the sturdiest buildings and their inhabitants within a four-and-a-half-mile radius.

If the bomb was detonated at ground level, the radioactive fallout would expose humans in the vicinity of the blast or downwind from it to possibly fatal radiation disease and would lethally contaminate more than a thousand square miles. In more specific terms, the same weapon detonated 8,500 feet above New York City's Empire State Building would gut or raze almost every structure within a radius of four miles. People in the structures would crash to the street; people in the street would be mashed by the avalanche of human and structural debris. In the broil of the explosion anyone caught in the open within nine miles of ground zero would receive probably lethal third-degree burns. Mass fires would likely break out within an area of 280 square miles, igniting everything flammable and leaving a smoking graveyard of melted-down cars, buses, lampposts, steel girders, glass store windows, and charred corpses. The weapon responsible for this would be ranked as medium-size in today's arsenals.

The longterm after-effects of a megaton-class explosion are necessarily more speculative. Here again, history suggests some guideposts. In June to July of 1946 the U.S. held its second weapons test after Trinity, exploding two atomic devices in the Marshall Islands' Bikini atoll. Navy personnel who participated in that series, Operation Crossroads, reported years later that they were never warned of the danger of radiation exposure. It was only after burns the size of silver dollars appeared on their limbs, forcing amputation in some cases, that they sensed what may have happened. One veteran of Crossroads, who lost both legs before contracting terminal cancer of the liver and colon, claimed to have been exposed at the time of the test to between 1,000 and 1,800 rads. "It was just as if the enemy had aimed at you point-blank and shot you with a gun," he recalled shortly before his death in 1983. "Our injuries didn't show up until thirty, forty years later." U.S. soldiers and civilians were exposed to the radioactive fallout from more than a hundred tests conducted in the Nevada desert between 1951 and

1962. And in 1984, after studying evidence that reported incidences of cancer 50 percent greater than normal among residents living near the test area, a federal judge ruled in favor of the claims for damages made by relatives of 375 cancer victims—victims of the delayed effects of *kiloton*-class bombs. A ten-thousand-*megaton* bombing, according to the National Academy of Sciences, would over the following twenty to thirty years dose every person in the Northern and Southern Hemispheres with enough radiation to cause a rise of 2 percent in the death rate from cancer and a worldwide increase in serious genetic disease.

The environmental impact of nuclear war has fomented even more dire predictions: the scalding and killing of countless crops; the blinding of birds and beasts throughout the world; the extinction of aquatic species; the pollution of the whole ecosphere with nitrogen oxides; the permanent alteration of the world's climate. The theory of a nuclear winter, transforming the earth into a darkened, frozen planet, has created such controversy that the U.S. government has undertaken a multimillion-dollar study to determine its validity. Could the unleashing of even a small fraction of the world nuclear arsenals spread such a pall of smoke and soot from mass fires that sunlight would be blotted out indefinitely, causing temperatures to drop by as much as 75 degrees, reducing drastically the oxygen-supplying photosynthesis of plant life, virtually eliminating food production in the Northern Hemisphere, freezing reservoirs and other freshwater sources, effectively collapsing the societies of the survivors and their life-support systems? Would a world so ravaged be *worth* surviving in?

The Soviet leadership is not unaware of such apocalypse. But their fear of the bomb is shadowed by national security concerns over what they perceive to be a hostile Western military presence backed by an American technological establishment that has continually forced the qualitative pace of the arms race, moving it via new weaponry relentlessly forward and frequently out of equilibrium. Similarly, in the U.S. there is a conflict in perceptions between the acknowledged danger of nuclear immolation and the known menace of Soviet expansionism. Those who stress the *nuclear* danger and call for an arms freeze, mutual or unilateral, tend to ignore the relevance of geopolitical dangers—East-West disputes, global patterns of Soviet misconduct—at levels far removed from nuclear confrontation. Their vision, as potential victims of holocaust, is circumscribed by disbelief that any other issue could rival that of mankind's survival. Those who magnify the *Soviet* danger tend to view nuclear weapons not as summonses to our final dissolution, but as guarantors of our right to live in freedom. They decry as alarmist or moralistic any demands for a weapons-free peace that is not related to justice or respect for human dignity, pointing out that such a peace might lead to domination of the world by the most ruthless. Working in a classified world of documents, graphs and hard-edged calculation, all emotion computerized out of their rationales, they see themselves as realists or rationalists, their opponents as accommodationists or Armageddonists.

Neither danger is of course exclusive of the other, and neither camp has a lock on ultimate wisdom.

The nuclear danger has been abetted by missed opportunities to halt the arms race and by a flawed psychology that believes the race, and our security, can be won through technological one-upmanship. It is, says McGeorge Bundy, the White House national security adviser under Presidents Kennedy and Johnson, the fear that if you don't deploy a new strategic weapons system, your enemy will. "That fear has greatly exceeded the comfort we obtain in doing something to meet it." For forty years American technology has scored a succession of weapons "firsts": the atom bomb, the intercontinental bomber, the thermonuclear bomb, the ICBM, the missile-firing submarine, hardened missile silos, the solid-propellant ICBM, the MIRV. Each new system increased the danger; each system was matched or bettered within four to six years by the Soviets. The arms race, someone has observed, is like a piece of iron: heat one end of it, and very soon the other end will be the same temperature.

The Soviet danger is no more intense, only more arresting because the evidence suggests unwanted and possibly imminent military-political consequences. For twenty years the Soviets have been modernizing, expanding, and developing their military capability across the board, outspending the U.S. by wide margins, attaining a superiority in ICBM throw-weight and accuracy that not only jeopardizes the deterrent credibility of the U.S. strategic arsenal but the relative balance of military force between the superpowers. Only in recent years has the U.S. responded to this Soviet challenge to traditional parity, and not just because of military concerns. In democratic societies like the U.S., leaders are always haunted by an electorate that may perceive military weakness or impotence making their nation vulnerable to humiliation from abroad. "Logically, we don't need many weapons," explained Bundy, "only enough to insure that we have an adequately survivable second-strike force, which we have. But politically, the public won't be comfortable if we're perceived to be far behind."

So the twain, nuclear danger and Soviet danger, advance upwards separately on the same graph with little expectation that their lines will soon converge. For neither superpower has been willing to surrender a basic self-reliance on its own security and that is the eternal nightmare of those engaged in the modest but stabilizing arms control process.

The question about arms control, its validity, is not whether the dozen or so major treaties and agreements negotiated between the superpowers and others this past quarter-century have halted the arms race—they haven't—but where the world would be today without them. It took more than a dozen years, from the first treaty in 1959 banning nuclear testing in the Antarctic to the first strategic arms limitation talks and the resulting SALT I treaty in 1972, before the U.S. and USSR even agreed on an arms control document. Excepting SALT I and the later SALT II, virtually all the treaties to date have involved *test bans* rather than *arms control*. They have outlawed testing in geographic regions (Latin America), in environmental regions (the air, the oceans, outer space) and, in the 1974 Threshold Test Ban Treaty, above a fixed explosive yield (150 kilotons) underground. No comprehensive test ban has ever been negotiated, and to many observers the piecemeal record of arms control negotiation seems negligible to the point of failure.

In the real world, however, a comprehensive test ban is probably chimerical. Successive American presidents and Soviet premiers have recognized this and sought to link their administrations with at least one or two modest steps forward in the arms control process; their cumulative record suggests that the world is a safer place for their efforts.

The milestones in this record have been the Limited Test Ban Treaty of 1963, which followed hard on the Cuban missile crisis and compelled the two shaken superpowers to ban further testing in the atmosphere, underwater, and outer space; the Non-Proliferation Treaty of 1968–70, signed by forty-eight nations including the U.S. and USSR, which has successfully barred any new nations from joining the nuclear powers' club (still an exclusive elite of five since China became a member in 1964); and SALT I, the landmark Soviet-U.S. accord, concluded in 1972, that severely limited antiballistic missile defenses and the numbers of offensive missiles deployed by each side. The subsequent SALT II treaty of 1979 was even more comprehensive in setting limits on bombers and all MIRVed systems, including missile warheads and launchers. It was signed by the two nations, but fell victim to political fallout after the Soviet invasion of Afghanistan; an outraged U.S. Senate refused to ratify it. Significantly, the Limited Test Ban Treaty, while not slowing weapons development, has stopped all atmospheric testing by the superpowers since 1963. The Non-Proliferation Treaty helped forge an international consensus against the spread of nuclear weapons. SALT, the only negotiation to deal directly with strategic weapons, managed to return some predictability and control to the process by enshrining in its treaties the concepts of mutual assured destruction and strategic parity. But SALT I, achieved during the Nixon-Kissinger era of *detente*, did not lead to increased good will and mutual restraint; the geopolitical climate worsened in the late 1970s and with it the chances for further successful negotiations at the time. The Reagan administration's proposal in 1982 for strategic arms *reduction* talks (START) was met by Soviet suspicion, but the reality of Reagan's re-election persuaded the Soviets to resume arms negotiations by early 1985.

Blame for the failures of arms control negotiations has been variously ascribed to the complexities involved; the Soviets' penchant for secrecy and their closed political system that brooks no public debate; the division in U.S. policy circles over the efficacy of arms control and the U.S. political process, particularly its protracted Presidential campaigns, which inhibits the focused commitment to arms control success by any administration; and, most persistently, the issue of verification. Treaties must be verified, and the ability to verify whether the other side is abiding by the rules is fast diminishing due to the sophisticated mobility and covert deployment potential of the new weapons.

Some scientists question the very raison d'etre of arms reduction, citing the absurdity of trying to remove what is unremovable. "You can have a pact outlawing all bombs, but it won't erase the knowledge of how to build them," says one of the Trinity designers. "It's always there, that knowledge. You can abolish the bomb, but you can't ever erase that danger." Other scientists are convinced that the technology has dominated rational thought and that the gamesmanship of arms control negotiations, the quest for unilateral edge or gain, is what has impeded progress. I. I. Rabi sees the need for a new psychological approach. "Thinking about the arms race in moralistic terms doesn't get you anywhere," he told the author. "Nor does negotiating with the idea of giving it to the Russians in the eye. Our mind-set in these talks has lain in scoring political points off their failure, in treating failure as some kind of heroic confirmation that, 'See, you can't negotiate with those guys.' We haven't sent anybody recently to the negotiating table with the *will* to succeed."

The clash of viewpoints among the scientists themselves has further muddled the debate and vitiated any unified action to resolve the danger. The division is nowhere more acute than between the school of thought advocating sharper limits on weaponry, led by Rabi and Hans Bethe, and the school that argues for whatever weaponry it takes to assure an impregnable defense, led by Edward Teller. The rival paladins in this debate are men of towering stature, Nobel Laureates in their late seventies or eighties who command respectful attention from their fellow physicists or from the president and his advisers. Apostles of the Bethe-Rabi school tend to congregate in the great urban university centers and to talk to each other through the same newspapers, periodicals, and seminars. Having helped build the bomb forty years ago, they retain a proprietary concern for it and

315

remain frustrated that the problem of its control continues to elude mankind. Disciples of the Teller camp can be found largely in the Pentagon, the Department of Energy which now manages the nuclear weapons business, parts of the White House and State Department, and in the great weapons laboratories of Livermore and Los Alamos.

In separate interviews the rivals outlined their credos.

Rabi: "Our policy has been all too consistent. When we indulge in a race for powerful new weapons, we endanger the security of our national institutions. This race is changing these institutions from what the Founding Fathers envisioned, which was not a military-industrial complex. That complex has become so permeating that every state and district in the country has an investment in the Cold War."

Bethe: "What does nuclear superiority mean? It doesn't mean anything. If one side has a hundred weapons and the other side two hundred, it might make a difference. But at the level of one nation's ten thousand to the other nation's five thousand missiles, it makes no difference. We'll both be dead. NATO (North Atlantic Treaty Organization) should get rid of its nuclear weapons and both sides should reduce their land-based missiles. We simply don't need the number of weapons in our arsenal. It's overkill."

Teller: "It is *not* overkill. In a fluid situation every kind of defense has to be considered. First, the Soviets are much more powerfully armed than we are. Second, *we* are determined not to start a nuclear war. Therefore, we must be prepared to survive one and strike back. I was accused in the 1950s of helping develop a horrendous, destabilizing weapon, the hydrogen bomb. Now I'm accused of favoring destabilization because I want a workable nuclear defense system. Well, shields are more stabilizing than swords."

Tension between the two camps reached flash-point on the occasion of a reunion of the nuclear scientists at Los Alamos in April 1983 to celebrate the fortieth anniversary

316

of the laboratory's founding. It was to have been a folksy affair with shop talk and reminiscences of families and children, but no discussion of the bomb and the scientists' role. Teller had not wanted to attend, unsure of whether he would be welcomed by those of his former colleagues who had never forgiven him for testifying against Oppenheimer at the latter's security hearing. In the end he came, along with Rabi and others. Rabi broke the folksy mood by delivering an impassioned discourse on the bomb and the arms race, with intimations of the scientists' culpability. "We meant well," he concluded. But it was another physicist, Victor Weisskopf, who carried Rabi's theme to the limits of discomfort for many of the assembled bombmakers. Over a banquet of roast rib-eye Weisskopf gave an address that resonated with feelings of guilt and despair. The atmosphere in the banquet hall became electric. First one and then another of the former directors of Los Alamos rose and responded to Weisskopf's remarks with a ringing defense of the weaponeers' role. They were warmly applauded.

On the plane returning East after the reunion were Teller and Rabi. Neither had spoken to the other since the Oppenheimer hearings. As the plane began its descent, Teller walked back to Rabi's seat and for a few moments the two men exchanged thoughts about Oppie, The Hill, and the old times.

XIII

Omega

Los Alamos has braved four decades of adjustment, triumph and decline. The laboratory's identity crisis and search for a new mission after Trinity was short-lived thanks to Oppenheimer's successor, Norris Bradbury. If Oppenheimer was its founder, Bradbury was to become Los Alamos's savior, rescuing the laboratory from its post-war blahs, diversifying its mission to fit the peacetime requirements of the fledgling nuclear energy industry, and recruiting to its halls a new generation of brilliant young physicists. With the resumption of weapons activity, Los Alamos underwent a renaissance in the fifties. New laboratories and schools were built, roads repaved; the town acquired a community center, shopping arcades, and a sports park where the Los Alamos Atomic Bombers played ball. By 1958 the town's federally owned property had been transferred to private hands, the laboratory opened to tourists and the security gates removed—those same gates through which Klaus Fuchs had passed on his errands of betrayal.

In 1959 Fuchs was released from prison in England, and he returned to East Germany to continue his work in physics. History has not forgotten his treachery, but it has diminished the breathless claims of a Congressional joint committee at the time that concluded Fuchs had "accomplished greater damage than any other spy not only in the history of the United States but in the history of nations."

The Bradbury regnum from 1945 to 1970 endured setbacks and struggles for funding and public recognition. Los Alamos's younger sister laboratory, Livermore in California, set it a brisk competitive pace; the glamour and esteem once associated with the Trinity and thermonuclear weaponeers had shifted to space technology and the astronauts. But by the time Bradbury stepped down after twenty-five years, Los Alamos had been restored to its eminence as the nation's premier development center for nuclear weapons. The succeeding decade under new leadership transformed the laboratory further from a solely weapons-oriented mission to a thriving enterprise engaged in six hundred or more programs dealing with nuclear energy and basic science research as well as bombs. But the primary mission has remained weapons building and two-thirds of the nation's existing nuclear stockpile was designed and developed at Los Alamos. The Los Alamites' work, from testing and maintaining the reliability of their creations to perfecting accuracy and safety controls, has been a synchronism of the march of nuclear technology from Trinity to the present.

Today's weaponeers continue to probe areas of the unknown, seeking answers to the national security problems of the eighties and beyond. Very little escapes their curiosity and reach. They plumb the polar regions of the Arctic, testing the properties of pack ice under which Soviet nuclear submarines can hide. They tinker with deadly blocks of TNT, fashioning special insensitive high-explosive that resists nuclear detonation should the bomber or vehicle carrying it accidentally crash. They explore ideas for antiterrorist technology, investigate ways to counter threats of biological and chemical warfare. In the field of advanced weapons concepts, they talk of microwave warheads for battlefield use and their newest antisubmarine marvel—a nuclear depth bomb that is launched like a torpedo, flies like a guided missile, then descends via parachute to penetrate the ocean depths and explode on its quarry.

"We're trying to see how many of these ideas hold up beyond the comic-book stage," says Los Alamos's present director, Donald Kerr, a youthful looking forty-five-year-old Cornell physicist. A true believer, Kerr ardently commends the product turned out by his 14,000 employees. "It's clear that the existence of these weapons has made both the United States and the Soviet Union more conservative in the exercise of their foreign and military power," he says.

The peace of exurbia has settled on Los Alamos. The onetime community of dirt streets and bathroom faucets that sometimes dispensed worms instead of water has become a manicured cityscape of condominiums, traffic-clogged avenues and the inevitable totems of fast-food America. In this spot that Oppenheimer once reportedly said should have been shut down after the war, with a sign erected on the front gate reading "This Is a Monument to Man's Inhumanity to Man," the laboratories are humming and one can still hear the occasional thud of a small test explosion far up in the purple canyons. The inhabitants fish, golf, procreate, attend church, worry about their schools and drugs and alcoholism, suffer from ulcers, and continue to build enough bombs to incinerate their way of life and the world's in an instant.

In this still hauntingly beautiful setting, high above the baking plains and sprawls of modern Santa Fe and Albuquerque, there abides a sense of remoteness, of detachment from the concerns and neuroses over nuclear survival that grip so much of the outside world. One enters the small museum near the original Ranch School and is immediately lost in a 1940s time capsule: a diorama of the interior of the old Santa Fe Post Office and its mysterious Box 1663; the facsimile of a student's room pre-1942, with bed and college banners; copies of old *Life* magazines and yellowing packs of Camels.

The nucleus of Trinity veterans who reside here grows

smaller with the years. They were fuzz-cheeked GIs and apprentice physicists then. Now they are mostly retired septuagenarians, padding about their modest homes in flowered Hawaiian shirts and zippered Western boots, sporting the occasional hearing aid or crutch. They are men whose children are bankers or ballerinas, whose wives work in hospitals and worry about entering a room with a microwave oven, whose grandchildren are marrying. They are, many of them, men of inordinate, almost innocent gentleness and courtesy. And they are, some of them, stern fundamentalists who can equate visions of nuclear holocaust with the horrors of the Old Testament. In a world of increasing doubt about the virtues of unlimited deterrence, they remain the last true "hawks", not the bombastic nuke-'em-back-to-the-Stone-Age types, but men quietly proud of their role who blame the other side for the ills of the arms race. "We had every right to be considered heroes," says Herbert Anderson, who won the Fermi Award in 1982 for his role in the first chain-reaction test. "It was a tremendous feeling to think that we went in and stopped a war, just like that," snapping his fingers. After the war Anderson left weapons research and today is struggling to find a cure for cancer through the analysis of proteins in the human cell. He works closely with a young Japanese assistant and never more than a few inches away from a green oxygen tank to which he is attached by a plastic tube. Anderson suffers from berylliosis, an incurable lung disease he contracted long ago while working to unravel the mysteries of nuclear fission.

The Trinity veterans thought the bomb they built would be the ultimate weapon. Few if any of them envisioned today's state of the killing art, the numbing diversity of weapons. They believed they were saving the world for their children and found comfort in the knowledge that the war they were helping to end was a just one. Now they sometimes feel the searing accusations of a generation that has no knowledge of just wars, only an incomprehensibility of unjust weapons. Yet the sense of commitment to country and science, the high excitement of solving technical challenges, still engages those of them not yet retired. "People ask me why I work at Los Alamos," says one. "Why wouldn't I? If I were to stop what I'm doing and leave tomorrow, it would make no difference in the grand scheme. Except to me. I'd retire and stay home. And I'd die."

There is, too, the unextinguishable allure of the weapons themselves, their "irresistible glitter," in the words of physicist Freeman Dyson. "To feel it's there in your hands, to release this energy that fuels the stars, to let it do your bidding, to perform these miracles, to lift a million tons of rock into the sky—it's something that gives people an illusion of illimitable power and it is, in some ways, responsible for all our troubles."

The Trinity veterans at Los Alamos tend not to dwell on their handiwork and its consequences. They do not act like men imprisoned by the memories of Hiroshima and Nagasaki. Most of them recall that first test not with somber introspection but with the enduring enthusiasm of technicians who made a frightfully complex gadget work, and created an era in so doing. Some, perhaps trying to distance themselves from the event, belittle the scientific significance of Trinity, dismissing it as a mere engineering feat. But most recall it as the emotional high of their working lives, remembering it with passion, reliving, starry-eyed, their association with one of the signal events of history.

Beryl Brixner's rheumy eyes gleam, his weathered hands take on a life of their own, waving animatedly, as he recalls how he orchestrated the fifty-five movie cameras that recorded almost 100,000 exposures of the explosion that morning. "Nothing, nothing will ever compare with that first test. Even the first thermonuclear test didn't approach it.

325

There was no real suspense left. You knew by then how it would come out."

Norris Bradbury shares some of this lingering wonder along with grave doubts. In his trim Los Alamos home, snuggled amid a grove of pines and flowering Russian olive trees, he talks of Trinity and the future in the crisp, laconic tones of the Navy commander he once was. "That first time is an experience I'll never forget. We were so intimately bound to it in a technical sense that we felt it as a special triumph. It was an incredible thing. Now we've gone through forty years without nuclear war. But what worries me most is the thought that if we found ourselves in a conventional war and getting beaten, public opinion, American mothers, might urge us to use the bomb. We managed to lose Vietnam without invoking the bomb. Could we avoid escalation the next time?"

Bradbury remains the optimist. In his basement he has carpentered with loving care a king-size marital bed of white pine for his granddaughter and her new husband. He expects to build many more.

At night, seen from afar, Los Alamos twinkles peacefully on the mesa like some lost fairy village. By day the aspen still flames the Jemez hills with gold, and wild turkeys call in the canyons. Breezes waft the scent of juniper across the plateau. It is then sometimes that the scientists and the older inhabitants in the valleys below, who cherish the land and occasionally curse the city on the mesa, say to themselves that nothing men may do or make, not even the atomic bomb, can touch or change the essence of that country.

The rest of Trinity's survivors are mostly scattered about the country, and their remembrances of that first test and what has followed are as varying or contrapuntal as one could find in so small and elite a group. They range from Hans Bethe's conviction that he has never since worked so

hard or so purposefully to Robert Wilson's wish tha
had all worked harder to produce the bomb soone
thus saved untold thousands of more lives on both side

It has been an odd feeling to talk with the bomb's creators, intensely humane men who built the most inhuman of
devices: Oppenheimer, the student of Hindu philosophy;
Hornig, afflicted with sea fever and a yen for violin playing; Teller, the concert pianist; and Alvin Graves, a cellist
who cultivated zinnias. Cyril Smith, who shaped the bomb's
plutonium ingots, collected Japanese art. Marshall Holloway, who helped assemble the nuclear core, was a bird
watcher.

As a group the men of Trinity seem almost consciously
to have tried to bury the legend of themselves as brilliant
collaborators with death whose handiwork hastened the
war's end while causing the cremation of thousands. They
have done their best to blend into the placidity of middle
America. Yet they have never quite made the full transition.
The bomb has set them apart from their fellow men and
marked them for posterity. Some of them would have it no
other way. They want never to forget the excitement and
promise of Trinity, the wartime esprit and the thrill of
matching wits with the cosmos. Emilio Segré, from his eyrie
in Berkeley overlooking the Pacific, recalls with delight that
only the great natural phenomena like volcanic eruptions
or the aurora borealis could compare with Trinity. "Sure, it
opened Pandora's Box," he says, "but how could it have
been avoided? As for having helped make it, if I go to hell
it will be for something other than that."

Others in the group feel weighted by the truth of Oppenheimer's long ago observation that, "In some crude sense,
which no vulgarity, no humor, no overstatement can quite
extinguish, the physicists have known sin. And this is a
knowledge which they cannot lose."

Several strains run through the conversations of the scientists as they reminisce on Trinity and the decision to drop the bomb. One is the *inevitability* of the whole affair, from the first test to Hiroshima and Nagasaki. The word recurs over and over in the explanation that science was bound sooner or later to unlock the atom and that it was fortunate the first honors fell to America and not to Germany or Russia. It was *inevitable* that the atomic bomb would be tested and that it would be used in battle. The second strain in their conversations is the scientists' rationale that their creation was a wartime enterprise and that the bomb was conceived and used within the context of the most savage conflict of all time. It is a comforting rationale to most of them, and there is much validity to it. Whether it is enough to answer the ghosts of Hiroshima and Nagasaki is something else. For those Trinity veterans, many of whom in 1945 were either in uniform or too low in the laboratory's organization to exert any influence on their peers, it *is* enough. They were doing a duty in the service of their country—period. It is in the group of older, senior scientists that one hears modifications of the "it-was-war" rationale. Among them a third strain plays: It was necessary to use the bomb against Japan, but *not* in the way we did.

Cyril Smith believes like others that Trinity alone could not convey the universal horror of the bomb as Hiroshima and Nagasaki did. But that has not quite erased the remorse he expressed at one time, the doubts as to whether the bomb might not have been just as effective without using people as victims. "Sometimes I wake up at night," he said, "feeling the plutonium metal in my hands, metal that I personally helped fabricate for the bomb, and realize that it killed hundreds of thousands of people. It's not a pleasant feeling." A few of the scientists still chastise themselves for having pursued their work on Trinity after V-E Day when it was clear

328

that the major threat which had impelled the Manhattan Project—Nazi attainment of the bomb—was over. Assuming that Japan would be soon defeated through conventional means, they wondered then, as they do today, why they simply didn't abandon their work. "In terms of all that I believe in, before and after the war, I cannot understand why I didn't take that act," Robert Wilson, now at Cornell, told a television interviewer. "It was as though we'd been programmed to do one thing, and like automatons were doing it." Frank Oppenheimer, who until his death in early 1985 was director of a science center in San Francisco, remembers no one slowing the pace at Los Alamos after the German surrender. "We all kept working. The machinery had caught us in its trap."

The images of Hiroshima's and Nagasaki's dead, the plight of the still dying, the portents of holocaust are powerful energizers of conscience in hindsight. Indeed, Wilson and others argued in vain at the time that the military should bring in Japanese observers to witness the Trinity test as a persuasive demonstration of the horror that might follow. Still, history and most of their colleagues have argued forcefully on behalf of the decision to use the bomb in anger.

Two Trinity veterans who went on to achieve measures of eminence were Donald Hornig and William L. Laurence. Hornig graduated from his perch atop the Trinity tower to become, successively, chief science adviser to President Johnson, the president of Brown University, and today Alfred North Whitehead Professor of Chemistry at Harvard University's School of Public Health. "It is still a landmark in my life, one of the most esthetically beautiful things I have ever seen," he said years later of Trinity. Hornig now wishes he had the key to turn off the arms race, but he has not changed his views that the bomb's use against Japan was inevitable, given the moral rationale that it would terminate hostilities. Laurence, the only journalist at the birth of the

Atomic Age, won a second Pulitzer Prize for his eyewitness report of the Nagasaki bombing. "No moral force could have stopped it," he said some years before his death in 1977. "The decision to use the bomb was not a human decision at all but one predetermined by historic forces. We might easily have stumbled into nuclear war by now had we not known, through Hiroshima and Nagasaki, the ultimate horror of the bomb."

From his office in Cambridge, Massachusetts, where he is Professor Emeritus of Physics at Harvard, Kenneth Bainbridge surveys the world's nuclear arms condition from the perspective of eighty-plus years and declares it "probably worse today than at any previous time." But he, too, has not altered his views on how the bomb was employed. "It was important to find out if the bomb would work. If it hadn't, perhaps everyone would have been better off in the long run. But if it *was* going to work, then *we* had better be the ones to know it and develop it. We knew what would happen if an atomic bomb was used over a city and we knew it would not be a nice weapon if wars were going to come along every quarter-century."

Other Trinity participants have cited the friends they knew who were being killed every day in the war. "We considered Hiroshima a surgical operation," said one. "Damn it, it would be so bad it would stop the Japanese. With so much killing going on, we didn't worry about the ethics of killing more." General Thomas Farrell had no regrets. "War," he said years later, "is always a choice of killing and how to die." The conventional incendiary bombing raids on Japan that preceded Hiroshima and Nagasaki, it was pointed out, caused more devastation and casualties. Luis Alvarez, who was part of the Hiroshima mission and now works in Berkeley, remains philosophical: "Frankly, I'm much happier with all the tension and brinkmanship we live with than

I am with the spectacle of having ten million people wiped out every twenty years in conventional wars. And that's the schedule we were on before the atomic bomb."

For nearly twenty years after Hiroshima and Nagasaki, Harry Truman kept his silence on the private torments that accompanied his decision to drop the bomb. Then, in February 1965, he told a television audience:

"It was a question of saving hundreds of thousands of American lives. I don't mind telling you that you don't feel normal when you have to plan hundreds of thousands of complete, final deaths of American boys who are alive and joking and having fun while you are doing your planning. You break your heart and your head trying to figure out a way to save one life.

"The name given to our invasion plan was 'Olympic,' but I saw nothing godly about the killing of all the people that would be necessary to make that invasion." The casualty estimates called for 750,000 Americans—250,000 killed; 500,000 maimed for life. The estimates for Japanese civilians and troops who would probably perish defending their homeland ranged into the millions.

"I could not worry about what history would say about my personal mortality," concluded the former President. "I made the only decision I ever knew how to make. I did what I thought was right."

Two protagonists of the atomic years—Teller and Oppenheimer—disagreed on many things, most notably the decision to build the hydrogen bomb. But on two points both agreed: it was necessary and right to develop the atomic bomb; it was unnecessary and wrong to have bombed Hiroshima without specific warning to Japan and the world that the United States possessed such a weapon.

* * *

XIII: *Omega*

Before he died in February 1967, Robert Oppenheimer granted the author an interview in his sunlit study at the Institute for Advanced Study in Princeton. The Institute, which he had directed for nearly two decades, was a staging point of ideas from some of the world's foremost experimental physicists. The blackboard in Oppie's office was adorned with equations, and his younger disciples shuffled reverently in for advice and encouragement. He moved as always lithely but with increasing caution, for the years and events had bent him. As he talked of Trinity and the bomb, his blue eyes still pierced and the voice softly vibrated. Listening to him, one was reminded again of the contradictions and torments that had been the lot of this remarkable man.

"We had to test at Trinity," he reflects, "because there were too many uncertainties. We felt as scientists that we had better try to prove that the bomb was possible and not let it hang over us, an unknown. Even had the Japanese surrendered without Hiroshima and Nagasaki, we would have continued testing and developed the bomb." Not long before, following a speech he had given in Geneva, Oppenheimer had been asked by a priest in the audience about his role as the "father" of the atomic bomb. If he had the choice, would he do it all over again? "Yes," Oppenheimer had answered. Another voice from the audience had angrily cried, "Even after Hiroshima?" And Oppenheimer had looked out with his steady gaze and again answered steadily, "Yes."

Such experiences, however, had taken their toll. Oppenheimer was not the same man who twenty years ago could sit in the highest councils of Washington and agree that the United States could give no warning demonstration spectacular enough to convince the Japanese that they should surrender. "I don't think we imagined what that first bomb at Trinity would really look like," he said, "and this was a grievous error. The awesome light that resulted had not been given adequate consideration. If there had been any demon-

332

stration that would have had a considerable effect on the Japanese, a pyrotechnic display over Tokyo Harbor might have been it."

"I have no remorse about the making of the bomb and Trinity. That was done right. As for how we used it, I understand why it happened and appreciate with what nobility those men with whom I'd worked made their decision. But I do not have the feeling that it was done right. The ultimatum to Japan was full of pious platitudes. It wasn't a pretty world and it is always easy to enjoy another man's bad conscience. But our government should have acted with more foresight and clarity in telling the world and Japan what the bomb meant."

The bombing of Hiroshima was a conscious political decision to shock the Japanese into surrender. The bombing of Nagasaki, however, was a decision that appears to have been assumed and carried out by the U.S. government without widespread debate. It was as inexorable as a state execution that proceeds on schedule, barring a last-minute reprieve. Thus, the issue of whether Nagasaki's destruction was militarily and morally justified is still argued.

To most Americans Hiroshima's obliteration seems excusable on the grounds that it saved untold numbers of American as well as Japanese lives. The bombing of Nagasaki, however, posed the question of whether the United States was needlessly cruel and precipitate in allowing the Japanese only three days in which to respond to the Hiroshima raid. Considering the dazed condition of the Japanese after Hiroshima, the considerable time it took them to realize the full devastation the bomb had wreaked on that city, plus the time span needed to concur on and forward to the Allies a decision as grave as the surrender of the Empire—the three-day respite the United States gave Japan between Hiroshima and Nagasaki may well seem inadequate.

There appears to have been little or no protracted discussion by U.S. leaders on the question of launching the second bomb attack on Japan. There is no evidence that U.S. political and military authorities ever seriously considered delaying it. In this additional holocaust 74,000 Japanese died.

Yet the reasons for this seeming callousness are explainable. There *was* no debate on the follow-up atomic-bomb raid. The great debate had come months earlier on the question of whether to use the bomb as a military weapon or not. Once that argument was settled, the fate of Nagasaki became simply a matter of military strategy. General Groves, one of the principal architects of the second-bomb strategy, described how it came about:

"There was never any decision reached to drop *only* two bombs. As far as I was concerned, there was no limit to the number of bombs that would be used. There was no debate ever on the matter of dropping a second bomb. The debate had all been on whether to use the atomic bomb as a weapon at all."

According to Groves, it was Rear Admiral William R. Purnell, a member of the influential Military Policy Committee, who first broached the idea of dropping a second bomb. Purnell and Groves discussed the idea at length, and it was proposed at a meeting of the Committee in December 1944. By that time the other members of the Committee—chairman Vannevar Bush; his alternate, James Conant; and General Wilhelm D. Styer, chief of staff of the Army Service Forces—had relegated much of the authority for bomb policy to Groves. After listening to Purnell's theory, Groves agreed that two bombs could end the war: the first would show the Japanese the power of an atomic weapon; the second would show them that we had the capacity to make more than one bomb.

"I gave my conclusions to General Marshall, Secretary of

War Stimson and President Roosevelt," said Groves. "None of them appeared to question them as being unreasonable." Roosevelt heard of the idea during a briefing by Groves at the White House just before F. D. R. departed for the Yalta Conference in February 1945. Later Groves apprised Harry Truman of the second-bomb strategy. Said Groves: "There was never any definite approval of this conclusion and there was no limitation placed in our plans on the number of bombs to be used." In other words, it appears that the decision which led to Nagasaki's demise was the result of a general acquiescence by U.S. political leaders to a military blueprint rather than of any formalized command on the part of the President and his advisers.

In late July, Groves prepared a one-page order for General Carl "Toohey" Spaatz, newly appointed commander of the 20th Air Force. The order called for initiating the use of atomic bombs on Japan. There was to be no limit on the number of bombs Groves would furnish Spaatz or on the number of bombs Spaatz would drop. Groves personally handed the order to General Thomas Handy, acting chief of staff of the Army, who forwarded a copy of it to General Marshall in Potsdam. Marshall cabled his approval back to the Pentagon, where Handy signed the order and turned it over to Spaatz, who was about to depart for Guam.

A week later Hiroshima lay in ruins. The follow-up raid was already planned and waited only on the weather, the twenty-four hours needed to assemble the bomb on Tinian, and more detailed reports on the extent of the Hiroshima destruction. "We had little information as to the damage the first bomb had inflicted on Hiroshima," recalled Groves. "The original release on that bombing emanated from the White House. I was responsible for its wording, including a statement to the effect that Hiroshima had been destroyed. However, at the time of issuance we had no definite proof of this. All I really had was a statement from the plane and the

335

observation planes that the bomb seemed to be of a power similar to the one exploded at Trinity. The release was issued as it was primarily to enhance the psychological effect on the Japanese High Command."

The effect of the White House release and American propaganda leaflets dropped on Japan—warning in no uncertain terms that the United States would use the bomb again unless the Japanese capitulated immediately—was enough to compel the enemy High Command to at least consider surrendering. Indeed, all sorts of peace feelers from the Japanese were rumored to be in the offing. Why, then, could the United States not have waited a few more days before sending the "Bock's Car" on the mission that destroyed Nagasaki? And was no effort made at all to delay the mission?

According to Groves no one authority ever considered allowing more time. "If the President had spoken to Stimson or Marshall at any time about this, or had Stimson even spoken to Marshall, I would have had the order almost immediately. The obvious reason they didn't was that we did not know then whether Japan would surrender promptly if only one bomb were dropped." In addition, Groves had the soldier's natural disposition to allow the enemy no quarter. "Once you get your opponent reeling, you keep him reeling and never let him recover," he explained.

As for the Japanese surrender feelers, Groves feels there was no reason why anyone in the U.S. government should have been impressed by them. History shows that it is common for nations facing defeat to make peace proposals which may not be concluded until many months later. In the interim, hundreds of thousands of lives may be lost in battle. "My mission was to bring the war to a conclusion and save American lives," said Groves. "If the war had continued without the use of the bomb, it is reasonable that there would have been at least ten million Japanese casualties.

The number of these casualties from our conventional bombing attacks alone would have approached those of Nagasaki in a few weeks' time."

It is perhaps a small irony to contemplate that, had the Trinity test failed—and caused even a week's delay in the follow-up raid—the Japanese might have surrendered during those extra days and Nagasaki might have been spared. Many of the scientists devoutly believe this. "If the Trinity test had failed," declared Hans Bethe, "we would not have dropped the plutonium bomb on Nagasaki."

Military sources point out that another test could have been held shortly and that sooner or later the second strike on Japan would have been made. But the fact remains that the Fat Man bomb sittting on Tinian that August day in 1945 would probably *not* have been risked over Nagasaki if Trinity had not produced some guarantee of effective performance. And if just one of the myriad components of the Trinity gadget had fizzled, the resulting delay might have saved the city and 74,000 Japanese lives.

A few weeks after Hiroshima General Groves wrote Kenneth Bainbridge: "Nothing the future may disclose can dim the splendor of the results attained through our ability to make military use of these forces." Years later he said of Trinity: "Those of us who saw the dawn of the Atomic Age that morning knew that when man is willing to make the effort, he is capable of accomplishing virtually anything. Was the development of the atomic bomb by the United States necessary? Unequivocally, yes. The atomic bomb is what has kept the peace since 1945."

Leslie Groves died in 1970 at the age of 73.

Hans Bethe, who headed Los Alamos's theoretical division and the crew that fashioned the bomb's critical initiator, is probably the most famous of the surviving principals

337

in the Trinity project. Today he is one of the foremost critics of the arms race, a leader with Rabi in the Union of Concerned Scientists. "The arms race is a long-range problem," he has said. "The Second World War was a short-range problem. And in the short range I think it was essential to make the atomic bomb."

He welcomes visitors to his cluttered third-floor office in Cornell's Newman Laboratory, a casually attired *ancien* with an elfish smile and tufts of unruly white hair sprouting from his head. "It still was the most exciting episode in my life," he says of Trinity in the faint accent of his native Germany. Bethe believes the U.S. could have warned the Japanese in advance of Hiroshima, but he himself at the time was not morally opposed to using the bomb. "I didn't think about these matters, I was too busy."

After the war Bethe advised the U.S. government on weapons and arms control issues, becoming the prime mover behind the 1963 Limited Test Ban Treaty. Today he urges a scale-down in U.S. nuclear arms, with the laboratories focusing on technologies that would lower the risk of nuclear war, rather than developing still another generation of advanced weaponry. "We thought we could control the genie," he muses. "It wouldn't go back in the bottle, but there were reasonable grounds for thinking we could contain it. I know now that this was an illusion."

Edward Teller, now in his late seventies and ensconced at Stanford University's Hoover Institute, remains the most formidable of America's scientific Cold Warriors. His militant views on the necessity for ever-stronger nuclear defenses have found receptive ears in Washington. His distrust of the Soviet Union, deep and abiding, also has struck responsive chords among U.S. policy makers. In a 1983 article Teller wrote for his Los Alamos colleagues, he noted that "the events of the past thirty-five years have demonstrated that while the danger from a ruthless adventurer named Hitler was more immediate, the danger from the patient, unrelenting leaders in the Kremlin is in reality greater."

It is one of the ironies of the nuclear odyssey that the older weapons builders of Los Alamos, who have been so personally unforgiving of Teller for his role in the Oppenheimer affair, philosophically cheer his stance in the arms race debate. That stance combines dour skepticism of arms control agreements with an unshakable belief that the road to arms reduction lies in producing more defensive weaponry. "If the Soviet Union knows that it is spending $100 billion on *offensive* weapons," reasons Teller in his heavily accented bass voice, "and we can destroy eighty percent of those in an attack, then it won't be worthwile for them to continue building such weapons. And if *defensive* weapons become cheaper to build than offensive ones, fewer of the latter will be built, the danger of sudden nuclear attack will diminish and perhaps disappear." It is a seductive argument unsupported thus far by the facts of recent history.

After forty years, too, the essential Teller remains intact and adamant on a base principle of the arms control issue. Writing to the late Leo Szilard in July 1945, Teller concluded, "I do not feel that there is any chance to outlaw any one weapon. If we have a slim chance of survival, it lies in the possibility to get rid of wars. The more decisive a weapon is the more surely it will be used in any real conflict, and no agreements will help."

Isidor Isaac Rabi, by contrast, has from the beginning espoused the view that nuclear weapons, not the Soviet Union, are the fundamental threat to peace and security. Almost immediately, the Trinity explosion became for Rabi symbolic of a potentially evil force unleashed—"awful, ominous and personally threatening." Four decades later, he recalled his feelings for his Los Alamos brothers: "I began to have gooseflesh because I realized it was the end of one world and the beginning of another, that we now had a power that put humanity at a new level of danger. I realized, too, for the first time how vulnerable people are to the instruments that scientists devise."

Ever since those first seconds after the blast, when Rabi sensed that the chill on him was not just the morning cold, he has acted as a contentious force within the scientific fraternity, seeking to reverse the arms race, to abort what he has called "this calculus of destruction." It is Rabi's gnawing fear that the epitaph of the Trinity scientists may one day read: *How Well We Meant.*

Few greater scientific achievements have been attained in so short a time, few greater tributes to human ingenuity ever written, than the creation in twenty-seven months at Los Alamos and Trinity of the atomic bomb.

Since that epochal July morning in 1945 the bomb has become the centerpiece of the world power struggle, the central determinant in our survival as a species, its mushroom cloud the universal symbol of fear and uncertainty. Half or more of the world's population may believe that starvation, already killing fifteen million souls each year, is the true present danger of our times, not the bomb. Starvation, however, endangers only a portion of humanity; the bomb threatens the extinction of the planet. With enough mates in stock now to approximate five tons of death for every living human, the bomb intrudes everywhere: into the discourse of our politics, our diplomacy, our cultural, environmental, and personal lives. It is the brooding specter in East-West relations, the cause of tension between otherwise loyal allies. Canadians wonder if their land will become one huge fallout receptacle in a nuclear standoff between U.S. interceptors and Soviet missiles launched over the North Pole. Western Europeans fear that in the event of Soviet-U.S. conflict on their soil, N.A.T.O., with its inferior conventional forces, may have to resort to nuclear weapons sooner than later.

T. S. Eliot wrote: *Between the idea/And the reality/ Between the motion/And the act/Falls the Shadow.* The shadow between man's effort to tame the nuclear beast and the reality of his failure to do so has been the shadow of distrust between nations or, perhaps worse, the illusion that man's security lies in his weaponry, that each new advance in the technology of his arms adds to his security rather than to the inevitability that one day, the world's last, these arms will be used. Even an unloaded gun will fire sooner or later, goes the Russian proverb. "The fact is there's no way to get what one wants with these weapons," Frank Oppenheimer, Robert's brother, said before he died. "Whatever it is you want—security, territory, natural resources—these weapons are not going to achieve it for you. Once used, they only leave you poorer or more wicked."

The bomb has traveled many leagues these past four decades. Nothing turned out quite as well as the exuberant young men at Trinity thought it would. Here would be a fresh start, a weapon so frightening it was inconceivable it could ever be used in anger again after Hiroshima and Nagasaki. It would cause a profound change in the psyche of the warriors, liberating them from the very idea of future war. But it didn't. For a while, before the novelty of its awesomeness faded, the bomb had shocked mankind into dismissing war as a sane national policy. Yet in parts of the world today conventional wars, employing tens of thousands of soldiers, are being fought. And the bomb has become yet another piece of inventory, albeit the prize one, in the warriors' arsenal.

A last hope remains for persuading governments to shut down the escalator to Armageddon, and that is the force of public opinion in which the legends of nuclear horror have

341

finally taken hold. Late in the day, that articulate segment of world opinion has finally absorbed and begun to revolt at the dimensions of the nuclear threat. Not since the early 1960s has there been such an outpouring of concern. Like the dissent of that time, it could prove to be shallow and short-lived. But this seems to be not the uninformed hysteria of earlier public protest, but rather a movement of people matured by the growing literature of the horror and truly sobered at the prospects of nuclear oblivion. It is a movement grounded not in the fatalism that afflicted the generation of the fifties through the seventies, but in the urgent ideals that infused those early days after Trinity when one young physicist could write these words to an elderly woman who had befriended him at Los Alamos:

"We worked passionately for the great end we achieved, knowing that it was really no end but a means. In that work we changed. We had to learn again in all its meaning how strong is the bond between science and the life of men. We shall never forget our time on The Hill. It was made of long night hours, of busy desert days and patient waiting in the laboratory. It held the terrible suspense of the last minutes at Trinity. . . . We take the hope that people of intelligence and goodwill everywhere can understand and share our sense of crisis. In that hope lies the world's best assurance."

Oppenheimer tried to express that sense of crisis when he told his colleagues just before he left Los Alamos for the last time: "Our pride must be tempered with a profound concern. The peoples of this world must unite, or they will perish. This war, that has ravaged so much of the earth, has written these words. The atomic bomb has spelled them out for all men to understand. If atomic bombs are to be added as new weapons to the arsenals of nations preparing for war,

342

then the time will come when mankind will curse the names of Los Alamos and Hiroshima."

And, he might have added, of Trinity.

The cathedral still stands on the Jornada. The wind plays hymns about the shrine where it all began.

To reach the site of Trinity from the laboratories of Los Alamos one descends by car from the Jemez hills, like an earthling returning from Mount Olympus, to the torrid lowlands that stretch from Santa Fe to the Mexican border. At the National Atomic Museum in Albuquerque, a replica of the "Fat Man" bomb, sired by Trinity, squats amidst an array of prototypical atomic weaponry. There is something faintly comical about "Fat Man," so much grief in this bulbous little dirigible of death with its quaint-looking buckles and its bustlelike tail fin, the remnant of some H. G. Wells fantasy. Two hours further southward, one enters the Army's White Sands Missile Range which encompasses the 51,000-acre birthplace of the atomic bomb, now a national historic site.

Far below the drifting clouds the site resembles some huge sundial etched in the desert by prehistoric tribes. It is a perfectly inscribed circle slashed by a single arrow-straight line, the old road from Base Camp to Zero, where the bomb was exploded. A larger road has intruded on the scene to accommodate the invasion of several hundred tourists each fall when the site is officially opened to the public for a day. But one can still picture the caravan of cars with the bomb bumping down the graded dirt road that summer morning, hub-deep in sand and trailing whorls of dust. They would have just left the McDonald ranch house, now painstakingly restored by the government to its original condition on the day the bomb's core was assembled inside it. They would have reached ground Zero in minutes. The scientists would have unloaded their cargo, then watched the Gadget's ascent

343

to the top of the tower, as slow and torturous as a condemned man's march to execution. And now, only the remains of one of the tower's four metal footings thrusts defiantly out of the hard earth.

Where the tower's base was stands a cairn of black lava blocks, fourteen feet high, the only official monument to the test. The bronze plaque on it reads simply: "Trinity Site, Where the World's First Nuclear Device Was Exploded on July 16, 1945."

The crater has long been filled, the ground picked clean of the last bits of trinitite. The radiation at Zero is still ten times that of normal background radiation, but well within the harmless range. Just outside the chainlink fence enclosing Zero lie the remains of Jumbo, victim of an abortive demolition attempt years ago that succeeded only in blowing out both ends of the old jug. On the nearby perimeter, vultures circle above the long-deserted bunkers now sinking beneath the drifted sand and tumbleweeds. Antelope still gallop through the sagebrush by the old Base Camp, its cistern and two rotting adobe huts all that is left. Gradually, Trinity is surrendering itself to nature.

Beyond, there are only memories and the fears. Of a summer evening when electrical storms sweep in, the thunder may roll down from the Oscura peaks, echoing across the valley under that vast sky, sounding not unlike the ominous thunder of that first atomic dawn.

Bibliographical Note

Index

BIBLIOGRAPHICAL NOTE

A story like that of Trinity relies in its telling on a range of sources as varied as the cast of characters who built the bomb.

This book is the sum and distillation of more than one hundred interviews with persons, official and unofficial, who played a part in the drama of that test. It is also a compound of several-score books, magazine and newspaper articles, television scripts and private and semiprivate papers, of which the most prominent are listed below. I spent several months perusing official Atomic Energy Commission documents which had never before been released to a journalist. The Commission reviewed my manuscript in detail for references to classified matter. In addition to reading, interviewing, and even monitoring old films of the test, I solicited and received dozens of personal letters from Trinity participants, some of whom provided maps, weather charts and other pertinent data. Finally, I visited the main locales treated in this story: Los Alamos and the Trinity site.

Well aware that the span of two decades has either dimmed or embellished some individuals' memories of that event, I have tried to weigh conflicting accounts of certain incidents and have used only those which either evoked some consensus or appeared to be supported by public documents. In several instances, conversations have been reconstructed according to my best efforts to honor the spirit in which they were told me by participants or eyewitnesses. Where a firsthand account was clearly unobtainable, my conjectures were based on interviews with others who were involved or on extensive reading and research.

Day of Trinity was written against the backdrop of the early atomic years, and for the chronicle of that period I relied heavily on Richard Hewlett's and Oscar Anderson, Jr.'s excellent *The New World, 1939–1946*. For technical authenticity, Volume One of David Hawkins's *Manhattan District History, Project Y, the Los Alamos Project* is probably the most detailed and accurate account of the scientists' ordeal at Los Alamos. I also found William L. Laurence's *Dawn over Zero* and Robert Cahn's *Saturday Evening Post* article "Behind the First Atomic Bomb" especially helpful in confirming accounts of the final hours before the Trinity test.

The following articles, books and documents provided guidance in preparing this story:

Alsop, Stewart, and Ralph Lapp, "The Strange Death of Louis Slotin," *Saturday Evening Post*, March 6, 1954.

Amrine, Michael, *The Great Decision*, New York, G. P. Putnam's Sons, 1959.

Bainbridge, Kenneth T., *The Reminiscences of Kenneth T. Bainbridge*, Oral History Research Office, Columbia University, New York, 1960.

Barnett, Lincoln, article on J. Robert Oppenheimer, *Life* Magazine, October 10, 1949.

Bundy, McGeorge, George F. Kennan, Robert S. McNamara, and Bernard Smith, "Nuclear Weapons and the Atlantic Alliance," *Foreign Affairs*, Spring 1982.

Bush, Vannevar, *Modern Arms and Free Men*, New York, Simon and Schuster, 1949.

Byrnes, James F., *Speaking Frankly*, New York, Harper & Brothers, 1947.

Cahn, Robert, "Behind the First Atomic Bomb," *Saturday Evening Post*, July 16, 1960.

Church, Peggy Pond, *The House at Otowi Bridge*, Albuquerque, University of New Mexico Press, 1959.

Churchill, Winston S., *Triumph and Tragedy*, Boston, Houghton Mifflin Co., 1953.

Clark, Ronald W., *The Birth of the Bomb*, London, Phoenix House, Ltd., 1961.

Compton, Arthur H., *Atomic Quest*, New York, Oxford University Press, 1956.

Curtis, Charles P., *The Oppenheimer Case*, New York, Simon and Schuster, 1955.

Department of State, *Foreign Relations of the United States, Diplomatic Papers, The Potsdam Conference, 1945*, Vols. I and II, Washington, U.S. Government Printing Office, 1960.

Dyson, Freeman, *Weapons and Hope*. New York, Harper and Row, 1984.

Eisenhower, Dwight D., *Mandate for Change: 1953–1956*. New York, Doubleday & Co., 1963.

Feis, Herbert, "The Secret That Traveled to Potsdam," *Foreign Affairs Magazine,* January 1960.

Fermi, Laura, *Atoms in the Family*. Chicago, University of Chicago Press, 1954.

Fitzpatrick, George, "Atomic Bomb Sightseeing," *New Mexico Magazine*, January 1946.

Gowing, Margaret, *Britain and Atomic Energy, 1939–1945*. London, Macmillan Co., 1964.

Groves, Leslie R., *Now It Can Be Told*. New York, Harper & Brothers, 1962.

Hawkins, David, *Manhattan District History, Project Y, the Los Alamos Project*, Vol. I. Los Alamos, New Mexico, University of California and U.S. Atomic Energy Commission, 1945.

Hewlett, Richard G., and Oscar E. Anderson, Jr., *The New World, 1939–1946*, Vol. I, History of the U.S. Atomic Energy Commission. University Park, Pennsylvania State University Press, 1962.

In the Matter of J. Robert Oppenheimer: Transcript of Hearings Before Personnel Security Board. Washington, Government Printing Office, 1954.

Joint Committee on Atomic Energy, *Soviet Atomic Espionage*. Washington, Government Printing Office, 1951.

Jungk, Robert, *Brighter Than a Thousand Suns*. New York, Harcourt, Brace & Co., 1958.

Knebel, Fletcher, and Charles W. Bailey II, "The Fight over the A-Bomb," *Look* Magazine, August 13, 1963.

——, *No High Ground*. New York, Harper & Brothers, 1960.

Koop, Theodore F., *Weapon of Silence*. Chicago, University of Chicago Press, 1946.

Lang, Daniel, *Early Tales of the Atomic Age*. Garden City, New York, Doubleday & Co., 1948.

Laurence, William L., *Dawn over Zero*. New York, Alfred A. Knopf, 1946.

——, *Men and Atoms*. New York, Simon and Schuster, 1946.

LeVien, Jack, and Lord, John, *Winston Churchill: The Valliant Years*. New York, Bernard Geis Associates and Random House, 1962.

Life Magazine, issues of August 20 and September 24, 1945.

Los Alamos Scientific Laboratory *Community News*, July 1960; January and June 1963.

Moorehead, Alan, *The Traitors*. New York, Harper & Row, 1952.

Morison, Elting E., *Turmoil and Tradition*. Boston, Houghton Mifflin Co., 1960.

National Broadcasting Company, "NBC White Paper: The Decision to Drop the Bomb." New York, January 5, 1965.

New York Times, The, issues of July 11 through August 10, 1945.

Nuclear Weapons Data Book. Cambridge, Mass., Ballinger Books, n.d.

Oppenheimer, J. Robert, "Niels Bohr and Atomic Weapons," talk delivered at Los Alamos Scientific Laboratory, May 18, 1964.

——, "A Talk in Chicago," *Bulletin of Atomic Scientists*, October 1963.

Pilat, Oliver, *The Atom Spies*. New York, G. B. Putnam's Sons, 1952.

Public Broadcasting Company, "The Day after Trinity, J. Robert Oppenheimer and the Atomic Bomb," a documentary film by John Else, 1980. Transcript.

Purcell, John, *The Best-Kept Secret*. New York, Vanguard Press, 1963.

Reuben, William, *The Atom Spy Hoax*. New York, Action Books, 1955.

Schell, Jonathan, *The Fate of the Earth.* New York, Alfred A. Knopf, 1982.

Smyth, Henry DeWolf, *Atomic Energy for Military Purposes: The Official Report on the Development of the Atomic Bomb.* Princeton, Princeton University Press, 1947.

Stimson, Henry L., "The Decision to Use the Atomic Bomb," *Harper's Magazine*, 1947.

Stimson, Henry L. and McGeorge Bundy, *On Active Service in Peace and War.* New York, Harper & Brothers, 1948.

Strauss, Lewis L., *Men and Decisions.* Garden City, New York, Doubleday and Co., 1962.

Szilard, Leo, *The Voice of the Dolphins.* New York, Simon and Schuster, 1961.

Teller, Edward, with Allen Brown, *The Legacy of Hiroshima.* Garden City, New York, Doubleday & Co., 1962.

Thomas, Charles A., "Epoch in the Desert," *Monsanto Magazine*, 1945.

Time Magazine, issues of August 13 and August 20, 1945.

Truman, Harry S., *Year of Decisions.* Garden City, New York, Doubleday & Co., 1955.

U.S. Atomic Energy Commission, Vol. 24 LAMS, Documents LA-1012, 1013, 1024, 1025, 1026 and 1027, December 1947.

Warren, Stafford, *Radiology and the Atomic Bomb.* Forest Glen, Maryland, Historical Unit, Walter Reed Hospital, U.S. Army, 1964.

West, Rebecca, *The New Meaning of Treason.* New York, Viking Press, 1964.

York, Herbert F., "Bilateral Negotiations and the Arms Race," *Scientific American*, October 1983.

The following newspapers and wire services were also used in preparing this book: *Alamogordo News, Albuquerque Journal, Albuquerque Tribune, El Paso Herald-Post, Sante Fe New Mexican,* Associated Press and United Press.

INDEX

353

Index

LANSING LAMONT, born and brought up in New York City, educated at Harvard College and the Columbia University Graduate School of Journalism (with a stint in the army as an Infantry officer in between), is currently director of Canadian Affairs for the Americas Society. He has been a journalist with the *Washington Star* and was *Time* magazine's national political correspondent from 1961-1968, reporting more than fifteen cover stories from their Washington bureau, including the astronauts' space shots, the 1964 and 1968 Republican and Democratic party conventions, and the Kennedy assassinations. During this time he also wrote *Day of Trinity*, which became a nationwide best-seller in both its hardcover and paperback editions. He went on to become deputy chief of *Time*'s London bureau, chief Canadian correspondent and Ottawa bureau chief for *Time* and *Time*'s United Nations bureau chief before leaving the magazine to become a free-lance writer. His second book, *Campus Shock*, a report on the dark side of American college life in the 1970's was published to critical acclaim in 1979, and his numerous articles have appeared in *Life, Fortune, People,* and *Connoisseur* magazines, as well as on the *New York Times'* op-ed page. In 1981 he was hired by the Americas Society to organize the first national forum in the United States on Canadian-American issues.